Seminole Burning

Seminole Burning
A Story of
Racial Vengeance

DANIEL F. LITTLEFIELD, JR.

University Press of Mississippi
Jackson

Manufactured in the United States of America
99 98 97 96   4 3 2 1
The paper in this book meets the guidelines for permanence and durability of the
Committee on Production Guidelines for Book Longevity of the Council on Library
Resources.

Library of Congress Cataloging-in-Publication Data

Littlefield, Daniel F.
    Seminole burning : a story of racial vengeance / Daniel F. Littlefield, Jr.
      p.   cm.
    Includes bibliographical references and index.
    ISBN 0-87805-923-7 (cloth : alk. paper).—ISBN 0-87805-924-5 (pbk. : alk.
paper)
      1. Seminole Indians—History—19th century.   2. Seminole Indians—Social
conditions.   3. Seminole Indians—Land tenure.   4. Indians, Treatment of—
Oklahoma—Pottawatomie County.   5. Lynching—Oklahoma—Pottawatomie
County—History—19th century.   6. Pottawatomie County (Okla.)—History—
19th century.   7. Pottawatomie County (Okla.)—Race relations.   I. Title.
E99.S28L573   1996
976.6'36004973—dc20   96-16413
                                                                              CIP

British Library Cataloging-in-Publication data available

Contents

Preface

My first knowledge of the episode known as the Seminole burning came from an undergraduate course in Oklahoma history taught by Angie Debo in the summer of 1959. The context in which she presented it became lost to me in time, but I could not forget the incident itself. Perhaps a decade later, I obtained a microfilm copy of "Violence on the Oklahoma Territory-Seminole Nation Border: The Mont Ballard Case" (1957), a master of arts thesis by Geraldine Smith, whose work at the University of Oklahoma was the first attempt to write a detailed history of the event. That film remained in my files until recently, after my interest in the Seminole burning had been sparked once more and I was well into the process of researching it.

In one of my frequent rummagings among the inventories and records in the National Archives, I found the Justice Department files relating to the case. As I read them, I realized that the story that emerged differed significantly from the one Smith had told. It was the discrepancies between the stories that caught my attention and led to this book.

Heretofore, historical treatment of the event has rested largely on newspaper articles, published federal documents, and the transcript of the Mont Ballard trial. The result has been an extremely inaccurate rendering of the facts in the case and some erroneous conclusions about its causes. Smith's work is flawed in that respect, though it was an attempt to go beyond the event itself and place it in a larger historical context of frontier lawlessness. Edwin C. McReynolds took Smith's work a step further in *The Seminoles* (1957), hinting briefly at the racial overtones of the affair. Since their work, the topic has lain dormant except for an occasional piece in the pulp press. My work expands on the contexts Smith and McReynolds introduced, with emphasis on the latter, and explores others that bear significantly on the event, such as questions of criminal jurisdictions in Oklahoma and Indian Territory, white renters in Indian Territory, the public perception of lynching in that era, and the personal agendas of individuals involved in the case.

Smith and McReynolds relied on limited sources in their work. They did not take into account the evidence that exists in the extensive files of the Justice Department in the National Archives in Washington, D.C.; the records of the U.S. Court for the Western District of Oklahoma or the Melven Cornish Collection in the Western History Collections at the University of Oklahoma; the records of the U.S. Court for the Northern District of the Indian Territory at the National Archives-Southwest Region at Fort Worth, Texas; or the Horace Speed Collection at the Oklahoma Historical Society. This work draws heavily on these and other primary sources as well as on newspaper articles and printed sources, some of which Smith's work was useful in ferreting out.

My thanks go to the archivists and staff at the above named institutions. But I must give a special thanks to Herman Kirkwood of Oklahoma City and Guy Guinn of Edmond, indefatigable researchers on the topic who provided me much information and many leads to sources regarding the oral history and family histories of participants in the event.

Finally, I thank those members of the Seminole Nation who encouraged my work or read my manuscript, especially Tedd McGeisey and other members of the McGeisey family, Melinda Micco, Ted Underwood, and Jim Burgess.

Seminole Burning

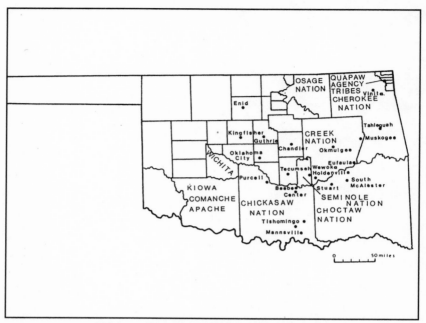

Oklahoma Territory and Indian Territory, 1898

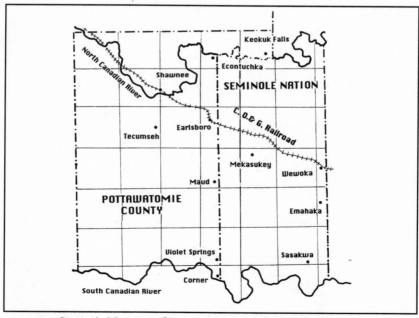

Seminole Nation and Pottawatomie County Oklahoma, 1898

(Maps by G. T. Hanson)

ONE

A Celebration

In early May 1906, the small farming community of Maud, Oklahoma
Territory, learned that one of its own, Mont Ballard, had gained release from
the federal penitentiary at Leavenworth, Kansas, and was returning home
after seven years. This news was momentous for Elias Riddle and other
of Ballard's friends, who quickly raised money and planned a welcoming
celebration for their former neighbor, who had figured prominently in their
small town's history.

At eight o'clock in the evening of May 7, hundreds of people jammed
the high school auditorium for the welcoming ceremonies. The local band
played "Home, Sweet Home" and "America," and Riddle, H. A. Bolinger,
and the Reverend James D. Hodges, a Methodist preacher, made speeches.
The formal program was followed by a feast, all in honor of Ballard and his
wife, Sarah Jane, who had worked steadily for his release.[1]

The celebration was a display of community solidarity, though Maud had
changed a great deal since Ballard went away. It had been only a post office
and general store when he left but was now a village with a business district,
schools, and churches, located a half mile east of its original site. The town's
growth had attracted newcomers, and among its people were many who did
not know Ballard and had no firsthand knowledge of the events that resulted
in his imprisonment. Thus his official welcomers painted a picture of his
crime that hardly fit the facts. In their speeches, they presented Ballard as

a scapegoat, wrongly prosecuted and convicted, innocent of complicity in the one event that had put Maud on the national map and had become, to some, its mark of distinction and, to others, a blot on its reputation—the burning of two Seminole Indian teenagers at the stake on a cold, moonlit night in early 1898. Because of a reward—"offered for blood," the speakers said—and "nefarious prosecution . . . by a band of carpet-baggers" who, they claimed, had interfered in a local affair, Ballard had "paid the penalty for the crime of others." The community was not welcoming home a criminal guilty of murder; it was welcoming home a sacrificial lamb.[2]

At least the speakers admitted that burning the Seminoles was a crime; that was more than the community had admitted in 1898. And though Ballard had been an active participant in events leading to the burning, the speakers were correct in asserting that he was less guilty than some. But he was also guiltier than others, and many in the crowd of celebrants knew it. One of the speakers—the Reverend Hodges—and doubtless numerous of his listeners had been a part of the mob. More than a hundred had participated in it during the course of a week, and perhaps that many more had witnessed the burning, including the prominent and insignificant, the substantial and the shiftless, the self-righteous and the wantonly vicious, preachers and saloonkeepers, lawmen and outlaws, outraged seekers after justice and ghoulish onlookers, all who crowded around the fire and, standing elbow to elbow, formed a brotherhood and sisterhood in crime. Spurred by the murder of a white woman by an Indian, presumably a Seminole, in the Seminole Nation just east of Maud, the mob invaded the Seminole Nation and terrorized Seminole men and boys for more than a week before selecting two, whom they took across the territorial boundary into Oklahoma to burn at the stake in a Baptist tabernacle a short distance southwest of Maud. The event had involved members of many households, especially in the hamlets of Maud, Earlsboro, and Violet Springs, all near the Oklahoma-Seminole Nation line.

The celebration of Ballard's return gave Maud citizens an opportunity, after the passage of years, to repair its image by putting the best face on the burning. After it occurred, the citizens of eastern Pottawatomie County, most of them not accurately informed of the facts, had conspired to thwart justice by refusing to cooperate with lawmen and prosecutors, hiding the identities of participants, and unwittingly helping to perpetuate a fabricated version of what had led to the burning. Though grand juries indicted nearly seventy of the mob members, only six, including Ballard, received prison terms. With Ballard's return from prison, the community could reaffirm its public position and present once more a united front against the reputation for lawlessness and mob rule that the burning had earned it, and which it felt it did not deserve. Thus Ballard, the speakers claimed, was not a criminal but a martyr "in defense of American womanhood." The crowd applauded loudly at their "every reference" to what the burners had done, expressed their "wholesale sympathy" for Ballard, acknowledged his "unstained citizenship," and hailed him "an honorable fellowman" and "a highly respected neighbor" who had been reclaimed. The ladies of Maud reinforced these sentiments by presenting Ballard with "a floral offering."[3]

This social occasion contrasted sharply with the reality of the event it indirectly celebrated—the deliberate and premeditated burning of two human beings. A majority of the citizens of Pottawatomie County, Oklahoma, were honest, hardworking, and law-abiding, but they allowed a few men from outside the community to use the citizens' desire for law and order to involve them in an act of personal vengeance. In 1906, the Maud community was blatantly pretending that some of its members had not given in to appeals to their basest passions. Their celebration of Mont Ballard's return sanctioned the actions of their relatives, friends, and neighbors. Some, without question, privately disapproved of what had happened, but few would make their feelings known. When they read the story of their celebration in the local newspaper, did any of those who had witnessed the burning pause after the editor's statement that the band's rendition of "Home, Sweet Home" and "America" had "kindled the fires of love and patriotism"?[4] Did any of them think about another fire that the mob had kindled no more than half a mile away one January night in 1898?

That such a crime against humanity could occur is not surprising. But how could the people celebrate it years later? On the surface, the mob's action appeared to be a form of violence familiar to most Oklahomans in eastern Pottawatomie County. To them, the burning seemed like the lynchings by mass mobs common in the United States, particularly the South, during the previous two decades. That was what the instigators of the burning wanted the public to think, and it was certainly the context into which federal authorities and local newspaper editors placed it. It is understandable why they presented it in that light. A majority of the people in eastern Pottawatomie County were from the South and border states and had only recently settled in Oklahoma, having arrived principally by way of Arkansas and Texas, through the Indian Territory, most of them during the 1890s, the decade of the greatest number of lynchings.

Given the southern heritage of the majority of the mob members, it seems easy to assign as a cause for the burning one of those commonly put forth by historians to explain mob violence in the South: racism, violence bred of economic or other frustrations, psychological tensions regarding gender and sexuality, or a culture-based sense of honor.[5] There was, without question, some degree of most, if not all, of these motives at work in the burning at Maud, but, as historian W. Fitzhugh Brundage points out in his recent study of lynching in the New South, such explanations of lynching are limited. "No explanation of the butchery of lynch mobs," he says, "can be entirely satisfactory unless it is sensitive to the historical and regional variations in mob violence."[6] In this case, the victims were Seminoles, not African Americans, and the lynching and its aftermath were products of their setting in both place and time.

Though Brundage's study deals with the lynching of blacks, particularly in Virginia and Georgia, his theory applies to the New South in general, which produced large segments of the population in Pottawatomie County, and is useful in helping to explain the dynamics of the Seminole burning. Mobs in the South, he finds, had certain shared elements: their pretext was to punish those who broke the law or violated local customs; they showed little or no regard for proving guilt or innocence of their victims; they were a form of racial repression; and they assumed "a degree of community approval." Brundage classifies mobs into four categories "based on size, organization, motivation, and extent of ritual."[7]

At first, the mob at Maud assumed the characteristics of what Brundage calls private mobs. These were "closed groups, secretive in nature," made up of relatives, friends, and neighbors of the victim to be avenged, "bound together by a shared sense of personal injury." Because they engaged in "a form of private vengeance," they were less given to ritual and "lacked the legitimacy that broad local favor might have given them."[8]

At the core of the mob leadership at Maud were relatives and friends of the murdered woman and her husband who came to the scene of the crime from Indian Territory and parts of Pottawatomie County some distance from Maud. They were strangers to most of the mob members from Maud. Though they made no attempt to disguise themselves, some hid their identities behind aliases, and they later sought to keep their roles in the affair from being made public. At their head was one who presented himself to the local folk as a professional burner by virtue of previous lynching experience in Texas. He and other mob organizers were calculating in their methods and sought to cover their wanton violence and their intent on vengeance with the guise of seeking justice. Nine days elapsed between the murder and the burning. During the first six days their harassment of the Seminoles was a family matter.

As days passed and they became frustrated in their efforts at finding the killer, the leaders changed their tactics and transformed the mob into one with the surface characteristics of what Brundage labels a mass mob. Such mobs, large in numbers and made up of anyone who was willing to take part, had "widespread local approval" and were fraught with ritual, such as public confession, prayer, and selection of symbolic lynch sites.[9] "Communal participation in mob violence," Brundage writes, "ensured that no single individual would be held responsible for the execution because mass lynchings became the expression of communal values of law and order, family honor, and white supremacy rather than personal vengeance. Mob members did not suffer wrenching guilt; rather, they rejoiced that they had punished a deserving victim."[10] If the mob leader had lynching experience as he claimed, he probably understood these social dynamics.

But in this case, there were obstacles to raising a mass mob. The murdered woman did not live in a white community but in the Seminole Nation, so the outrage against local white community values was lacking. To participate in a mob, the white citizens of Oklahoma had to enter a different federal jurisdiction in which local affairs were governed by the Seminoles, whose values—not those of the white community—informed the society. Murder was an outrage against local Seminole values, just as it was among the whites; the difference was that Seminoles did not resort to lynching to express that outrage. Because the crime occurred in the Seminole Nation, the mob leaders, in effect, had to "import" white outrage. They resorted to circulating rumors of rape. They sent out public notice of their intent to burn two Indians at the scene of the crime, though only one had committed the murder, but the unexpected arrival of a Seminole policeman disrupted their plans and caused them to delay. Two days later, they sent out another public notice. Both times, they drew perhaps as many people from outside the Maud community as they did from Maud. Most knew little of the circumstances of the crime, had no emotional attachment to the Maud community, and went to the scene mainly out of curiosity. Thus in preparation for the burning, the mob leaders ritualized the activities for the crowd's sake. Immediately after the burning, they left Maud, returning to their home communities and leaving the local residents to deal with the aftermath. To garner wider public support for what they had done, they circulated false stories through the newspapers, not only of rape but of necrophilia, to incense the general public in Oklahoma. Because they had truly believed those stories—or chose to in order to salve their consciences—the people of Maud could celebrate Mont Ballard's return in 1906.

Thus there were forces at work in the event that most citizens of Maud, even some of the mob members, and most federal officials did not seem to recognize. The burning had not been the work of a mass mob that gathered in emotional reaction to an outrageous crime. The local people had been manipulated by mob leaders, relatives of the dead woman and her husband and their allies, who had come from outside the Maud community, intent on lynching from the start, and had capitalized on a lack of adequate local law enforcement to give vent to their racial hatred. The harassment of the Seminoles and the burning of two of them reflected the propensity for wanton viciousness and malicious violence on the part of the murder victim's family and friends as they sought vengeance for her death. The mob leaders had contrived to make it appear to be a communal act to cover their part in more than a week of harassment, of searching for victims to burn, and finally selecting them on the basis of personal grudges. They were able to carry out their private scheme of vengeance because of the peaceful conditions that prevailed in the Seminole Nation, the unsettled conditions in Indian Territory owing to the impending dissolution of the tribal governments, and the confusion over criminal jurisdiction as federal courts assumed control of affairs in the territory.

Many who followed the mob leaders did not know the truth: that only one Indian, not two, had committed the crime for which two burned, that one of those was certainly, and the other probably, innocent of the crime, and that there had been no rape or sexual violation of the corpse. Those who knew the truth or learned it later refused to utter it, continuing to tell the story that the mob leaders wanted told and handing it down to subsequent generations, some of whom today are reluctant to discuss the episode with strangers or even talk about it among themselves except in hushed tones. What follows is an attempt to give an accurate account of the Seminole burning, to explain why and how it happened, and to show how, in its aftermath, Justice Department officials in Oklahoma and the Indian Territory struggled to see justice prevail but, at most, won only a minor victory over lynching in Oklahoma.

TWO

Borderlands

The post office and store that constituted Maud when Mont Ballard went to prison in 1899 sat within sight of the boundary between Oklahoma Territory and Indian Territory—at that point, Pottawatomie County and the Seminole Nation. West of the line, the landscape had dramatically changed since the creation of Pottawatomie County a few years earlier. The open landscape of the former Potawatomi and other tribal lands was now laid out in neat squares, marked by wire fences that enclosed fields of corn, cotton, and wheat, orchards and gardens, pastures and hay meadows, and home places with recently constructed frame houses and barns. Roads followed some of the lines that bounded the mile-square sections of land. From their side of the territorial boundary, Oklahomans looked east into a world that, for the most part, was culturally, economically, politically, legally, and racially alien to them. In an age driven by the concept of "progress," white Oklahomans found the Seminole Nation objectionable. Like the other Indian republics of the territory with their large land masses, it represented an impediment to the "progress" driving the American nation. From their side of the line, Seminoles witnessed the "order" that the Americans had imposed upon the former Potawatomi, Kickapoo, and Sac and Fox domains, and many of them feared—rightly so—the imposition of such "order" upon them. In 1897, the borderlands where these two radically different worlds met were remarkably peaceful, but the prevailing social and cultural opinions held about Indians by the whites in the region would provide much of the impetus for, and later justification of, the violence that occurred near Maud in the early days of 1898.

The creation of Pottawatomie County had been another step in the attrition of the Indians' land base during the preceding thirty years. On the eve of the Civil War, the Cherokees, Chickasaws, Choctaws, Creeks, and Seminoles, commonly called the Five Civilized Tribes, owned all of present-day Oklahoma except a disputed area between the north and main forks of the Red River, the panhandle, and a tiny region in the northeastern corner held by a number of tribes. Because factions of each of the Five Civilized Tribes fought for the Confederacy, the United States levied penalties at war's end, mainly in the form of land cessions. By treaties in 1866, the tribes gave up almost the western half of their territory, on which the United States later settled tribes removed principally from the Midwest, Great Plains, and Southwest. In the center of the territory, however, was an area that the government had not assigned to any tribe. A clamor soon arose for the opening of these Unassigned Lands, as they were called, to non-Indian settlement. Public appeal prevailed, and at noon on April 22, 1889, the area was opened by a land rush and became known in 1890 as Oklahoma Territory.

During the next five years, lands belonging to various Indian tribes opened in response to the continued agitation by American farmers for more land. Congress had passed the General Allotment Act in 1887, providing for the dissolution of the common tribal titles to the land and for the allotment of parcels to tribal members. The government began to apply the provisions of this act to the tribes surrounding Oklahoma Territory, allotting lands, opening surplus, unallotted lands to non-Indian settlement, and attaching the lands governmentally to Oklahoma Territory. Potawatomi and Shawnee, Iowa, Sac and Fox, and Tonkawa lands opened in 1891; Cheyenne and Arapaho land and Pawnee land in 1892; and Kickapoo land in 1895. In addition, the Cherokee Outlet, which the United States purchased from the Cherokees, opened in 1893. Pottawatomie County was created from lands formerly held by the Potawatomis, Shawnees, Kickapoos, Sacs, and Foxes.

Meanwhile, the Five Civilized Tribes, who still held their lands in common, were also under pressure to take individual allotments and open their surplus lands to non-Indian settlement. These Indian nations had been exempt from the provisions of the General Allotment Act; thus in 1893 Congress established a commission, chaired by former Senator Henry L.

Dawes of Massachusetts, to negotiate allotment agreements with the tribes. The Dawes Commission, as it was called, met stiff resistance from tribal leaders who insisted that former treaties guaranteeing their sovereignty be honored. At first, their resistance was effective, but Congress began to make legislative inroads that destroyed the tribes' ability to hold out. In 1895 it provided for a survey of the tribal lands and expanded the federal courts' jurisdiction in Indian Territory, and in 1896 it gave the Dawes Commission authority to create tribal rolls.[1]

These inroads on the nations' autonomy helped achieve the Dawes Commission's purpose—to negotiate away the tribal titles, to obtain agreements to allot lands, and to prepare the way for statehood and U.S. citizenship for the Indian population. By the spring of 1897, only the Choctaws and Chickasaws had negotiated, signing the Atoka Agreement on April 23. Congress increased pressure on the other tribes by enacting legislation providing for dissolution of the tribal courts on January 1, 1898. The Seminoles reached agreement with the Dawes Commission on September 17, 1897, and the Creeks on September 27. Only the Cherokees were outstanding. However, of the nations who had negotiated agreements, only the Seminoles ratified theirs. Despite the failure of the Cherokees to negotiate and the other tribes to ratify their agreements, the fate of the Indian republics was sealed. Congress was already deliberating legislation that would become the Curtis Act in 1898, providing for the allotment of lands without tribal approval if necessary.[2]

The Dawes Commission's success with Congress was owing in large measure to the propaganda campaign it had undertaken to shape public opinion regarding conditions in the Indian Territory. The commission had been created in response to demands by the American public and politicians that the Indian Territory be opened and brought into the Union. The public policy aimed ostensibly at securing the rights of not only the common Indian folk but the Americans who, by that time, were living in Indian Territory. However, the hidden motive was acquisition of more Indian land and natural resources. By the early 1890s, not only were thousands of Americans living in Indian Territory, but their numbers were increasing daily. After the Dawes Commission arrived in Indian Territory, the national press engaged in a propaganda war against the tribes and in behalf of these Americans. According to the picture painted by the press, the tribal governments were corrupt, and a few educated, "enlightened," influential Indians and intermarried whites in each tribe controlled huge quantities of the tribal domain to the detriment of the rank-and-file Indians. There was a good deal of truth in such reports, but the Indians were not the press's real concern. The thousands of Americans in Indian Territory, it claimed, had no political rights or educational privileges and were living in a state of lawlessness—a virtual reign of terror—which prevailed because of the ineffectiveness of the tribal governments in maintaining law and order.[3]

Views held by Oklahoma citizens regarding Indian Territory were a microcosm of national opinion. In their annual reports to the secretary of the interior, the governors of Oklahoma Territory had joined the clamor for allotting any remaining Indian reservations and nations and opening surplus lands to non-Indian, preferably white, settlement. Sentiments expressed in 1893 set the tone for subsequent reports: "The portions of the Indian Territory not yet opened to settlement are very wild and the Indians see only the worst side of civilization, and their progress will be very slow until they come in closer contact with the white man. Where lands have been taken in severalty the Indians have generally made an effort to accommodate themselves to civilization and have gone to work and are doing very well in agricultural and mercantile pursuits."[4] Oklahomans believed that the Indian governments were inefficient, corrupt, and incapable of maintaining order. In 1893 the governor wrote, "The condition of affairs in the Indian Territory is certainly very deplorable, and with the crudity of their forms of government it will always be difficult to suppress crime."[5]

Perhaps none of the arguments for dismantling the Five Civilized Tribes had caught the American public's attention like this last one—the allegations of general lawlessness and inadequacy of the tribal governments to maintain law and order. Although there was ample evidence that native citizens were no more lawless than the citizens of any western state, the rampages of Indian outlaw bands such as the Cook Gang in 1894 and the Buck Gang in 1895 made national headlines and contributed to Congress's determination to expand federal court jurisdiction in Indian Territory. Before legislation went into effect on September 1, 1896, felony cases involving whites in the Indian Territory, either as victims or perpetrators, were tried at Fort Smith, Arkansas, and at Paris, Texas. Law enforcement fell to U.S. marshals attached to the two courts. Congress had created a federal court at Muskogee, Creek Nation, in 1889 to handle lesser offenses. The congressional act of 1895 created two new courts in Indian Territory with jurisdiction to include cases previously heard by the Fort Smith and Paris courts, expanded the jurisdiction of the court at Muskogee to match that held by the other two, and gave jurisdiction over lesser offenses to U.S. commissioners, who held court at various places in the territory. The legislation left the tribes' courts intact to deal with cases that involved only their citizens. However, Congress dissolved the tribal courts on January 1, 1898, and took the final step toward judicial control over the Indian. By then, the publicity of outlawry in Indian Territory had become so commonplace that whenever an outlaw was tried and convicted in Kansas, Missouri, or Texas, the public often assumed that he was from Indian Territory.[6]

To Americans, the code of law enforcement and judicial process in the Five Civilized Tribes seemed simple if not crude by contrast to their own. In the Seminole Nation, for instance, the two main forms of punishment were flogging and execution by firing squad. Because there were no jail sentences, there were no jails. When the lighthorse police captured offenders, they held them for trial, without legal counsel, before the national council and the chief. The punishment meted out depended upon the severity of the crime. Two capital offenses were murder and repeated acts of theft, for which those convicted were whipped. The number of lashes given for other crimes varied according to the offense.[7]

The Seminole code, though simple and rigid, was effective and well enforced. During the three decades following the Civil War, the Seminoles earned a reputation for deep concern for law and order within their boundaries and for swift, unwavering execution of the law. Pressure from the band chiefs and active patrolling of their small nation by the lighthorse police maintained order. The people respected the law and feared the lighthorse policemen, widely acclaimed for their effectiveness as law enforcers. Seminole law enforcement had implications for outsiders as well. In the mid-1880s, the Seminoles received federal permission to shoot to kill any whites who were caught stealing from the Seminoles and resisted arrest.[8]

Outsiders viewed the laws of not only the Seminoles but the other Indian nations as "strongly tinctured with race customs—a mingling of the barbaric and English common law."[9] The Seminole code seemed particularly so. Even the Creeks, who were governed by a constitution, bitterly complained about the lack of trial by jury in the Seminole Nation and the swift and summary execution of Seminole laws.[10] Americans, whose idea of due process of law included trial by jury and the right to appeal, found the Seminole code brutal. Only Seminoles who committed criminal acts against whites or members of other tribes in the Seminole Nation or committed crimes outside its jurisdiction had the luxury of a trial by jury in the federal courts of Indian Territory or in the courts of Oklahoma Territory.

Although in general Oklahomans considered themselves law-abiding, their territory had matched or perhaps outstripped the record of Indian Territory for lawlessness during the first half of the 1890s. The land runs that opened the first few districts of Oklahoma Territory were themselves wild affairs, attended by violence and followed by vigilante law. Terrorism associated with townsite speculation had followed the run that opened the Cherokee Outlet in 1893. The territory provided the bases of operation at various times for some of the West's best-known outlaws. It was not until the mid-1890s that the U.S. marshal's office in Guthrie, the territorial capital, brought outlawry under control.[11]

Still, in some areas of the territory, Pottawatomie County especially, outlawry was slow to die. For years after it had been opened by a run on September 22, 1891, the county was known for horse stealing, murder, and other violent crimes. The county spawned its own gangs of well-known outlaws such as the Christian brothers and the Jennings gang. With the lingering outlawry in the county, there was also a persistent antagonism between local and territorial officials, especially the U.S. marshals, who Pottawatomie County citizens thought treated them unfairly, even persecuted them.[12]

Geography made the southeastern part of the county a common habitation for many of the last outlaw gangs, such as the Christians, and a general gathering place for rather undesirable characters, whose criminal activities spilled over into the Indian Territory. The county had been isolated until the late 1890s. Bordered on the east and south by Indian Territory, until 1895 it had neither railroad nor telegraph crossing it. Old trails, most of them branches of the Chisholm Trail, crossed the county from north to south, to fords on the Canadian River. Even before Oklahoma Territory was established, rustlers used these trails to drive stolen horses to Texas to trade for whiskey.[13] Simply crossing the river into the Chickasaw Nation or crossing the border into the Seminole Nation took criminals into not only different federal jurisdictions but different local jurisdictions as well. Criminals who congregated in southeastern Pottawatomie County had a number of possible routes to escape the federal authorities, whose headquarters were at the territorial capital at Guthrie.

A major contributing factor to crime in the region during the 1890s was the whiskey trade. Though the sale of alcoholic beverages to Indians was illegal, the saloons in Pottawatomie County provided much of the whiskey that found its way into the Seminole and other Indian nations. By 1894, the county had sixty-two saloons and two distilleries. Saloonkeepers in towns close to the line—particularly Keokuk Falls, Earlsboro, Violet Springs, Young's Crossing, and Corner—known primarily as "whiskey towns," were deeply involved in this illegal traffic. Saloonkeepers and merchants cultivated the lucrative Indian trade. Proprietors and clerks at key trading points in the county developed enough proficiency to conduct business in the language of the tribe whose members made up the bulk of their Indian trade: Seminole, Creek, Potawatomi, Sac and Fox, Shawnee, and Kickapoo.[14]

Like most Americans, not just those who lived near the boundaries of Indian country, the whites of Pottawatomie County had a sense of cultural and racial superiority to their Indian neighbors. Such attitudes, in fact, had been a mainstay among the population that settled Oklahoma Territory, which was born of the farmers' movement of the late nineteenth century. From the beginning, men such as David L. Payne and W. L. Couch, who had founded the boomer movement from their home bases in Kansas, had portrayed their followers as the "real" settlers who were locked in a political and economic struggle with corporations, whom they considered monopolists and speculators. Their mission, as they presented it, was to wrest control of public lands—which they considered the Unassigned Lands to be—from the corporations, especially cattle companies and railroads. Their rhetoric took on a decidedly anti-Indian cast as they argued that if the tribes who claimed title to the Oklahoma lands had land enough to rent to the cattle barons or to grant to railroads for rights of way, they had more land than they could use. In the boomers' view, Indian land title should give way to American economic necessity. The land should not be controlled by Indians under treaty title or the corporations for monopoly or speculation but by the "real" settler, the farmer.[15]

After the founding of Oklahoma Territory, propaganda that greeted travelers as they arrived at times added to the anti-Indian bias by depicting the Indians as uncivilized and lazy. A good example is the brochure for travelers published by the Atchison, Topeka and Santa Fe Railroad, which had put a line across Oklahoma from north to south. In its 1892 edition, the company prepared travelers for culture shock as they traveled south from Arkansas City, Kansas: "Keep your eyes wide open, and a short distance south of Arkansas City, where one of Fred Harvey's inimitable meals has made the inner man contemplative and happy, there is such a sudden transition from richness to poverty, from civilization to barbarism, that it is difficult to at once comprehend what the quick landscape change means. A group of Indians, lazily moving along the road on their patient ponies, explains the transformation. You are in a territory that belongs to our brother in red, who is always behindhand, except when it comes to a pretty fight."[16] Though the brochure announced that American civilization had entered the age of the chain restaurant, it failed to mention that the age of the Indian wars had passed, and many future Oklahomans entered the territory with a preconceived bias about the Indians they would see.

By the late 1890s, there was a popular feeling on the border that the Indians received special treatment from the government to the detriment of advancing American—especially white—society. The government was dominated, one Pottawatomie County editor argued, by policy makers who believed the Indians were abused and in need of government guardianship to protect them from the whites.[17] Such feelings ran high in Pottawatomie County, where whites who rented Indian allotments found their leases in jeopardy in 1895 as a result of a shift in federal regulations regarding leasing of Indian lands. The Indians, one editor argued, were capable of fending for themselves, but federal bureaucrats maintained them as wards simply to preserve their jobs. "This pack of emaculate [sic] saints," he wrote, "love the poor Indian, it has suddenly become a ruling passion with them, and the honest settler, who has put his land in cultivation, must lose his all."[18]

The anti-Indian bias took other forms. A general perception that the Indians were idle prevailed in the county. That idleness had been fostered, some claimed, by a governmental policy that fed and clothed the Indians and furnished them with spending money. Pottawatomie Countians, like many whites who rented land in Indian Territory or elsewhere lived along its borders, harbored a smoldering resentment at the Indians' occupation of good land, not using it "adequately" in their opinion. The government bought tracts of land from the Indians, they claimed, allotted the best land, tax free, to the Indians, and opened the surplus lands to settlement but made the settlers pay $1.50 an acre for it. The result was that the Indian had use of the land without paying taxes while the whites had to work poorer land and pay taxes to support the Indian. There was also the belief that government policy fostered lawlessness. The government's protection of the Indians, it was said, made the whites on the border vulnerable to depredations but powerless to protect themselves. Whites erroneously believed that Indians could commit crimes with impunity because of their ward status.[19]

Cultural biases concerning land use were reinforced when the Oklahomans looked east, across the border into the Seminole Nation. In only a few years, they had transformed their own landscape. The northern two-thirds of Pottawatomie County, particularly, had been well suited to farming and ranching. Neat farms producing corn, cotton, and wheat covered the landscape. Where the terrain permitted, straight roads ran north and south and east and west along the section lines, cutting the earth's surface into one-mile squares. Frame homes and farm buildings were everywhere, and permanent towns with regular street patterns and public edifices were rapidly developing. At the county's eastern border, all of that ended.

There were no towns such as Americans knew in the Seminole Nation until the late 1890s. Social structure was not based on where one lived but the tribe or town to which one belonged. Thus there were clusters of log houses, known as "towns" or "settlements," and trading centers that appeared on the maps as Wewoka, Sasakwa, and Heliswa, but it was not until the spring of 1897 that the Seminole National Council authorized the incorporation of the first—Wewoka—and platted an American-style town-site as a trading center on the railroad recently built across the nation. Most of the Seminoles lived in log cabins scattered throughout the countryside, where they farmed small patches of corn and vegetables and ran their hogs, cattle, and ponies on the public domain.[20]

Though the Seminole Nation had been surveyed in 1895 and 1896, there were no open section lines. Wagon roads connected Wewoka and Sasakwa, both near the eastern national boundary, and crossed the nation from Sasakwa, westward to Violet Springs, and from Wewoka, northwest to Heliswa and Mekasukey Mission and the Oklahoma border east of Earlsboro. In 1895, the Choctaw, Oklahoma, and Gulf Railroad built a line to connect South McAlester in the Choctaw Nation and Oklahoma Territory. It entered the nation at Wewoka and went northwest into Oklahoma, crossing the line near Earlsboro. But the common mode of transportation for the ordinary traveler was horseback. A network of trails webbed the nation, going wherever the terrain allowed horseback riders to pass and connecting the Seminole settlements throughout the nation.

The land of the Seminole Nation was not well suited to agriculture on a large scale. It was the smallest of the five Indian republics of the Indian Territory, less than forty miles long from north to south and about sixteen wide, bounded on the south by the Canadian River and on the north by the North Fork of the Canadian. Numerous tributaries that fed into those streams cut the landscape. Gently rolling hills in the north gave way to more rugged, broken land along the watersheds of Wewoka Creek in the central region and Little River and its major tributary, Salt Creek, in the south. Prairies with timber stands, where the land broke away to streams, dominated the northern section. In the south, particularly the southeast, timber dominated, with prairies on the upland areas.[21]

This terrain, though ill-fitted for large-scale farming, was good for livestock production. The Seminoles were herders long before they removed from Florida, and in the late nineteenth century most raised enough livestock for subsistence or to sell as a basic source of ready cash. Only Chief John Brown engaged in ranching on a large scale in the 1890s. In reality, he was simply the owner of record for thousands of cattle that Texas ranchers pastured in the Seminole Nation. His cattle ran on the open range through the winter, feeding on the prairie grasses that had cured on the ground. In the spring, huge roundups occurred, the cattle separated by owners' brands. To prevent Seminole cattle and horses from crossing into Oklahoma and devastating the farmers' crops, Brown had a barbed wire fence built on the Seminole Nation-Pottawatomie County border from the Canadian to the North Fork. Gates were built at points where main travel routes crossed the border. In the southern half of the nation, the gates were at Maud and Violet Springs.[22]

To Pottawatomie County citizens looking east, the fence that separated the two landscapes was a symbol of the demarcation of two extremely different cultures and worldviews. The line formed an equally startling view to Americans going from the Seminole Nation into Oklahoma. Paul McKennon, a young member of the team that surveyed the Seminole Nation in 1895 and 1896, wrote in mid-November 1895: "We crossed the Oklahoma line Friday at 4 o'clock. It looked real odd to us as we came across an immense prairie for ten miles without a sign of civilization and then to come in sight of the OK line three miles away. We could follow the line easily as far as we could see by the big wheat and corn fields and nice cottages. Every field ran down to the Seminole line and stopped. We were on a high ridge three miles off and could see it plainly."[23]

Obviously to this Arkansan, the fence represented the end of advancement of American society and culture from the west. However, the Seminoles, like members of the other Indian republics, were under mounting pressure to accept that progress, allot their lands, and open their territory to Americans. Before the 1890s, the Seminoles had been perhaps the least touched of the five tribes by the importation of American-based social, religious, and economic practices. During that decade, the Americans had encircled them and had brought American society to their western border. Their common border had been remarkably peaceful. The Seminoles minded their own business, and the Americans restrained their anti-Indian sentiment, sought the Indians' trade, especially in whiskey, and looked forward to the day when the tribal governments would be dissolved.

THREE

Landlords, Renters, Intruders, and Fraud

Despite the American public's general feeling of racial and cultural superiority to the Indians, the lure of economic gain to be extracted from "undeveloped" Indian land and resources made the Indian Territory appealing to thousands of whites and blacks. By 1897, nearly 300,000 were there. The landholding system among the tribes had contributed to this invasion of the tribal domains. The people of each tribe owned their lands in common, but individuals could occupy as much land as they could improve. Improvements included structures, wells, and fenced fields and pastures. These improvements were the property of the individual, who could sell them, rent them, or pass them down to heirs. Land not fenced was public domain, accessible to all, and livestock roamed freely upon it. To landless Americans, particularly poor whites and blacks from the South, so much open land was irresistible. Most of those who came rented land from the Indians or intermarried white or black citizens of the nations, but many of them were there illegally and were known as intruders. Whether renters or intruders, these people were mainly the castoffs of American society, who lived off the Indian resources, let their children grow up in ignorance, and raised the loudest cry for the government to dismantle the Indian nations. Because the intruders who occupied Indian land illegally lived on the fringes of society, they were subject to few laws, for which they had little regard.

From the ranks of these intruders would come the leaders of the Seminole burners as well as the hard core of the mob members.

The invasion of Indian Territory by poor Americans was abetted by members of the Indian nations who realized that they could make good incomes from rents on improvements. At first, this process was controlled somewhat by a system of official permits that allowed noncitizens to live and work in an Indian nation. By the late 1880s and early 1890s, however, influential members of the Chickasaw, Choctaw, Cherokee, and Creek nations began to claim large tracts, which they broke up into small farms and rented to Americans, without any pretense of working the land themselves. In effect, they became landlords, who merely collected rents. The practice of leasing became so common in the 1890s that a writer for one national magazine called the Five Civilized Tribes "a race of landlords," and his assessment had some merit.[1]

The practice had not at first been popular in the Seminole Nation. The Seminoles had been isolated until the early 1890s, more than a hundred miles from the Union Agency that served them at Muskogee and surrounded on all sides by Indian nations or tribes. The Seminole government had engaged in an aggressive policy of paying their lighthorse policemen to drive unwanted whites out of the nation, which was small enough that they could patrol it with some ease. In 1895, when Agent Dew M. Wisdom assessed Seminole affairs, he found them prospering and believed they had advanced in material wealth because of an absence of whites. The 1890 census listed ninety-six whites in the Seminole nation, and the agent reported the following year that the last intruder had been expelled. By the mid-1890s, however, with large numbers of renters and intruders in the other nations and whites on their western border, the Seminoles were renting, though whites never moved there in large numbers. Leases were made for varying lengths of time, but in the Seminole Nation they were usually long-term, five or ten years. If the lands contained no house, the renter might agree to build one in return for the use of the land. If log buildings already existed, the agreement might include construction of frame houses, excavation of wells, continued upkeep of the farm and clearing of farmland, or a share of the crop.[2]

Though this system of renting in Indian Territory attracted people of all sorts from the United States, one class dominated: poor farmers, mostly whites. To be sure, the Indian country attracted merchants, missionaries, confidence men, attorneys, and others looking for fruitful fields, but for the most part the Americans who flooded into the Indian Territory were a shift-less lot, most of them displaced by economic conditions in southern states, particularly Texas, Arkansas, Mississippi, Alabama, Georgia, Tennessee, and Kentucky. Most found their way to Indian Territory through Arkansas and Texas, which became the staging grounds for the invasion of the territory. These people, in general, were so ignorant that one Cherokee whose pen name was "Truth" wrote in 1882 that the government should remove them from the Indian Territory so that they could be civilized through mission work, much like that conducted by American benevolent societies among blacks of the South. If they were not removed, "Truth" predicted, they would resort to claiming citizenship in the territory by whatever means necessary to gain access to the land.[3]

These Americans, over whom the Indians had no jurisdiction, except to collect rents from some of them, were the source of much of the lawlessness that the American press complained about. As one writer put it in 1889, there were thirty-five thousand people in the Indian Territory who had no right to be there and were "morally unfit to live anywhere outside of prison walls." The Indian Territory became a place where people could go to escape their home jurisdictions and leave their pasts behind. So many did so that the schoolchildren of the territory sang a little song:

> Oh, what was your name in the States?
> Was it Thompson, or Johnson, or Bates?
> Did you murder your wife
> and fly for your life?
> Say, what was your name in the States?[4]

Most who came, whether honest or not, arrived with little more than a few personal possessions, their work teams, and some farming implements. Many were sharecroppers who had probably never owned land or had any expectations of doing so. The Indian Territory offered the prospect, at least, of a place where they could make a crop and, perhaps, improve the lot of their families. In 1892, the Indian agent at Muskogee reported that most new farms were being opened by noncitizen whites and blacks, who were the source of most of the intruder problems. As time passed, more and more failed to go through the formality of renting and simply squatted on the public domain of the Indian nations. This tendency reflected the growing disregard for Indians' rights and the mounting demand that the Americans be given legal access to the land they occupied. In 1896, the Cherokees asked and answered some significant questions regarding this class of Americans who, by that time, were overrunning the Indian Territory, in effect, usurping and using up its resources: "What would these same white men do if it were not for the Indian country? Who or what has caused their wanderings and drifting around in covered wagons,—homeless and poverty-stricken? They are your Tennesseans, Georgians, Carolinians that the worn-out lands of those states have set adrift—they are pure Americans for generations back who have been crowded west by a more frugal and industrious emigration."[5]

Despite what the Indian nations' records revealed and what arguments their leaders made, the American press claimed that the shiftless represented only a small percentage of the renter class. "The average renter is industrious, intelligent, and honest," said one writer. "But for him," he continued, "the five civilized tribes would be wearing gee-string and breech-clout, with no source of income but government annuities and the cattleman's grass money. The landlord class owe all they possess to his patient toil and enterprise."[6] Of course, the objective of such fallacious arguments, which ignored the history of the tribes, was to dissolve the tribal title to the lands and open them to non-Indian settlement.

The writer was correct, though, in suggesting that it was mainly the Indian landlords who welcomed the noncitizens into the Indian nations. Those Indians who objected to their presence or, by culture, did not understand them viewed the ever-growing presence of these Americans with alarm. The economically prosperous and educated classes of Indian citizens looked at these whites with disdain, forming conclusions about their character from their shiftless nature, their dishonesty, their poverty, and their willingness to let their children grow up in Indian country without an education. On their part, the white renters, inheritors of the racist attitudes of the southern and border states from which most of them derived, looked down upon the Indians and harbored a resentment at their ownership of the land. By 1896, the Cherokees believed that racism was inherent in the relationship between Indian landlord and white renter, the whites considering it "almost criminal that an Indian should rent to, and in that manner dictate terms to, an American citizen." The Cherokees spoke prophetically for Indians of the territory: "This very disposition to consider the Indian lower than the American citizen is what makes the Indian so tenacious of his lands and his separate government. He dreads the day of an association with the whites when his blood will be despised and himself oppressed because he is an Indian."[7] It was the dependence of these white renters upon members of the various Indian republics that the Dawes Commission had used to label the Indian nations impediments to American progress.

The subservient relationship of renter to landlord may have been particularly difficult for whites in the Seminole Nation. The close military, economic, and social alliances between the Seminoles and blacks since the Red Stick War had resulted in a great deal of racial intermingling. In the post–Civil War era, enrollment of blacks as tribal members and participation of the freedman bands in the national council and other Seminole affairs led to a public perception of the Seminoles that was particularly unflattering by late nineteenth-century American standards. In the 1890s, a decade of race separation, Jim Crow legislation, and legislative debates over how much blood quantum was required to make one black, the popular press stereotyped the Seminoles as all but universally "negroized," with only a few Indians that could "boast of blood uncontaminated by that of the African."[8] That opinion certainly prevailed in Oklahoma.[9] To most white renters in the Seminole Nation, the reversal of economic roles based on race was probably not only humiliating but galling, not necessarily because the Seminoles might have been mixed with Africans but because they were less mixed with whites than were the other tribes and were, therefore, considered less "civilized." Also, the aggressiveness with which the Seminoles had removed intruders and the tenacity with which they resisted the renter system no doubt contributed to resentments harbored by those on their borders who wanted to gain access to the land.

Prominent among the rising landlord class in the Seminole Nation was Thomas S. McGeisey, a man of growing prominence in Seminole affairs. Though McGeisey had had brushes with the law in earlier years, by the late 1890s he had a good reputation in the Seminole Nation. He was about forty-five years old, well educated for his time, and in 1894 was elected one of the three school commissioners for the Seminole Nation. In 1897, the national council named him one of the commissioners to lay out the townsite of Wewoka. That same year he was secretary of the Seminole National Council and secretary of the Seminole commission that negotiated with the Dawes Commission. He was selected to be secretary of the Seminole delegation who would be traveling to the American capitol early in 1898. McGeisey had five children: Martha by Lowiza, the daughter of Passack Harjo; Lincoln, Nora, and William by Seney, also the daughter of Passack Harjo; and James by his current wife, Mallosey. He wanted his children educated and sent his oldest son, Lincoln, to school in the Seminole Nation and to mission school in Pottawatomie County. McGeisey hoped that his teenage son would soon be able to relieve him of some of his business affairs. Lincoln, no doubt to his father's dismay, developed a taste for whiskey, the bane of many young Seminoles of that day, and was known in the Oklahoma saloons at Earlsboro and Violet Springs and by peace officers who broke his whiskey containers when they caught him.[10]

Thomas McGeisey had a substantial improvement, by the standards of the day, about three and one half miles east and somewhat south of the post office at Maud. The most common Seminole dwelling was a single-room house made of logs chinked with mud. On the McGeisey improvement, however, the main or "big" house had a central room, sixteen by seventeen feet, with a one-room half story above it. Attached to this hewed log section was a large frame room on each side, and the entire structure was covered with shingles. About twenty feet from the main house sat a fourteen-by-fourteen-foot kitchen with a large side room, all made of hewed logs and covered with clapboards. Nearby were other structures: a smokehouse, a dug well and well house with a shed attached, a barn, a wagon shed, and cribs. A rail fence enclosed the house and attached structures, and another enclosed the barnyard.[11] Southwest of the farmstead was a large field, enclosed by a rail fence, where McGeisey raised the corn to feed his livestock. In 1895, McGeisey decided to rent the farm, perhaps because as a salaried employee of the Seminole Nation, he was required to give time to the nation's official business.

His renter was a white farmer, a native of Mississippi, named Julius M. Leard.[12] Leard was at ease in Indian Territory, having spent most of his life there. He belonged to that class of shiftless farmers whose frustrations mounted as the years passed without any real hope of gaining title to the Indians' land. Leard was, in fact, part of the second generation of his family to be intruders on Indian land. His grandparents, James M. and Zora P. Lewis, had migrated from Lincoln County, Mississippi, to Arkansas in 1869. Poor and lacking teams, they and the families of their older children stopped near Clarendon in eastern Arkansas long enough to make a crop and then moved on up the Arkansas River, settling between Enterprise and Hackett City, just south of Fort Smith and within a mile of the eastern boundary of the Choctaw Nation. There they remained until the old man died in 1875. Meanwhile the older of their seven children and their families had moved into the Choctaw Nation, where their mother and younger siblings joined them.[13] Eventually, the whole Lewis clan would become a part of the ever-growing population of whites who overwhelmed the Indian nations during the next two decades. There were probably some decent folk in the Lewis clan, but there were a large number of rotten apples in the family barrel.

The year they arrived in western Arkansas, the older men in the family began to engage in criminal activity in the Indian Territory. During the next twenty years, the names of James Lewis's sons and sons-in-law appeared on the U.S. criminal court dockets at Fort Smith: David, John B., Thomas, and Edward Lewis, Preston Early, and David Leard. Charges varied widely—larceny, arson, violation of the tobacco law, and, most frequently, liquor trafficking in Indian Territory.[14] In fact, the Lewis clan became known as whiskey traders.

In the late 1870s, the Lewis family escalated their nefarious activities to include an attempt at fraud, along the lines that the Cherokee writer "Truth" predicted would become popular among such interlopers. Some of the Lewises had tried to get permits from the Choctaw Nation to remain legally in the territory as laborers and farmers, but they were refused, perhaps because of their growing criminal records. As U.S. citizens without permits, they were vulnerable to ejection by Choctaw authorities, but even more so because of their criminal activities. Thus, typical of many of the shrewder whites, in 1878 they laid claim to Choctaw citizenship on the basis of alleged Choctaw ancestry. They based their claim on depositions by Marcus and Sarah Lewis, a couple also claimed to be Choctaws but who in reality were blacks, whom the Lewis clan paid $300 in money, cotton, and other goods to go to Fort Smith to make their statements. Marcus claimed that his grandfather's uncle was also the uncle of the deceased James M. Lewis, whose mother was supposed to be part Choctaw.[15]

Armed with these depositions, the Lewis clan tried to present an application for citizenship to the Choctaw National Council in 1879 as well as to subsequent councils. However, they did not get so far as a review of their application by the Choctaw citizenship committee, their claim was so flimsy. The Choctaws had a clear-cut criterion for admission to citizenship: the applicant must be listed on a roll recognized by the nation or have a progenitor on such a roll. For the Lewis family, there were two possibilities. They must trace their ancestry to someone who enrolled to remove with the tribe after the Treaty of Dancing Rabbit Creek or to a recognized Choctaw who elected to stay in Mississippi. The Lewises could demonstrate neither. Besides the depositions of Marcus and Sarah Lewis, they had little other "evidence" to make a case. With the elder Lewis dead, they would ask the Choctaws to take their word that their father's mother was part Choctaw and that their father looked like an Indian. Marcus and Sarah Lewis disappeared after making the depositions, allegedly going back to Mississippi, but no one knew that with certainty.[16]

Whites like the Lewis family realized that claims such as theirs, no matter how spurious they might be or how disputed by tribal authorities, could create legal entanglements that would make their ejection difficult, if not impossible. If it looked as if the legal snarls might be untangled, they simply moved on. At first, some of the family had rented from Choctaws, but others had simply taken up land at will on the Choctaw public domain. After they applied for citizenship, they dropped all pretense of renting and simply squatted, farming and raising livestock and—especially in the case of Thomas and David Lewis—running whiskey on the side. Ironically, their application for citizenship may have called the attention of Choctaw authorities to them. Two years after the Choctaw Council refused to hear their flimsy claim, the Choctaws declared the Lewises intruders and called on the federal government to remove them from the Choctaw Nation. Though the Lewises went to the Indian agent at Muskogee to protest, the agent reaffirmed the Choctaw request that they leave.[17] Unlike many whites who tended to hang on despite orders to leave, the Lewis family complied. The Choctaws apparently had a strong case against them not only as intruders but as undesirable ones at that.

The clan scattered. Samuel and Rhoda Lewis Cowart went to Texas, but their older children remained in Indian Territory with the rest of the clan, who for the most part went to other Indian nations. Two families went to the Cherokee Nation, but most went among the Creeks. Only Thomas Lewis remained in the Choctaw Nation after the order to remove, but after two years, he went to the Creek Nation as well. In recent years, they had squatted on the Choctaw domain under the pretense of being Choctaws. Now, without any claim to citizenship, they squatted or rented in the Cherokee, Chickasaw, and Creek nations, most settling in the latter along the Canadian River.[18]

Among those who moved to the Creek Nation were Susannah Lewis Leard, who settled with her children Angie, Julius M., Rufus, Joseph Herschel, Madison, and Jackson. Her marriage to David Leard had ended in divorce, with Leard returning to Mississippi. In 1882 she married William Early, an Arkansan, whose brothers Preston and Hiram had married her sisters. Why Leard abandoned the family is uncertain, but the Lewis family may have cast him out, as they did those members who did not go along with the wish of the majority. Hiram Early had refused to be a part of their fraudulent claim to Choctaw citizenship, and the family forced him out. He and his wife went to Colorado, where they ultimately divorced. It was about the time of the claim that David Leard returned to Mississippi, leaving his children by Susannah Lewis to spend their growing-up and adult years in Indian Territory.[19]

Always the opportunists, some of the Lewis family members tried their luck at staking a claim in the great land rush that opened the Unassigned Lands on April 22, 1889: Thomas and Edward Lewis, Henry Clay Roper, Virgil Cowart, and Julius Leard. Only the Lewis men were successful. Both claimed town lots, but neither moved onto them, and all returned to the Creek Nation after a short time in Oklahoma Territory.[20]

Susannah Lewis Leard Early died in 1890, setting her family adrift once more. By that time, some of her children and other families of Lewis relatives had moved into the western part of the Creek Nation near present-day Hanna and Holdenville, Oklahoma, close to the eastern Seminole border, where they became the second generation of their family to engage in the illegal whiskey trade. In 1891, Indian agent Leo E. Bennett at Muskogee wrote, "Year by year the Territory seems to become a more inviting field to the avaricious vendors of the various kinds of intoxicating beverages, and it is with regret that I have to report that, despite the determined efforts of the courts and this agency, the introduction of intoxicants is increasing." By then, Julius and Rufus Leard were well established in this illegal activity and were known locally to "sell whiskey for a living." Bass Reeves, the well-known black deputy U.S. marshal, whose beat included the Creek and Seminole nations, described the Leards that year as "regular" whiskey peddlers who had been in business for "some time." Their uncle Thomas Lewis and their cousin Virgil Cowart were also known to the U.S. marshals at Fort Smith as whiskey peddlers, as was Cowart's brother-in-law H. Clay Roper. When law enforcement officers attempted to build a case against one of their members, the Lewis clan closed ranks, testifying to one another's innocence and swearing at times that the whiskey belonged to another member of the family who was not in custody or lived in some other jurisdiction and would be difficult to find.[21]

Ever moving, most of the families in the Lewis clan tried their luck in Oklahoma Territory once more. The lands of the Potawatomi and

Shawnee, Sac and Fox, and Iowa tribes opened to settlement by a run in the fall of 1891. A few members of the family took up homesteads, but most straggled in during the succeeding months and bought land or rented. By the mid-1890s, most had settled in Pottawatomie County near the western border of the Seminole Nation. Julius and Herschel Leard lived near Maud, but most, bearing the surnames Lewis, Early, McKibbon, Cowart, Roper, Adams, Guyer, and Clark had settled over twenty miles farther north along the North Fork of the Canadian near the northwest corner of the Seminole Nation. Meanwhile, some of the Lewis families had stayed in Indian Territory, which still remained a strong attraction even to those who had left. Members of the Cowart and Leard families had begun to backtrail into the territory by 1895, when Julius Leard rented the improvements of Thomas McGeisey in the Seminole Nation.[22]

By then, Julius Leard was in his late twenties and had a growing family. At Eufaula in 1888, he had married Mary Catherine Martin, whose family history in Indian Territory was similar to his own. The Martins were Tennesseans, who had migrated to the Indian Territory by way of Texas and Arkansas. Mary's father, Edward Martin, moved to Mannsville, Chickasaw Nation, where he was a merchant. Her brothers, however, remained close to Leard's family. Thomas W. and Will Martin lived at Beebe, Chickasaw Nation, where some of the Lewis clan lived, and John Stoke Martin lived near other of Leard's relatives at Holdenville in the Creek Nation.[23] By the time Julius and Mary Leard moved onto the McGeisey improvement, they had three children: Frank born in 1889, Sudie born in 1891, and Nannie born in 1892. After they had made their second crop on McGeisey's place, they had a fourth child, Cora, born in early 1897.[24]

By that time, Julius and Mary Leard and their family had joined nearly seventy other members of the Lewis clan and thousands of other whites and blacks in one of the largest attempts at fraud to be perpetrated against the Indian republics of the Indian Territory. The door opened for such fraud with the congressional act of June 10, 1896, which authorized the Dawes Commission to make rolls of tribal members. Though they were to accept the existing rolls maintained by the tribes, they also could take applications from persons who claimed tribal citizenship but whose names did not appear on the rolls. The commission could receive applications in the form of affidavits and other documents until September 10 of that year and must render all decisions by December 1.[25] The Lewis clan saw this law as a means to revive their old spurious claim to Choctaw rights by virtue of their alleged Choctaw blood. For years, they had illegally occupied Indian land and used its resources; now they intended to possess it.

Like thousands of other opportunists, they had to work fast. Because most of them resided in Pottawatomie County in 1896, Shawnee became their center of operations, while those in the Indian Territory went to McAlester, Choctaw Nation. They were assisted in making their affidavits by an infamous family of professional claims makers named Arnold, who had apparently encouraged them in making their claim to Choctaw citizenship in the late 1870s. The Arnolds were former slaves whose roots were in Virginia and Georgia and who had made their way to the Indian Territory by way of Arkansas. Whites had chased them out of Logan County, and they fled to the Choctaw Nation, where, to outsiders, they passed as Indians and began making claims, first to Cherokee and then to Choctaw citizenship. Along the way, they became associated with the infamous W. J. Watts and his citizenship association, which had plagued the Cherokees with citizenship claims for two decades.[26] The affidavits that the Arnolds helped the Lewis family generate, as well as others they made themselves, did little more than establish their kinship to each other. Their claim to Choctaw citizenship rested on the same two affidavits of Marcus and Sarah Lewis that they had used in their spurious claim before the Choctaws in the late 1870s.[27] Their association with the likes of Watts and the Arnolds measured them as a part of the hordes who were determined to undermine the tribal nations at any cost.

The Dawes Commission's decision no doubt displeased the Lewises. About 75,000 people had filed claims with the commission before the deadline. The commissioners realized, of course, that if all the claims were just, there were more people excluded from membership in the tribes than currently belonged to them. When the decision process ended, the commission had admitted only 2,075 people to the rolls, and not a member of the Lewis family was among them.[28]

Though thwarted once more, they were persistent in their opportunism and refused to give up. The congressional act of June 10, 1896, had provided for appeal of the commission's decisions to the federal courts of the Indian Territory. Thus in early 1897, the Lewis family, their case consolidated under the name of the matriarch, Zora P. Lewis, appealed their case.[29] Some of the family, especially those finding life difficult in Oklahoma, began to backtrail to the Choctaw and Chickasaw nations, for while their case was under appeal, the Indian authorities were powerless to molest them. In the fall of 1897, Julius Leard harvested his third crop on Thomas McGeisey's farm in the Seminole Nation. No doubt he and the other Lewis family members looked forward to a settlement of their citizenship claim, which the federal court would soon hear.

The relationship between McGeisey and the Leards was apparently good. Julius Leard felt at home in Indian country, having lived there since childhood. He could speak the Muskogee language sufficiently to conduct affairs related to his whiskey trade and farming in the Creek and Seminole Nations. He had made an effort to "blend" in by virtue of the claim not only to Choctaw citizenship but, by 1897, to one-quarter Choctaw blood.[30] McGeisey may not have known about Leard's whiskey running or the ruthlessness and dishonesty of the family to which he belonged, but he certainly knew the type of shiftless renters that Leard represented. Still, McGeisey apparently trusted Leard. He had left his furnishings in the rented house: heating stoves, bedsteads, a rocking chair, kitchen table and chairs, kitchen utensils, and even his clocks. In one of the side rooms he had stored his family Bible and his library of some forty books, including treaties, histories of the Indians, works on medicine, geographies, and other school texts. Also stored in the side room were six trunks, two containing the clothing and personal items of McGeisey's deceased wife and the others the clothing of McGeisey and his children.[31]

By the Christmas season of 1897, Leard's prospects looked good. Thomas McGeisey then lived about a mile east of the Leard farm, but the Leard's had no white neighbors nearby. However, they had many friends and relatives who lived in the Maud community, just west of the Oklahoma line. Julius's brother Joseph Herschel, five years his junior, had married Roena, the daughter of David and Mary Guinn, the parents of a large family of hardworking farmers living near Maud. Like Leard's family, the Guinns had gone to Oklahoma by way of Arkansas and the Creek Nation, but unlike the Lewises, the Guinns had made no claim on Indian land and had been successful homesteaders in Pottawatomie County. Julius and Mary Leard counted the Guinns among their close friends. On Christmas Day 1897, they and their children were guests at a large gathering for dinner at the home of David Guinn. The men hunted squirrels, sixty-eight of which the women cooked and served up as the main course.[32]

On the Seminole side of the line, the Seminoles also began to celebrate the holidays. In the Creek and Seminole Nations, American-style dances, referred to as "fiddle" dances, were commonly held during the week from

Christmas to New Year's Day. As people in the borderlands began to celebrate the festive season, they could not have envisioned, in their wildest imaginations, the terrible events that would occur at the Leard farm east of Maud only a few days later.

FOUR

Murder and Riders
after Vengeance

About half an hour before sunset on Thursday, December 30, 1897, an Indian rode up to the yard gate at the Leard farmhouse on a bay pony with a roached mane. He dismounted, hitched his horse, came into the yard, and approached Mary Leard. He was a stranger, a big man with a scar on one cheek. He told her that he had stopped to borrow a saddle. She could see that he had no saddle but had thrown something that looked like an old quilt over the pony's back. She refused him, saying that her husband was not at home and "I do not know you." He told her that he lived three miles down Salt Creek, but she stood firm: "I cannot loan you the saddle; Mr. Leard is away from home." The stranger then asked for a drink of water, went into the kitchen, which stood about twenty feet from the main house, got a drink, turned around, and walked back out onto the porch. Strangers stopping by and expecting hospitality were not unusual in isolated regions of Indian Territory, but there was something about this man that Mary Leard did not trust. From inside the kitchen, where she had followed him, she watched the stranger. Perhaps he lingered too long, or, as her son, Frank Leard, said, "Mama saw him do something." For whatever reason, she became suspicious of him. She went out, let loose a bulldog the family kept tied in the yard, and tried to sic it on the Indian, but instead of chasing him, it went after some hogs that were running loose in the yard.

Mrs. Leard ran into the big house and got a gun. When the Indian saw her come out with it, he mounted his pony and rode west.[1]

As she went about the chore of getting supper, Mary Leard no doubt wished that her husband, Julius, would return. He had gone to Oklahoma that morning to help his brother Herschel gather corn on a farm about three miles south of Maud. When he left, he intended to return in the evening, for Herschel's farm was only about six miles away. Thus as evening came on, Mrs. Leard had no reason to think that her husband would not be home that night. However, "a friend" stopped over at Herschel's house, and Leard decided to spend the night, apparently with few worries about leaving his wife and children alone in the Seminole Nation.[2]

About half an hour after the stranger left, Mary Leard and Frank, who was eight years old, were busy carrying the food she had prepared from the kitchen to the big house. Frank had carried one load and had started back to the kitchen when he spied the man standing at the corner of the house. Frank ran to the kitchen and told his mother that the "Indian boy was back," just as the stranger came through the east door and began to say something to Mrs. Leard. She picked up baby Cora and ran out the south door. The Indian grabbed the rifle, which Mary Leard had brought into the kitchen, and chased her through the yard. He tried to shoot her twice, but the gun only snapped, apparently because it contained no cartridges. From the front porch of the kitchen they ran in a circle, and when Mary Leard was about eight feet from the porch once more, he caught up and hit her over the head with the rifle. She went down without making a sound, falling on the baby. The Indian went back to the big house, threw the rifle on the bed, returned to Mary Leard, and turned her off the baby. He picked Cora up by one arm and threw her onto the floor of the house. "I want some money," he told Frank Leard. "We haven't got any," the boy replied. "You are a liar," the killer said. "You have got the money." "No, we haven't," Frank responded. "Papa has got the money and gone with it, he has all the money we have got." The Indian said nothing else, stepped off the porch, walked past Mary Leard's lifeless body, and went out the gate he had come through when he first appeared. He disappeared and did not return. He was apparently alone, for Frank listened intently but heard no one else around.[3]

The Leard children spent a harrowing night. Frank held the door ajar, keeping watch to see if the killer returned. Unable to drag their mother's body inside, the children watched as the hogs that were loose in the yard became attracted to the body. Knowing that hogs feed readily on dead flesh, the children kept them away from the corpse until the cold forced them to close the door. During the night, the hogs began to feed on the body.[4]

When daylight came on December 31, the Leard children went for help. Though their landlord, Thomas McGeisey, lived about a mile east of them, the children did not go that direction but toward Maud, probably because that was where their father was or because it was more familiar territory where relatives and friends lived. Frank, six-year-old Sudie, and five-year-old Nannie walked to Maud to give the alarm, carrying the severely injured baby, Cora, who would die from her injuries a few months later. They arrived at Maud about ten o'clock.[5]

David O'Bright, a plasterer working at Maud, and local residents George Pettifer, Bert Catron, and Jim McPhail mounted their horses and rode quickly toward the Leard home. About two hundred yards from the house, they overtook Julius Leard, who was returning from his overnight stay at his brother's house, and told him what had happened. At the house, they found Mary Leard's body lying in the yard. The hogs were still eating at it, having nearly devoured the head and neck. Catron later said that it was difficult to say even if she had been murdered, "the way she was eat up." The men covered the corpse with a sheet and carried it into the house, and a short time later several women arrived to dress the body, which was laid out in the kitchen.[6]

Julius Leard and his friends, who gathered as the news spread, at once undertook to find his wife's killer. He sent word to Thomas McGeisey, asking him to come at once to help him. McGeisey was preparing to visit his mother, who lived some distance away, to bring her to his house so she might attend New Year weekend church services, but sent word that he would go to Leard's upon his return. As news spread at Maud, people continued to gather, and groups formed to go out in search of a likely suspect. Leard had a good description of the killer, which he had obtained from Frank. They were looking for a "big" Indian with a noticeable scar across one cheek.[7] Though both man and horse, a bay with a roached mane, had distinctive features, Leard knew no man who fit that description or who rode a horse of that type.

The groups of white Oklahomans who were scouring the countryside, mainly close friends and relatives of Julius and Herschel Leard, were in an angry mood. If Leard had given them a description of the killer, they ignored it and attempted to arrest any Indians they met in the vicinity, perhaps not so much on suspicion of murder but to find if they had any information about the killer. Six of them ambushed two young Creeks and a Seminole, Billy and Chippy Coker and Cobley [Copeler] Wolf, who were riding about two miles southeast of Maud. From their hiding place behind a knoll, they sent bullets whizzing past the Indian youths' heads and shotgun pellets splattering into tree limbs nearby. Billy Coker and Wolf, though unarmed, charged the whites and demanded to know why they were being fired on. The men, who included George and Russell Guinn, brothers-in-law of Herschel Leard, denied that they had fired the shots. Apparently unnerved by the charge, they did not attempt to arrest the youths but tried to persuade them to go with them to Leard's to view Mary Leard's body. The boys refused and went on their way to Passack Harjo's settlement, a few miles further south, to attend a fiddle dance that night. Chippy Coker, who was only about twelve years old, had continued to ride when the shooting started and did not go with them.[8]

Meanwhile, Kinda Palmer, a Seminole lighthorse policeman who lived near the scene of this incident, heard about Mary Leard's murder and went to investigate. Even though he had no authority because the victim was white, he went because an Indian was allegedly involved. Even if both victim and perpetrator had been Seminoles, his authority would have been questionable because the tribal court authority was due to end the following day, when the federal courts would assume all jurisdiction in the Indian Territory. Palmer took with him Tulmasey [James Wise], who was working as an assistant lighthorseman during the holidays. At Leard's house, Leard, Russell Guinn, Jesse Guinn, and three others ordered them at gunpoint to dismount. Tulmasey was unarmed, and Jesse Guinn disarmed Palmer. Some of the whites held them under guard in the house while Leard appropriated Palmer's horse and saddle and Jesse Guinn his pistol for their own use during the day. Palmer and Tulmasey, who did not understand English very well, did not know exactly why they were receiving such treatment. "We were scared," Palmer said, "and suspected that the white men may have thought we were guilty of the murder of the white woman." Tensions were running high in the gathering crowd, which included, from the Maud community, Russell, George and Dave Guinn, George Cash, George Pettifer, Philip H. Cooper, and John Malloy, some of whom had earlier waylaid Billy Coker and Cobley Wolf.[9]

Backed by the crowd, Julius Leard began to talk about revenge. He started for Thomas McGeisey's place shortly before noon. Having gone for his mother and brought her to his home, McGeisey had started for Leard's

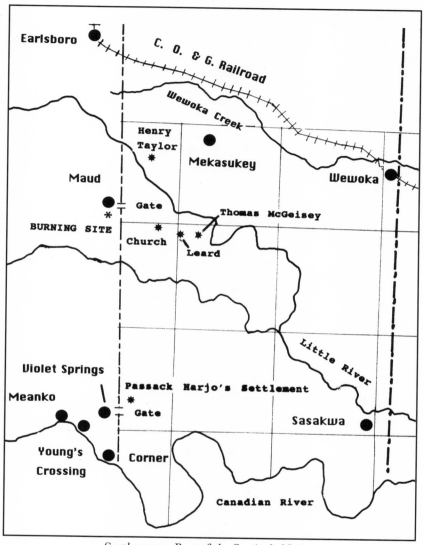

Southwestern Part of the Seminole Nation

(Map by G. T. Hanson)

farm and met Leard and two others on the road. They turned back with him, Leard appealing to McGeisey to help him find the Indian who had murdered his wife. McGeisey was due to leave for Washington in a few days as a tribal delegate, and though he wanted to help, he told Leard he had no time. McGeisey's response apparently did not sit well with the distraught Leard, who vowed revenge and told McGeisey, in McGeisey's words, that "if he didn't find the real murderer of his wife he would have to have revenge to kill two or three Indian boys, and two or three hours afterwards he was preparing to go out and hunt boys again, and while he was at the gate he said he would have to have revenge if he was to have to kill the whole tribe."[10]

The group that Leard was preparing to lead when he said this was acting on information supplied by Louis Graham, a black who lived on Passack Harjo's place about six or seven miles south of Leard. Apparently unaware of the killing, Graham had gone to Leard's farm to buy corn. For some reason, the men who had congregated by that time were interested in finding a twenty-two-year-old Seminole named Mose Tiger, whom Graham knew and had seen the night before at the dance at Passack Harjo's settlement. The mob decided that they should go in large force and set out for Passack Harjo's.[11] Meanwhile, the crowd held Graham prisoner with Kinda Palmer and Tulmasey.

The mob that descended on Passack Harjo's settlement was huge, about twenty in all. Among them were Leard, George Guinn, Cap Guinn, Russell Guinn, Herschel Leard, George Cash, Sam V. Pryor (alias Texas Ranger), Thomas W. Martin, George Pettifer, Joe Cherry, Joseph Williams, J. M. Dickerson, Jesse Guinn, Charley Woodard, and Dave Guinn. This group consisted primarily of Julius and Herschel Leard's relatives, either by blood or marriage. Dave Guinn was Herschel's father-in-law, and the other Guinns and Woodard were his brothers-in-law. All were from Maud except Martin, who was Julius's brother-in-law, and Pryor, the husband of his and Herschel's cousin, who lived in Texas but was there on business. Their purpose was ostensibly to pick up Mose Tiger, but on the way into Passack Harjo's settlement, they picked up his son Sam P. Harjo. They took the people at the settlement by surprise, for this was the first that anyone there had heard about Mary Leard's murder. The mob took into custody at gunpoint George P. Harjo, Johnson McKaye [Chauncy McGuire], Sever [Sefa], Parnoka (Sever's father), Lincoln McGeisey, and Mose Tiger, who had gathered at Passack Harjo's for a dance that night. Leard's gang had these in custody when Billy Coker and Cobley Wolf rode in after their earlier skirmish with the Guinns, and, unfortunately, into the hands of the mob.[12]

The mob returned to Leard's place with their prisoners under guard in a wagon loaned them by Passack Harjo. On the road about 4:00 p.m., they met Louis Graham, whom the guards at Leard's farm had released. Texas Ranger, apparently in command, ordered him to return with them, though Julius Leard protested, "He is all right; I know him." Texas Ranger insisted. On the road they also picked up Wiley Morgan [Markey] and arrived at Leard's farm about sundown. "We were all taken into Mr. Leard's house," the prisoners said, and, at Leard's request, "Mr. Leard's little boy passed around and looked at all of us good to see if he could recognize the man who had killed his mother, and he could not." The boy was excited but said that only Mose Tiger resembled the killer. Some of the men thought perhaps Frank was too excited to be certain and encouraged him not to be afraid and to look again. Still, he failed to identify Tiger positively. Then, said Louis Graham, "They made Mose Tiger pull off his slicker, and they told the boy to look at them again and after examining each one, including Lincoln McGeisey, the little boy said that none of them was the one." After an hour and a half to two hours, he still could not identify anyone; thus, said Graham, "They turned all of them loose only Mose Tiger and they kept him." They also released Kinda Palmer and Tulmasey, whom they had held all day. Said Palmer, "Seeing that the mob were very mad, we were afraid of our lives until we were turned loose."[13]

This roundup had brought no results. Frank Leard's failure to identify the killer among the captured Seminoles and Creeks put the mob in an ugly mood. According to Louis Graham, the general sentiment in the crowd was that they wanted to find the killer, but if they did not, they would kill four of the other "sons of bitches" and then "go to farming."[14]

At this point, U.S. officials in the Indian Territory became involved in the search. While he was at Passack Harjo's settlement that day, Julius Leard had torn the pasteboard back from a book and had written a note on it to deputy U.S. Marshal Nelson M. Jones. "My wife was murdered last night; I want you to come at once," he told Jones, and sent the note by Ben [Pin?] Harjo. Jones, whose jurisdiction embraced the Seminole Nation, was under the command of U.S. Marshal Leo E. Bennett, assigned to the court for the northern district of Indian Territory at Muskogee nearly a hundred miles away. Jones had had his appointment only a few months and at the time rented land from Passack Harjo a short distance southwest of his landlord. So far from headquarters, Jones was isolated and seemed uncertain what to do. He could hardly believe the note. He went to see his nephew, Jim Jones, who lived a mile away but across the border at Violet Springs, one of the "whiskey" towns in Pottawatomie County, to see if he had heard any details, but he had not. With George Moppin, a black who could speak the Muskogee dialect, they went to see Ben Harjo, who told him "that the woman was certain murdered" and that Mose Tiger was under suspicion. Instructing his nephew to follow him the next day, Nelson Jones took Moppin with him as his interpreter and arrived at Leard's house about eleven that night. He found about fifteen men there, including the Leards; Thomas W. Martin (whom Jones called Abraham or Abe); Tom King, who had come from the Chickasaw Nation with Martin; "Parson" A. E. Butterfield; Robert Ogee; and a man Jones knew as Morris and thought was Leard's cousin but who in reality was H. Clay Roper, married to his cousin. Besides Tiger they had in custody an Indian called Sam Waters, who was allegedly "crazy" but had established his whereabouts at the time of the murder. Thus Jones released him.[15]

Jones began an investigation that night. "I asked Laird," he said, "what description the children had given to him in regard to the guilty man in describing him, and he told me they described an Indian about the size of John Palmer and looks like John Palmer; but he says, John Palmer ain't the man. I says have you got anybody else that you know in this country that you think is the man? and he says, no, not but one man." Said Jones, "He said if that is not the man who is guilty of this crime that he did not know who to say was." Who this man was is uncertain, but Jones knew whom Leard referred to and responded, "Mr. Laird, that man is too big a man for to go with the size that your boy says; he is too large a man." Leard replied, "Well, he is kind of an onery [sic] fellow and it must be him."[16]

In an attempt to get a better lead, Jones questioned Frank Leard about the murderer. To Jones, Frank was a boy of "average intelligence," and "a pert boy for his age and having been raised out there in the country." Frank told the marshal essentially what Leard had reported from him: that his mother's killer was "a man that looks like John Palmer." He was big like Palmer, and wore black pants tucked inside his boot tops. Jones asked if George Harjo fit the description, but Frank, who knew George, said he was not the man. Leard asked Frank if Lincoln McGeisey fit the description, and Frank replied, "No, Papa, I know Lincoln McGeesey [sic], and I know he ain't the man." He pointed to a prairie about two hundred yards across that spread to the south in front of the house and said, "I would know Lincoln McGeesey across that prairie." Leard agreed with his son's statement; thus why he asked specifically about Lincoln is uncertain. Then Leard had another thought and said to Jones: "I don't know to save my life if it ain't the man that wanted to borrow 50¢ of you at Violet Springs one day; if it ain't that man I do not know who it could be." Jones knew to whom Leard referred but could not recall his name. He lived west of Wewoka, between there and the Leard place. Through his careful questioning of Frank in the presence of Julius and Herschel Leard, Jones learned that there had been only one Indian on the premises, that he was not drunk, and that after he had killed Mrs. Leard and demanded money from Frank, he left and did not return. Frank believed that the killer was alone, for he had not heard him talking to anyone else and he had seen no one else as he held the door cracked to keep a lookout.[17]

Jones looked for possible motives for the crime. He asked Frank as delicately as he could if Mrs. Leard had been raped, for earlier he had heard some speculation about its possibility. Frank said that the Indian had not touched his mother after he hit her with the gun except to turn her over to pick up the baby. Though Jones did not view the body, he obtained secondhand reports from Mary Guinn, who had dressed the body in preparation for burial. Her husband, Jesse, told Jones that Mrs. Guinn had found no evidence of sexual assault. Jones said, "I told him I wanted to know, I wanted to understand thoroughly, and he said, my wife don't find that she was disturbed at all after she fell on the ground." Jones concluded that Mary Leard's killer "did not foully treat her in any way" and that the object of the attack was not rape but revenge. "I would think," he said, "to speak in this way, that he got insulted about the saddle and her trying to sick the dog on him and trying to drive him away caused him to come back there and commit the deed he did. That is the way I have fixed it up."[18]

Jones may have had some ideas about possible suspects, given his pointed question about George Harjo, for Saturday morning, January 1, 1898, he and Moppin went home by way of Passack Harjo's. His object, he said, was to talk to "Indian boys" to see if he could "get any evidence of the guilty man." On the way, he met Dave Coker, a Creek who had served the Seminole lighthorse police. Coker, Billy and Chippy's father, had heard no talk about the murder. There was to be a dance again that night at Passack Harjo's settlement, and Jones had decided to attend to see if he "could find out if the guilty man was there." But Coker volunteered to go instead, arguing that if the guilty man was there, he had a much better chance than Jones of finding him. Coker, who had no authority of any kind, agreed to let Jones know if he heard anything. Satisfied with this arrangement, Jones went on home. A short time later, his nephew Jim Jones passed on his way to Leard's, where Jones had asked him to go the day before. Apparently changing his mind about his original intent to investigate at Passack Harjo's settlement, Jones returned to Leard's with his nephew.[19] Unfortunately, this kind of indecisiveness would characterize the way Jones conducted himself during the next few critical days of the investigation.

While Jones was absent from Leard's farm, the mob had fanned out in squads over the countryside, following the web of trails, searching for likely or unlikely suspects, and apparently ignoring the description of a large man with a scar on his face. That day they concentrated on areas north of Leard's farm. Two men arrested Billy Thlocco [also called Billy Harjo], a nineteen-year-old Seminole who lived near Mekasukey Academy. Billy was at the house of Henry Taylor about three miles southwest of Mekasukey and five from Leard's when he was arrested. He understood only a little English, so Taylor interpreted for him. "George Pettiford [Pettifer] and a man named Grant and a man named [George] Cash and a lot of others whose names I don't know arrested me," said Billy. "Tied my hands and feet, tied my hands down with my feet and then kicked me; George Pettiford kicked me about four times and he hurt too; they then said hurry up and tell who killed the woman; there was a one eyed man who kicked me and a man knocked me down and hurt me; then they took me down to Laird's house before the little boy." At Leard's, where they found Leard and a number of others assembled, Frank Leard looked at Thlocco but did not accuse him. They bound Thlocco's legs with a chain, brought it up and around his hands, passed it around his neck, and then fastened the end of it to a large staple in the floor.[20]

In the afternoon, another group brought in a man named Brown and Moses Davis, both in chains. After a couple of hours, Jones released them because the Leard children could not identify them. Some in the crowd objected to his releasing Brown, but they finally dropped their objections and let him go. Just before sundown Jones left the Leard farm once more, going home, where he had a prisoner held for assault with intent to kill. Jones planned to spend the next day looking for two witnesses in the case against the prisoner and then take him to Wewoka the day after that to appear before U.S. Commissioner Walter T. Fears.[21] Why Jones let a case of assault with intent to kill take precedence over a murder investigation is uncertain, but the decision was apparently typical of him.

Unfortunately, Jones was not a man of strong will or character and reputation. He drank heavily and, at fifty-two, was getting too old for the job he was doing. A native of Tennessee, he had lived in Texas from childhood until 1871. At that time, he moved to Burneyville in Pickens County, Chickasaw Nation, and then about 1889 to Purcell, where he farmed for four years. The move to Purcell may have been a result of his growing criminal record in Pickens County, where he was accused of large-scale cattle rustling in 1883 and of murder in 1886. By 1895 he was at Violet Springs and Young's Crossing in Pottawatomie County, running a grocery store and saloon. Then in February, 1896, he moved to the Seminole Nation, where he served as a deputy in the Indian Territory under Marshal S. M. Rutherford. When Leo E. Bennett was named U.S. marshal for the northern district of the Indian Territory, Jones was commissioned a deputy under his command on October 16, 1897.[22]

Jones's absenting himself suggested to the mob that they could do very much as they pleased. Late in the day, sometime before Jones left, Leard had released Mose Tiger, who had been among the group brought in from Passack Harjo's the day before. Tiger could not understand what Frank Leard had said about him during his interrogation. "They made us boys stand while the little boy looked at us and examined us," Tiger later said through his interpreter. "The little boy looked at me first, and when he looked at me he told his father and the crowd that I was the boy; I couldn't understand him but Lewis Graham he understands English told me then; he told me what the boy said. I was scared and thought they were going to kill me because of this boy's awful mistake." After they let the others go, they tied his hands with wire that cut into his wrists and kept him that way until, after twenty-four hours of terror, they let him go.[23]

About 7:00 p.m., Julius Leard, Jesse Guinn, Mont Ballard, and three others arrested Albert Washington several miles north of Leard's farm. They started back to Leard's with Washington walking ahead of their horses. His pace was apparently too slow, for they forced him to run, hitting him on the head and pushing his head with their pistols. Threatening to kill him, Leard ordered him to respond to their questions in English. By the time they arrived at Leard's place, the crowd had swelled, as it would every night, to about forty armed men, who were standing around a huge log fire that they kept burning day and night in the yard. They were in a mood to act. Someone in the crowd asked what Leard intended to do with Washington. Someone else said they had "better hang the God damned Indian." They brought Frank Leard out to look at Washington, but he did not identify him as the killer. The men nevertheless kept Washington under guard near the fire until about two o'clock the following morning, when, without explanation, they told him to go.[24]

Before breakfast the following morning, Sunday, January 2, the mob released Billy Thlocco, whom they had held since about ten the previous morning. Like Mose Tiger and Albert Washington, he had received rough treatment, chained all the time to a large staple in the floor of the upstairs room of the house. During his captivity, George Pettifer and others kicked him, punched him with their Winchesters and shotguns, cursed him, and threatened to kill him. Leard also harassed him, at times sitting in front of him and asking questions while a crowd stood around, saying that if he did not tell who killed Mary Leard, they would kill him. Now, after all that, they released him, simply saying that they had made a mistake.[25]

The viciousness with which Billy Thlocco had been treated reflected an ugly mood that by then had begun to grip the close group of mob leaders at Julius Leard's house. After Thlocco's release, they had no one in custody, and they were no closer to finding the killer than they had been at the start. The excitement had grown until there were fifty to sixty men at Leard's farm, most of them armed, in part because rumors circulated at Maud that forty Seminoles had encamped on the river, ready to ride on the Leard place to rescue the Indian captives.[26] Frustrated in his search, Leard had begun to think that the Seminoles could be more helpful in finding the killer than they had been and that they were, in fact, shielding the guilty man.

He made what appeared to be a half-hearted attempt to bring the Seminole authorities into the case. More than two decades earlier, the United States had established its authority in cases of crimes against whites living in Indian Territory. Enforcement fell to U.S. marshals assigned to the federal courts. Still, the Seminoles had had wide authority to hunt down criminals in their territory, and in an earlier day, the lighthorse police probably would not have tolerated Leard's and his men's actions. But now, there was little they could to. On the previous day, the federal courts had assumed jurisdiction in all criminal cases, and tribal jurisdiction had ceased.

Leard had to have known that. Nevertheless, on one of his hunting expeditions on Sunday, he and Cap Guinn met Peter Osanna [Osanna Harjo], a Seminole lighthorse policeman who lived southeast of Maud, whom Leard asked to help find the killer. Osanna agreed to ask the second chief of the nation for authority, which he must have before he could arrest anyone because jurisdiction in the case rested with the United States. Leard left the impression with Osanna that he had a good lead on the killer, based on the description his son had given. "It seemed like the parties were known," Osanna said. "He knew party that killed that woman because my son told me by description [i.e., Frank Leard told his father]. He said the boy described that one of them his chin was cut, off here a little this way—" Here, Osanna indicated the direction of the cut on the cheek. "He didn't say on which side but it was cut that way, right straight that way, but he didn't say on which side, and I told him that must be a notable person [i.e., easily identifiable]." In addition, Leard told him the killer rode a bay horse with a roached mane. "After he described that horse, . . . he said George P. Harjo and Dave Coker knew the parties that murdered the woman, and he says, they know it but they won't tell us, and if they don't tell us we are going to have them arrested and make them tell, and if they don't tell us we will go out and look for the guilty party."[27] Perhaps Leard's belief was based on the pointed question Nelson Jones had put to his son about George Harjo, or perhaps he believed that Coker had learned something at the dance at Passack Harjo's. Leard may have simply understood one of the realities of Seminole Nation life—that local communities were close-knit, informed by effective communications channels of their own.

Whatever the source of his suspicions about Coker and George Harjo, Leard by then believed that the key to finding the killer was somewhere in Passack Harjo's settlement, which was on one of the main travel routes in that part of the Seminole Nation. After the road came through the gate in the Seminole boundary fence at Violet Springs, it passed for several hundred yards between fenced fields into his settlement. He lived north of the road and Joe Grayson, a Seminole freedman, south of it. In his mid-sixties, Passack Harjo was known as a "Spanish-Seminole," who had removed from Florida in the 1840s, gone to Mexico with Wild Cat's band about 1850, and then returned to the Seminole Nation.[28] He was head of a large extended family, and from their strategic location on one of the main roads leading to Oklahoma, those at his settlement could easily observe who came and went. If Leard assumed that the killer wanted money to buy whiskey, someone at Passack Harjo's settlement might have seen the killer pass to or from the whiskey towns across the border. Leard may have known, as well, of Passack Harjo's relationship to the lighthorse policemen of the region and assumed he had access to information. Peter Osanna was the husband of Passack Harjo's daughter, and Kinda Palmer, the other local policeman, was his wife's brother. Thus Leard's request for Osanna's help may have been more of a veiled threat, an attempt at intimidation, than a genuine call for assistance.

While some mob squads went about the western part of the Seminole Nation looking for new suspects, Leard began to retrace his steps. Frustrated at his failure to find the killer, he and his squads began to round up some of the Seminoles they had captured earlier, concentrating on those who were associated with Passack Harjo's settlement. Charley Woodard, George Guinn, Russell Guinn, and another rider offered Thompson Brown, a Seminole who lived near Maud, a hundred dollars to find out who had killed Mary Leard. Later that day, Brown was at Achena Church, about a mile west of Leard's place, when those same Guinn brothers, W. H. Vansickle (whom Brown called Van Shipman), George Pettifer, Cap Guinn, John Malloy, and Ward Chievers—all from the Maud community—arrested Lincoln McGeisey again. They asked Brown to go along to interpret for them at Leard's.[29]

Why the mob picked up McGeisey again is uncertain. It may have been Leard's attempt to extort the truth from someone at Passack Harjo's settlement. Frank Leard had said categorically before witnesses that Lincoln had not killed his mother. Thus Leard may have been making good his threat to force George Harjo and Dave Coker tell what they knew. Both men were connected to McGeisey's family. Lincoln McGeisey was Passack Harjo's grandson, George Harjo was the old man's son, and Coker was married to Thomas McGeisey's cousin. The first Seminole Leard had turned to for help was his landlord, Thomas McGeisey. If Leard believed that the Seminoles associated with Passack Harjo were shielding the killer, perhaps he might force action by taking the teenage son of a prominent government official who also had kinship ties to the old man's family. On the other hand, Lincoln McGeisey's second arrest might have resulted from the fact that, as it turned out, he was suspected of having robbed the house of one of the mob members, Joseph S. Williams, who rented from Coker's wife. The mob action might simply have afforded the opportunity to settle a score.

The mob waited until they reached Leard's place to interrogate Lincoln McGeisey. Where was he, they asked, on the day Mary Leard was killed? He had been at his grandmother's place, helping to haul wood, he replied, and had then gone to Passack Harjo's, where he stayed the night and attended a dance. The mob took off McGeisey's pants and made him take off his shirt. On his undershirt near the waistband was a spot about the size of a quarter. Vansickle asked him where that "bloodstain" came from. McGeisey said that he did not know but said that a few days earlier he had hurt his nose, which had bled, and showed them the wound on his nose; perhaps it had come from that injury. Vansickle and Cap Guinn took the barrel and stock of a broken gun, the murder weapon, from under a bed and asked McGeisey, "Did you hit the woman with this gun?" McGeisey said, "No." Then Cap Guinn asked him to explain a tear down the front of his shirt. McGeisey said that he had torn it on his saddle horn. Guinn asked him if the saddle horn had put the blood on his shirt; again he replied, "No." Then someone asked if he had got drunk on Friday night. "Yes," was the answer. Throughout the interrogation, surrounded by a huge crowd of threatening men, the eighteen-year-old steadfastly maintained that he had nothing to do with the killing.[30] Frank Leard's earlier emphatic statements that Lincoln was not guilty meant nothing to the mob leaders, who were no longer relying on the Leard children to identify the guilty one but had begun to resort to their own tactics.

Thomas McGeisey arrived at the Leard place while his son was being interrogated. Lincoln asked Thompson Brown in Muskogee to go and call his father in. The mob members ordered Thomas McGeisey and Brown to speak only English to Lincoln. The elder McGeisey asked his son the source of the blood on his shirt, and Lincoln repeated what he had told his captors. Though the mob had brought Brown along to interpret during this questioning, McGeisey could speak English as well as Brown could, so at this point, sensing the mood of the mob, Brown went home.[31] The mob, intent on holding Lincoln McGeisey, kept him under guard.

The crowd dispersed, many of them going to Maud for Mary Leard's funeral, held that afternoon. Only a skeleton crew remained at Leard's: George Guinn, John Malloy, and one other, left to guard McGeisey. That evening, the crowd swelled again to fifty or sixty.[32]

Later that night, the actions of the mob leaders turned violent in their treatment of Lincoln McGeisey, as if they had been holding back until the funeral was over. Several men were inside the house when Mont Ballard, H. Clay Roper, and another came in and ordered them outside, where they and the rest of the crowd stood watching. Someone pulled the window curtains down, and after a time, Roper and another brought McGeisey out of the house with a rope around his neck. Ballard walked behind them with a Winchester in the crook of his arm. More than fifty armed men surged behind them as they walked McGeisey about two hundred yards across the little prairie glade in front of the house. They came to a little tree, someone threw a rope over a limb, and Julius Leard, apparently still convinced that he could force the truth from the Seminoles, ordered Lincoln to tell about the murder or they would hang him. He knew nothing. Julius Leard hoisted him up, keeping him there for some time. When he let him down, someone kicked him in the ribs three or four times. Leard strung him up again. Then he let him down. According to James Alfred Smallwood, a Maud farmer who watched, "Julius Laird, when he let him down, Julius asked him if he would tell it, and he says, yes, I will tell it." Joseph Williams asked McGeisey about some items that McGeisey admitted having helped to steal from the Williams home, but they got no information about the murder. After that, they took McGeisey back to the house. Though more than fifty people were around the Leard house that night, those who were most active in brutalizing McGeisey were Leard, Roper, Ballard, Williams, and his sons Charley and Hardy.[33]

Julius Leard spent the next day, Monday, January 3, riding at the head of a squad comprised of George Brown, Smallwood, Mont and Woodson Ballard, Joseph and Hardy Williams, and J. W. Wilson. Taking Lincoln McGeisey with them, they stopped first at Thomas McGeisey's house, where they let Lincoln dismount and go inside. While the other riders remained outside on their horses, he, Leard, and the elder Williams talked to Thomas McGeisey about recovering Williams's property, which Lincoln had hidden in his father's smokehouse. The elder McGeisey denied any knowledge of it, and while Williams and Lincoln went to the smokehouse to retrieve it, Leard and McGeisey talked.[34] Leard told McGeisey, regarding Mary Leard's murder, that "he was satisfied Lincoln was not guilty of it, but he was in danger because the men was increasing in number; they might take him out and hang him, but he said he would do all he can to save his life." McGeisey believed Leard was sincere, judging from his tone and demeanor. He summed up their conversation this way: "Well, I thought he was using a kind word at the time."[35] And Leard may well have been. The mood of the mob leaders had obviously turned the night before. Whatever he told McGeisey, however, Leard had no intention of releasing Lincoln until he was satisfied about the matter of the blood on Lincoln's shirt. In short, it appears that Lincoln was being held hostage while Leard continued his search for the killer.[36]

Leard and his mob began their day's search north of McGeisey's house. About seven or eight miles from Mekasukey, they stopped Shawnee Barnett, aged about twenty-five. They demanded to know where he was going, and when he told them that he was on his way to Tom Coker's place to work that day, they ordered him at gunpoint to go with them to Leard's instead, apparently for no other reason than an association with Passack Harjo. About a quarter of a mile from Leard's place, they asked his whereabouts at the time of the murder. He had been working at Coker's and had heard about the murder at Passack Harjo's settlement on New Year's Day. Leard then told Barnett that he could go.[37] This decision was practical. Tom Coker was a Seminole lighthorse policeman and the brother of Dave, who Leard believed knew something about the killing. Coker could verify Barnett's story, and Leard probably had second thoughts about rousting someone so closely connected to a lighthorse policeman because he and the other mob leaders had by that time settled on a new course of action that they did not want to bring under the scrutiny of law enforcement officials.

Meanwhile, Marshal Nelson Jones, the lawman who could have altered the course of events, stayed out of Leard's way. After leaving Leard's house on Saturday evening, he went home, where his prisoner, Marsh Wilson, was held under arrest. Wilson was to appear for arraignment before U.S. Commissioner Walter T. Fears at Wewoka. Jones took him by way of Sasakwa early Sunday afternoon to ask Chief John F. Brown's advice in the Leard case. According to Jones, Brown told him to use his "best judgment in protecting innocent people." Whether Jones made clear to the chief exactly what was taking place at Leard's is uncertain, for Brown seemed unconcerned. Any lack of concern may have sprung from two sources. First, Brown was preparing to go to Washington to make final the Seminole allotment agreement with the Dawes Commission and may have been distracted from the domestic scene. Second, the murder fell clearly under federal jurisdiction, and Jones was the responsible law enforcement official in the district. However, any trust he placed in Jones was misplaced.

Though Jones knew well what was going on at Leard's farm, he took his time getting from Sasakwa to Wewoka, driving his wagon only four miles before stopping for the night at a Seminole's home because he had made no arrangements to stay in Wewoka. Jones's son David met him and went on with him to Wewoka the next morning, when he informed Commissioner Fears about the events at Leard's. While there, Jones met Stoke Martin and Thomas Welt Martin, Mary Leard's brothers. The latter had been at

Leard's house since the day after the murder and was in Wewoka to meet his brother, who was on his way to Leard's from his home in Holdenville, Creek Nation. The Martins left Wewoka to spend the rest of the day rounding up suspects, and Jones made plans to arrive at Leard's either that night or the next day.[38]

As Jones prepared to leave Wewoka that afternoon, Thomas McGeisey arrived to make a desperate effort to get his son out of Leard's hands. After Leard and his cohorts left his house that morning, McGeisey went to Wewoka to ask Commissioner Fears to issue a warrant for the arrest of not only his son but George Harjo, whom the mob implicated with Lincoln in the burglary of the Williams house and whom they were apparently searching for once more. McGeisey told Fears and Jones about the recovery of Williams's property, emphasizing that he had had nothing to do with the burglary himself. At first, McGeisey's request baffled Jones and Fears because it appeared to them that McGeisey was simply trying to protect himself from being implicated in the stealing, but McGeisey said that he was afraid of what the mob might do to Lincoln. McGeisey was scheduled to leave for Washington, D.C., two days later with Chief Brown and others and was uneasy about going with his son in Leard's hands. Fears issued the warrants, and Jones and his son Dave started for Leard's, promising to return with Lincoln McGeisey. But Jones was more interested in catching the killer of Mary Leard than in serving the two warrants, so he decided to go to Leard's and serve the papers if or when he found Lincoln McGeisey and George Harjo. Accepting Jones's promise that he would return the next day with Lincoln in custody, and assuming that his son would be safe, Thomas McGeisey remained in Wewoka and left for Washington on January 5, as scheduled, with the Seminole delegation, of which he was to serve as secretary.[39]

Meanwhile, the mob squads had continued their work throughout the day. Near Mekasukey, the Martin brothers, one of the Ballards, and Jim Jones, the marshal's nephew, arrested John Palmer, the twenty-eight-year-old Seminole whom Frank Leard had said the killer resembled. They held him at gunpoint for fifteen or twenty minutes, demanding information about Mary Leard's death and threatening to kill him if he refused to tell. Then they made him sit on the ground for about an hour before releasing him.[40]

Also near Mekasukey, eight riders headed by Leard arrested John Washington, a Seminole about twenty-two years old. They broke down the door and entered with guns drawn while Washington was sitting at the table, eating his noon meal at the home of Bunny Wilson four miles north of Leard's. On the evening of the murder, he had been at a dance some eight miles from the scene and had remained at the dance, which had continued through the next night. Though Washington neither spoke nor understood much English, he understood the curses they hurled at him and their orders for him to go with them. They then went in search of George Kernel (Checufana) and Thomas Thompson, whom they arrested and took with Washington the nine miles back to Leard's, arriving about sundown. They ordered Kernel and Thompson to lie by the fire in the yard and brought Frank Leard out to look at them, but he could identify no one. The mob members then handcuffed Washington and Thompson together and sent all of the prisoners upstairs to be kept under guard.[41]

Meanwhile, another squad consisting of Joseph Williams and others had gone south of Leard's that day and arrested George Harjo, Mose Tiger, and Peter Tiger. All had been among those taken at Passack Harjo's the first day the mob rode. The mob had released Harjo and Peter Tiger the same afternoon but had held Mose Tiger for a day. They arrested Harjo the second time apparently because of his implication in the burglary of Williams's house or because Leard believed, as he had told Peter Osanna, he knew something about the killing. Why they took the Tigers again is uncertain. Though George did not speak much English, he understood the gist of the interrogation at Leard's. Williams claimed that Lincoln McGeisey had named him as the killer. George, of course, denied it. Williams then asked if McGeisey had done the killing. George said no, that he knew nothing about it. Williams and some others sent the Tigers to stand near the fire and took Harjo aside. "They threatened several times to kill me," he said, "and accused me of killing the woman. I said I never done it." They asked him if he would rather be shot or hanged, and he replied that he did not want either. Finally, he said, "They took me before the little boy and the little boy said I was not the one but the mob would not turn me loose and carried me up stairs."[42]

Leard and the other mob leaders were clearly still focusing a good deal of attention on Passack Harjo's settlement. Shortly after the mob picked up George, the old man had become concerned about his son and his grandson and asked Louis Graham by messenger to go to Leard's to see about the two teenagers. Graham arrived before the riders came in with their prisoners. H. Clay Roper ordered him to stay until they brought George in. Later that night, Stoke Martin asked Graham the whereabouts of Sam Harjo, another of Passack Harjo's sons who had also been arrested on the first day. Learning that he was at Passack Harjo's settlement, a squad including George Guinn, Cap Guinn, Jesse Guinn, Charley Woodard, and others took Graham with them to fetch Sam, whom they found at the house of his sister Anna Harjo.[43]

Back at Leard's, a "big fat man," who constantly threatened them, guarded Sam Harjo and Graham near the fire in the yard. "He was on one side of the fire, a log heap, and we was on the other," said Graham, "and this big fat man said, punch them boys up round there and make them tell about the killing of that woman, and someone said, no, don't to punch them, and he said, we will kill about four of you sons of bitches, and then you will tell." Graham believed they thought he knew something about the murder, for they kept up the threats: "If you fellows don't tell, some of you, we will turn in and kill about four of you and then we will go to farming again; . . . you haven't any laws over here in your country, but God dam you we have got some laws for you and after we kill about four of you sons-of-bitches we will settle down and farm but we won't until we do."[44] They kept Graham by the fire but took Sam Harjo upstairs and placed him under guard with the rest of the prisoners.[45]

Leard and his squad, who had been out all day with Lincoln McGeisey, brought in one other prisoner that night. Late, near Mekasukey, they rousted Indian Sam (Sam Ela), a Seminole about thirty-seven years old, out of bed. Bound in chains, he rode double with Lincoln McGeisey back to Leard's, where his captors bound his legs and kept him under guard.[46]

The mob now had in custody John Washington, Thomas Thompson, George Kernel, Lincoln McGeisey, George Harjo, Mose Tiger, Peter Tiger, Louis Graham, Sam Harjo, and Sam Ela.

When Marshal Nelson Jones arrived at Leard's late that night, he did not tell the mob that he had warrants for the arrest of McGeisey and George Harjo. The size of the crowd apparently frightened him. Dave Jones counted twenty-seven standing near the fire. Besides both Leards, Jones recognized Cap Guinn, "Parson" A. E. Butterfield, Ward Chievers, Stoke Martin, H. Clay Roper, George Pettifer, Charley Woodard, Robert Ogee, and Philip H. Cooper. He asked Leard whom they held. Leard listed the prisoners but admitted "he did not suspicion either of these boys but kept them because they had been brought in by some of the boys," meaning the squads. So Jones spent the night without serving the warrants and demanding the two prisoners. He was drinking, as was apparently his habit, and helped shackle some of the prisoners for the night.[47]

After they bedded the prisoners down, Jones suggested a plan to coerce a confession from John Washington, whom the children had said looked something like the killer. Leard and Stoke Martin would take Washington out and pretend they were going to hang him while Jones stood guard to keep the crowd from knowing what was going on or interfering. Leard instructed George Cash to bring Washington downstairs, saying that he and some others wanted to talk to the prisoner. Leard and four others took Washington out to a corner of the yard and made him sit down. First, they pointed guns at him as if to execute him. Then they got him up, tied his hands behind his back, took him to a tree, slipped a noose around his neck, and threw the end of the rope over a limb about twenty feet above the ground. They hauled him up, and he hung there with his feet off the ground until he became unconscious. He said through his interpreter, "I kind of died away; it seemed to me I hung there about a half hour; when I was let down my mind was gone, I do not know what they did with me, when I came to know any thing, I was lying on the ground." Leard and the others were kicking him, cursing him, and punching him with their guns. When he showed signs of rousing, one grabbed his hair and jerked him into a sitting position. Before and after they strung him up, they said a good many things to him that he did not understand, but he gathered enough to know that they accused him of killing Mary Leard and demanded that he confess. Meanwhile, Jones stood guard and apparently had some difficulty in keeping the others from interfering, for some were intensely curious about what was going on. Failing to torture a confession from Washington, they took him back upstairs and chained him with the others.[48] When Washington told the other prisoners what had happened, a guard angrily told him "to quit talking Creek." After that, during the next several hours, they deprived him of sleep, and men punched him with Winchesters and pulled his hair.[49]

About seven the next morning, Tuesday, January 4, Jones had McGeisey and George Harjo brought from the house to the fire in the front yard. In the presence of his son Dave and one of the Martins, Jones had the warrants read to the prisoners. McGeisey told him that he had burned a part of Williams's stolen goods, that he had done it all himself, and that his father had nothing to do with the theft. Jones asked McGeisey why Leard was holding him. He did not know. Then Jones took them to wash up before taking them back to the house for breakfast. He had Leard station Frank and his little sister so that they might see the two prisoners when he brought them to the house from the direction Frank had said his mother's killer had come, hoping that they might identify one of them. The children "said positively that neither of them was the man." Leard then told Jones, "I am satisfied that neither of these men are guilty." However, Jones decided that he could not take his prisoners away because he needed his wagon to haul them to Wewoka to appear before Commissioner Fears. Thus he informed McGeisey and Harjo that they were his prisoners and that he would be back for them the following day. Jones padlocked the prisoners together with a chain on their legs, sent them back upstairs, asked Stoke Martin to stay with them until he returned, and left. On the road, he met a group from the Violet Springs and Meanko areas, including Jim Castleberry and Calvin "Dad" Marcum on their way to Leard's from an expedition of Indian hunting.[50]

Changes were taking place in the makeup of the mob. The events at Leard's had dragged on until it had attracted the attention of men in the whiskey towns who had no personal concern in the affair but began to ride the countryside, picking up Indians at random. Another group from Violet Springs, including Jim Jones and Chesley Guinn, arrested Billy Thlocco again that day. Thlocco, released on Sunday morning, had spent the night at his home and the next day had gone to Joe Grayson's house, not far from Passack Harjo's settlement, and spent that night. The next morning, he was preparing to go to Passack Harjo's to deliver a letter from Grayson when the vigilantes rode up. They threatened to kill him, searched him, and started with him to Leard's. About two miles from Passack Harjo's, they found Sepa [Sever] Palmer, a twenty-nine-year-old Seminole, in the woods with his team and wagon, getting wood. They forced him to walk ahead of them to Passack Harjo's. Nelson Jones was there when they arrived. He and Passack Harjo convinced them that Thlocco "didn't have nerve enough to kill a squirrel," and they released him. They kept Palmer, however, and forced him to go with them to Leard's. Julius Leard looked at Palmer closely and said he was well acquainted with him. About three or four in the afternoon, the mob told Palmer he was free to go.[51]

During the day, Leard released other prisoners so that the mob now held only John Washington, George Harjo, and Lincoln McGeisey.[52] Apparently because of Jones's claim on McGeisey and Harjo as his prisoners, the mob leaders considered Washington their prime suspect. The mob kept up their mistreatment of him. Throughout the day, they kept him chained by one foot to a huge log outside the yard, releasing him only to go to dinner, during which they chained him, George Harjo, and Lincoln McGeisey together. That evening they stripped off all of his clothes and examined both them and his person, apparently looking for bloodstains. They let him dress and eat some supper and then took him upstairs and chained him again to George Harjo and Lincoln McGeisey.[53]

Jones returned for his prisoners shortly after dark, having gone by way of Violet Springs to get supplies and pick up William Poff, a hired hand about his place and his sometime helper. All seemed quiet at Leard's. "How is the excitement?" he asked Clay Roper, Cap Guinn, and Ed L. Martin, Mary Leard's father, who had arrived about noon that day and appeared to be in charge. Jim Jones, who had been there since his squad had brought in Sepa Palmer, told his uncle, "There is nothing to be excited over for they haven't found the guilty man." During the day, Leard's friends had moved his personal belongings to Oklahoma, so Jones took over the house and took charge of the prisoners. Leard was still out hunting Indians, and, in his absence, the crowd became suspicious of Jones, afraid that he might attempt secretly to take the prisoners away. Thus they built a bonfire at the back of the house and kept it and the one in front blazing high so they could detect any movement. About eleven o'clock, some of the mob became restless and declared that if they knew for certain that Washington was Mary Leard's killer, "they would have him if they had to burn the house to get him." Jones went outside and talked to them for about half an hour, finally convincing them to wait and determine Washington's guilt with certainty. Julius Leard came in about midnight or one o'clock from near Mekasukey, where he had been checking Washington's alibi, and the crowd quieted down. Jones spent the night in the house, part of it upstairs with the prisoners, who he assumed were under his authority. For guards, he used Poff, Ed King, Jim Castleberry, John Damron, and Chess Guinn. The last four were on the scene when Jones and Poff arrived, and he asked them to help him, apparently because they were from near Violet Springs and he knew and trusted them.[54]

Early the following morning, Wednesday, January 5, Jones decided to move and make camp about half a mile from the house to separate himself from the crowd and to prepare for taking McGeisey and Harjo away. As he made preparations, he heard some talk in the yard that the crowd would not allow him to take John Washington. He approached Ed Martin. "I asked him, I says what have you got against this man Washington," Jones said, "and he says, I don't know as we have anything." Leard agreed: "I traced Washington up all day yesterday . . . and last night found out that he, on last Thursday in the fore part of the day was helping another Indian haul some wood and they went to a dance on Thursday night," the day of the killing. Still, Martin told Jones "that they wasn't satisfied to give up Washington." Jones asked, "What do you think you could do if I wanted to take them away from here?" Martin replied, "I ain't agoin' to do anything but I have a crowd of people here who are going to do a whole lot."[55]

What about McGeisey? Jones believed now that it was Ed Martin who had the final word in determining the prisoners' release. He proposed that they question him once more to try to establish his guilt or innocence. Martin and Leard agreed. While guards Ed King and William Poff were at breakfast, they went upstairs and questioned Lincoln McGeisey again about his whereabouts when Mary Leard was killed. Jones urged McGeisey to tell the truth because he wanted to prove his innocence. About four o'clock on the previous Thursday, McGeisey said, he was on the road from his father's house to Passack Harjo's when, about halfway there, he met his grandfather. The old man was on his way to Leard's to sell some yearlings. McGeisey told Passack Harjo where he was going and continued to Anna Harjo's house, where he saw Peter Osanna and his wife, who were there to get a stray hog. He talked with them about half an hour and went on to his grandfather's house, about a quarter to a half mile away and stayed there with Passack Harjo's wife and sons Duffie, Jim, and George. When Passack Harjo returned about dark, McGeisey and Duffie helped the old man unsaddle his horse and put it up, and they had supper together. Later, McGeisey, George, Duffie, and Sam attended a dance at a house nearby, and afterwards, McGeisey spent the night at Passack Harjo's.[56]

In addition to Lincoln's denial, Jones had evidence that Lincoln had not killed Mary Leard. Frank Leard had maintained from the start that McGeisey was not the one and "still told me," Jones said, "every time I talked to him." Frank had been unable, in fact, to identify any of the Seminoles that the mob had brought in, reaffirming his original statements that the killer was a stranger. Also, during his initial investigation, Jones had found a set of tracks in a corn field that began about fifteen steps west of the house. Someone wearing a pair of number-six boots, one of which was run down a little, made the tracks, which led southwest. Jones believed he made them after dark because he had walked over some corn stalks and big weeds, something a man would not do in broad daylight. The tracks disappeared at a fence a hundred and fifty yards southwest of where they entered the field. Leard said that the tracks did not belong to anyone at his place. Jones took a measurement, and he and Leard made McGeisey and the other prisoners walk to make tracks to compare. None matched. The track in the field was three quarters of an inch shorter than McGeisey's.[57]

And then there was the matter of the stain on Lincoln McGeisey's shirt, which some of the mob members believed incriminating and which Jones believed was the reason for holding the youth. McGeisey had made no effort to hide the spot, which was a little below the waistband of his pants. "I told him to pull his shirt off and he pulled it off," said Jones, "and I said Lincoln is this the same shirt you had on Wednesday evening when I broke your whiskey over here in the Seminole?" Lincoln replied, yes, it was the same. Jones examined the stain with an eye glass but could not tell if it was red mud or blood, but it had stained through his top shirt and onto his undershirt. "I looked through his clothing for further stains," Jones said, "but I found none, and he had on the same old pants for drawers that he had on when I took the whiskey out of his clothes." Jones asked McGeisey how the stain got there: "You see this skinned place on my nose?" Lincoln asked. "I run against a limb and my nose bled and I skinned my nose, and I cleaned it on my shirt; I was hurt pretty bad and I took my shirt and cleaned my nose." Jones believed the story because of the wound on his nose and was confident that Leard, Ed Martin, and others could place no significance on the stains.[58]

In order to avoid trouble and attempt to settle the question of McGeisey's guilt with certainty, Jones suggested that he and Leard check out his story. They went to Passack Harjo's, where, starting with the old man, they questioned the family separately. "Passack Harjo states the same as Lincoln did exactly," said Jones. "Jim Harjo corroborated him; Duffie, George and Sam the same." As they left Passack Harjo's house, Leard said, "I am perfectly satisfied that the boy has nothing to do with it." According to Jones, Leard said of McGeisey, "I am satisfied that he is an innocent man and we do not want to fool with him any more." From Passack Harjo's they went on what Jones called "an exploring expedition" to another Seminole settlement twelve miles east to search for information or clues. At Passack Harjo's, they learned the name of an Indian who had borrowed Lincoln's coat at the dance. Eager to find why someone that far away had been in the vicinity of the dance, they decided to investigate, but their trip was fruitless. Thus Jones and Leard returned to Leard's house about an hour before sundown and reported what they had learned to the mob.[59]

Jones and Leard agreed that it might be better for Jones to move the center of his investigation to his own home. Seminoles in the vicinity of Leard's farm had been scared out of the area, and Jones believed he would have more success with his investigation if he moved. Also, the move would relieve him of the expense of feeding a number of men who congregated at his mess. In addition, he wanted to try to capture two brothers, Abe and Mose Johnson, in the southern part of the nation and take them with McGeisey and George Harjo to the commissioner at Wewoka. Thus Jones prepared to take his prisoners and leave. "I talked to old man Martin," he said, "and asked if he was satisfied that these men were not the guilty men, and he said yes, they were satisfied, and was willing for me to take them away, and I harnessed my team." But while Jones was doing that and packing up his camping equipment, the mob leaders held a conference. As Jones started into the house to get his prisoners, Martin said, "We don't want you to take these men away from here. Everything is satisfactory that this McGeesey is innocent; there are men here that are not convinced." An estimated forty men were there at the time. Jones said, "I am going to take them." Martin replied, "You will be killed if you make an attempt just as sure." Nevertheless, Jones said that he was going to try. "I went to the door of the house, and there were as many as fifteen guns leveled on me right then." Jones told them that he did not understand how they could keep the prisoners from him. Robert Ogee of Maud said that as long as they had guns and ammunition they could do so. "There isn't a one of you who believes that you have got the guilty one," Jones said; "why do you want to hold them?" Then, according to Jones, "Julius Laird got up, and said Lincoln McGeisey, and Washington are innocent men, and he says I know George Harjo has nothing against him, and he wanted them to let me have them, as they were innocent men, and not the men they were after." The armed men refused. Jones warned them that they were taking something on their shoulders that they could "never be shut of" if the prisoners were harmed.[60]

When the prisoners returned from supper, the crowd would not let Jones or his guards go near them. Jones made only a feeble effort to assert his authority, and no attempt to arrest the men for interfering with him in the discharge of his duty. He simply told them that they had violated the law by stopping him at gunpoint but that he was "perfectly helpless" to oppose them. They said that they did not care about his authority. He was too weak. Jones sent Poff upstairs to get his grip, but when Poff stuck his head through the stairway into the loft, two men cocked their guns and put them against his head. When he told them what he wanted, they cursed him and drove him down the stairs. Jones concluded that it was time to go, given the mood of the mob.[61]

Jones made one last appeal. You do not really believe that either man is guilty, he told them. Here was Leard, he said, who had been with him all day and could make a statement that would satisfy them concerning Lincoln McGeisey if he would. Instead, Leard told him that the men were all "riled" up and had given their orders, and the best thing for Jones to do was to follow them. Jones was apparently afraid to resist them, for he was now shorthanded. Jim Jones had left for Violet Springs about noon, taking Henry Moore and Dad Marcum with him, leaving Jones only two guards he trusted. Let him have any *one* of the men they had nothing against, Jones begged. They gave him George Harjo, and he prepared once more to leave. Ed Martin and Julius Leard told Jones that they took responsibility for the lives of McGeisey and Washington. If they considered them innocent, why would they not let him take them, Jones inquired. There were too many men, they replied. "Old man Martin told me," Jones said, "he was satisfied that neither of these men were guilty men and for me to be contented that they would send these men to me as soon as the crowd got away." Jones named those that stood him down, besides Leard and Martin, as Parson Butterfield, Jim Hodges, George Pettifer, Herschel Leard, Stoke Martin, Chesley R. Guinn, Jim Morrow, Ward Chievers, Philip H. Cooper, Charley Woodard, and Robert Ogee.[62]

Despite Martin's promise to send the prisoners to Jones, it soon became apparent that Leard, Martin, and other mob leaders, especially Sam Pryor (Texas Ranger) and H. Clay Roper, had other plans. Before Jones could get away, Martin and Leard came to him again. "I didn't mean what I said when I agreed to be responsible for these men's lives," Martin said, and he asked Jones to release him and Leard from their oath of responsibility. Jones refused. Martin then said, "I take them, but I no longer wish myself considered responsible for their lives, for I have men here who would have taken them from you anyhow." The chain and locks that held McGeisey and Washington together by their legs belonged to Jones, who had loaned them to the mob during their Indian hunting expeditions. If they could replace his chain and locks with theirs, they could say that Jones released the prisoners to them. They asked him for the key. He refused to remove the chain and retained the key, apparently as a symbol of his claim to the prisoners: "I says if you take the men away from me you must take all I have on them." A little after sundown, Jones, William Poff, and Ed King left with only George Harjo in custody. Afraid that the crowd might still try to take George Harjo away from him, Jones asked some others from southeastern Pottawatomie County to ride with them. Chesley R. Guinn, a man named Meyer, and Jim Castleberry followed them for some distance before finally turning and going another direction.[63]

Jones himself was in a large measure to blame for his failure to take Lincoln McGeisey and John Washington away. He and those with him had been drinking throughout the week. It may have been the effects of alcohol that had made him leave the impression with Leard and others that they had some quasi legal authority to round up Seminoles at will. His comings and goings and long absences from the scene may have left the impression with the mob that he cared little what they did. Jones had apparently told the Martins and Leard when they planned to string up Washington that, if they were satisfied he was guilty, he would go off and "have business" elsewhere and they could do with Washington what they pleased. On another occasion, when Jones was questioning prisoners, he apparently warned them to tell all they knew of the murder, or the mob would burn them to make them confess.[64]

Thus having abetted the mob, could he have taken McGeisey if he had really wanted? Some of the mob leaders later claimed that they believed he could have. But whether from inexperience, cowardice, or a realistic reading of the odds at the moment, Jones himself did not believe that he and his two guards could have taken McGeisey against the will of Leard, Martin, their relatives, and other mob leaders. They would surely have killed him. Whether or not Jones truly believed that, some members of the mob thought that he appeared to and that he talked as if he did.[65] And in this case, apparently, thinking made it so.

As he rode away from Leard's farm, Jones knew well the implications of his leaving Lincoln McGeisey and John Washington. The mood of the mob had turned the previous night when they wanted to lynch Washington. Jones knew what the mob leaders had in mind; he had, after all, been with them for nearly a week. He knew how intent Leard and Martin were on vengeance. Yet despite their night riding and bullying, harassing, torturing, and illegally detaining the Indians, they were no closer to finding the truth than when they started. A week had passed since Mary Leard died. Their frustration was growing. The hasty conference among the mob leaders and the reversal of Ed Martin and Leard regarding the release of the prisoners indicated that the mob was taking a new direction.

That new direction had resulted, in part, from the federal authorities' legal claim to jurisdiction over Lincoln McGeisey and George Harjo. For several days, Indian hunting had been more or less a private affair. The mob was comprised of three main groups: Mary Leard's brothers and, later, their father and close associates from the Chickasaw and Creek nations; citizens of the Maud community, particularly the Guinn family, related by marriage to Herschel Leard; and the Leards' relatives, members of the Lewis family from northern Pottawatomie County and elsewhere. In addition, as time wore on, they attracted curiosity seekers who came and went from Maud and the whiskey towns along the border. A fourth group consisted of Nelson Jones and his hangers-on. As long as Jones had not interfered and had gone along with the private mob's tactics, they apparently had little concern for him. However, once he presented himself as a representative of federal authority by attempting to serve his warrants, he became a liability to their cause. To defy a local law enforcement officer was usually of little consequence to such a group; defying federal authority was another matter. If they harmed their prisoners now, federal authorities would know whom to blame. The fact that the events were taking place in the Seminole Nation had prevented the congregation of large numbers of whites. In fact, the numbers had commonly fluctuated from eight or ten to forty or fifty. There was nothing here to resemble a mass mob, ready to take action. Nothing was happening to keep up their interest. Thus the mob leaders embarked on a course to bring larger numbers into the mob, at least to give the event the appearance of mass mob action, which ostensibly would gain, in turn, the appearance of wider public approval of what the mob leaders had in mind.

Those leaders had, in fact, already taken the first step to increase participation in the affair to make it appear the action of a mass mob. While Leard and Jones were out checking McGeisey's alibi that Wednesday, word went out to Oklahoma, especially to the whiskey towns, that two Indians would be killed that night at Leard's farm. What transpired at the farmhouse just before dark that Wednesday evening made it clear that the mob leaders were determined to add this one last lawless, vicious act to the list of those that they had committed during the previous week. In its premeditation, it was more chilling and vicious than the murder of Mary Leard, which had set the chain of events in motion. The mob leaders had decided to *burn someone* in revenge for the killing of their kinswoman, and it apparently mattered little if, by their own admission, the ones they burned were innocent.

FIVE

Seminole Burning

The mob would burn *someone*. The leaders had decided that by Tuesday night, perhaps even sooner, but the decision became firm after Edward L. Martin arrived from the Chickasaw Nation. But how many would they burn? Though Leard, those close to him, and the Seminoles knew that only one Indian had been involved in the killing, Leard had vowed vengeance if he could not find that one. Nearly a week had passed, and he had no likely suspect. As matters stood, one victim would evidently not be enough to satisfy him and Ed Martin. But who would the victims be? For a time, George Harjo and Lincoln McGeisey had been likely candidates. While Harjo was in custody, mob members had brought hay in, scattered it in the room and threatened to light it. After his release, the intended victims became McGeisey and John Washington. The mob leaders had apparently selected McGeisey early on and left him alone but had continued to torture Washington. They came in from time to time and pointed their guns at him as if to shoot; each time, he closed his eyes, expecting to be killed. They told him it was just a matter of time until they burned him.[1] By Wednesday, as important to the leaders as deciding whom to burn was the problem of finding some means of giving "legitimacy" to what they were about to do. They had to do something to involve more people, for there was safety in numbers. The action of Leard and a few others to settle a private matter of vengeance might lead to retribution, but action of what appeared to be a mass lynch mob was less likely to be challenged, given the commonality of lynching in recent years. Because they knew that McGeisey and Washington were innocent of the killing, the mob leaders had to find another—the "right" man—someone they could pass off as the young Indian the Leard children had described as their mother's killer, the stranger whom they had not seen since.

Plans for a burning, which had evolved during two or three days, had the approval of Leard and the Martins and involved others allied to the Leard and Martin families. They were, for the most part, members of the Lewis family to which the Leards belonged and had, like the Martins, come from outside the Maud community to act as mob organizers and leaders. Some of them had been members of the squads from early on, had had a hand in stringing up Lincoln McGeisey, and had led the resistance against Nelson Jones when he weakly proposed to take George Harjo and Lincoln McGeisey to Wewoka.

The captain of the mob, whose job was to control the men, was Samuel V. Pryor, a man with a shadowy, disreputable past. Born in Mississippi in 1866, Pryor lived in Texas, where he claimed to have been a Texas Ranger at one time.[2] Pryor was married to Olivia Cowart, Leard's cousin, and was apparently in the Indian Territory because the appeal of the Lewis family claim to Choctaw citizenship was due to be heard by the federal court at South McAlester in early January. He was at Maud when the murder occurred. Julius Leard had stayed the night at his brother's house because an old friend had arrived. That friend was apparently Pryor, for on the day following the murder, Pryor was at the head of the mob that descended on Passack Harjo's settlement and appeared to be giving orders when they picked up Louis Graham on the road. A stranger to the Maud community, whose members made up the squads at first, Pryor became known to local mob members during the next few days simply as a dark, heavy, bearded man who emerged as leader and whom his followers called by one of his nicknames—"Texas Ranger," "Texas," or "Tex." From the beginning, he was intent on burning some Indians in retribution for the murder of his relative's wife, and it apparently made little difference to him *which* Indians. He was the one who suggested a burning, claiming that he had been involved in mob activity in Texas and "that nothing had come of it."[3] From the start, his intent was apparently to commit a criminal act and get away with it. Early in the search for Mary Leard's killer, Pryor sent word to others, Lewis family members and friends, in the Chickasaw and Choctaw Nations and in northern Pottawatomie County to come and help him direct the burning, which he had originally planned for Wednesday night. By that time, most of his cohorts had arrived.[4]

Among these outsiders were Thomas P. (Tom) King and Pryor's half-brother, George Bird Ivanhoe, who arrived early in the search. King, a friend of Mary Leard's brothers, had gone to the Indian Territory in 1883 and moved around, settling in the Seminole Nation in 1892, where he served as a deputy U.S. marshal. Ivanhoe, twenty-two years old, became known to the local mob members simply as "a little light complected man." When Ivanhoe arrived is uncertain, but he was in the mob for days.[5] Though the opposite of his half-brother in appearance, Ivanhoe could match Pryor in his ruthlessness. In addition, Edward L. Martin, Mary Leard's father, had arrived from the southern part of the Chickasaw Nation about noon on Tuesday.

Another group of mob leaders, also strangers to the Maud community, came from northern Pottawatomie County, more than twenty miles north of Maud. Some of these were members of the Lewis family. When word of the murder reached their neighborhood, a large group organized immediately to go to the Seminole Nation. Though their number is uncertain, they included H. Clay Roper, Andrew J. Mathis, Jesse McFarland, and perhaps L. Hiram Holt, who was a Baptist preacher and local personal property assessor and who lived near the others. They stopped at Earlsboro on their way to Leard's farm, laying in a store of supplies and buying guns and ammunition.[6] They had arrived at Leard's farm by the night following the murder and, collectively, proved to be among the most vicious element in the mob. Though all acted as mob organizers, practically nothing is known of McFarland. Somewhat more is known about Roper, Mathis, and Holt.

Roper, like most of the mob leaders, was a drifter. Born in Kentucky in 1858, he had moved to the Creek Nation in 1879 and settled near Eufaula. He married Zora Cowart, Leard's cousin and sister to Pryor's wife. Like most of the Lewis family, they rented farm land from the Indians or squatted and scratched out a living, Roper supplementing his income by engaging in the illegal whiskey trade. Also like most white renters, they moved frequently—to Arkansas, back to Indian Territory, and, by 1894, to Oklahoma. In early 1896, Roper bought land from the McFarland family in Pottawatomie County.[7] In the days following his arrival at Leard's, he became recognized by mob members from the Maud community as the second in command, or "lieutenant," to his brother-in-law, Sam Pryor.

Mathis and Holt were in some ways worse than Roper because of their pretended self-righteousness. Andrew J. Mathis was a thirty-two-year-old farmer who lived near Roper and other of Leard's relatives. Born of Texas stock, he had spent his childhood in Arkansas, living in the same community as the Lewises. Like them, he had been a drifter, living in the Indian Territory, moving to Oklahoma Territory in 1896, finally settling in Pottawatomie County near the Lewises, members of his own family, and other families from their old neighborhood in Arkansas. The son of a Presbyterian minister, he often pretended to be religious, especially in the presence of his neighbors, but he had a reputation for not taking good care of his large family. There were hints as well that he was engaged in criminal activities, for he would frequently mount up and leave home with a .45 Colt revolver in his belt and return with money. When word of the murder reached his neighborhood, he joined the party that organized to go to Maud. L. Hiram Holt, the preacher, was forty-seven, a Missourian who had made his way to Oklahoma after a number of years in Arkansas. He was active in hunting Indians and tried to lend a high moral tone to the viciousness of the mob.[8]

In addition to these outsiders, others became attracted to the scene. At first, the crowd that came and went, varying greatly in number from day to day, had consisted mainly of farmers and businessmen from near Maud who were friends, relatives, and neighbors of Julius and Herschel Leard. As days passed and word spread, men came and went from more distant communities, particularly Earlsboro, Violet Springs, and Meanko, simply out of curiosity. In their numbers were many who had bad reputations or were associated with the whiskey trade. Among the latter were Mike Lawless and Sam Norton from Earlsboro, and from the southern part of the county were Andrew J. Morrison and the Marcums, father and son. Others with less than stellar character from the southern section were James Castleberry and Ed Garrison, who were under indictment at the time for murder. Castleberry, whom Nelson Jones had used as one of his guards, had often been at cross purposes with the law. Besides Castleberry, Ward Chievers and George Moppin had been witnesses for the defense in the Christian brothers' trials in 1895. Others such as Ed King and Nelson Jones himself had been involved in criminal cases in the southern part of the county over the years.[9] The presence of such men who had at times skirted the law would prove convenient to Leard, Martin, Pryor, Roper, and the other mob leaders in helping to change the demeanor of the mob, and, without doubt, they were the source of much of the whiskey that found its way to Leard's farm. In time, however, Leard and the other leaders would find that involving people who had no stake in the Maud community was a mistake, for they would be less inclined to remain silent about what they had witnessed at the Leard farm.

These mob leaders planned to get more people involved by creating excitement in Pottawatomie County. From Saturday through Tuesday, the size of the mob at the Leard farm had varied from only a handful to fifty or sixty; its membership was not consistent except for the core of men close to Leard. Apparently in an attempt to create high feelings and increase the size of the mob, Leard and others began to cast what they were doing in terms of the rituals that commonly attended lynchings in the South during recent years. First, they had to enhance the "reason" for their action by making allegations that a vast majority of mobs in the South had used to justify their actions: sexual assault. It was common, too, for mobs to find a scapegoat if the perpetrator of the alleged crime could not be found. Leard and the other mob leaders began to lay the groundwork for that as well. They began to circulate falsehoods about the circumstances of Mary Leard's death. Though Frank Leard had insisted that only one man had committed the crime and that he was alone, by Tuesday the mob claimed to be looking for *two* Seminoles who, they said, had not only killed Mary Leard but *raped* her as well, though early on, Nelson Jones and others had determined that no sexual assault had occurred. In addition to these intentional falsehoods, rumors of an impending attack from the Seminoles to rescue the prisoners also helped to keep tension high. On Wednesday, to stir excitement, the mob leaders spread news throughout eastern Pottawatomie County that a burning might occur that night if they found the guilty Indians. As they expected, people from Earlsboro north of Maud to Violet Springs in the south responded to this obvious invitation and openly discussed the possible burning. Fear spread among residents of the Seminole Nation. Louis Graham, whom the mob had detained three times, left the area that day for Sasakwa. "I went down there to keep them from catching me and burning me up," he said.[10] Graham knew that Leard and the others were apparently not particular regarding victims.

Curious Pottawatomie County citizens who had no emotional stake in the affair made their way to Leard's that day so that by the time Nelson Jones confronted the crowd late that afternoon, it had already swelled to forty or fifty, the result desired by the mob leaders. Many of the outsiders had gone to see a spectacle and frankly admitted it. Part of the hostility that Jones sensed in the crowd resulted without doubt from their fear that he might take the intended victims away. With Jones out of the way, the mob leaders went ahead with plans for the burning and informed McGeisey and Washington that they were to die. By Wednesday night, then, the mob had entered a new phase in its evolution. It was no longer what it had been at the start—a group of farmers, neighbors and friends of Leard, excited over the murder and guided by impulse.[11] Too much time had elapsed for impulse to carry events. The burning would be a deliberate, premeditated act of vengeance, which the mob leaders would carry off under the guise of a lynching of the sort common in the South.

Plans for burning McGeisey and Washington on Wednesday night changed unexpectedly, however, when news of the plan reached the wrong ears. Younger Bowlegs, a Seminole, was buying supplies at Earlsboro that day when store owner A. W. Anderson told him about widespread talk that the mob planned to kill two Indian boys at Leard's that night. Though a number of people from Earlsboro were going to see the burning, Anderson would have no part in it. Bowlegs saw small crowds in the street, gathering to go to Leard's farm. On his way home, he reported what he had heard to Thomas Coker, a Creek serving as a Seminole lighthorse policeman. Coker, whose brother David had promised to help Nelson Jones gather information at Passack Harjo's settlement, decided to go to Leard's to investigate, though he had no official jurisdiction in the case. His family's kinship to McGeisey, however, might carry some weight. The Cokers also had some important political connections. Their father was a half-brother of Isparhecher, the chief of the Creek Nation, and their sister was the widow of Chief John Brown's brother. Though Thomas Coker understood English, he did not speak it well and asked Bowlegs to go with him as interpreter to find why the mob intended to burn the boys. That night, Coker, Bowlegs, Bowlegs' brother Cookey, Harry Brown, George Kernel, and Albert Washington started for Leard's, seven or eight miles south. Brown was white, a longtime resident of the Seminole Nation, and Cookey Carbitcher, Dave Coker's brother-in-law, had married Thomas McGeisey's cousin.[12] Kernel had been arrested with John Washington, and Albert Washington was John's brother.

They soon learned that this undertaking was risky. On the road, they met seven or eight armed white men who were also on their way to Leard's and who demanded to know where they were going. When Kernel told them, the men warned against going there. W. H. Kuykendall, who lived near

Earlsboro, pointed a gun at Coker and demanded to know who "that big man" was. Coker did not respond because he did not want them to know, apparently uncertain what they might do if they found out that he was a lighthorse policeman. Kernel told them simply that Coker wanted to talk with Leard. Satisfied with that response, they rode on. When Coker and his party arrived at Leard's close to 11:00 p.m., about one hundred well-armed men were standing around the fire in the yard, but most of them quickly faded into the darkness as the riders approached.[13] Having gathered to witness a burning, they were no doubt afraid someone might identify them as part of the mob.

Through Bowlegs, Coker told Ed Martin that he wished to see Leard. He took Coker and Bowlegs inside while the rest of their party stayed outside the yard fence. When they entered, only Leard was in the room. Coker learned that they held McGeisey and Washington upstairs. "I told Julius Laird not to kill the boys," Coker said, "but to leave it in the hands of the law. If they are guilty of the crime, leave it in the hands of the law. I told him that McGeesey had been a good boy ever since he was born; never stolen anything; never been whipped, and never murdered anyone, and told him that Lincoln McGeesey had been over to his grandfather's, Passack Harjo's during the afternoon of the day the woman was murdered. . . . Julius Laird told me that he was satisfied that the boy, Lincoln McGeesey, was not guilty of the murder of that woman and said he was going to turn him loose the next morning. He said that he will and I was not uneasy about them." But Leard was plainly lying to Coker; he had no intention of turning the captives loose. He later frankly admitted that he held McGeisey and Washington because he had not found the killer. Trusting Leard to be truthful, Coker left, feeling somewhat assured about McGeisey's safety.[14]

While Coker and Bowlegs were inside with Leard, the men outside were in an ugly mood as they huddled in groups around the fire and in the shadows, talking. Coker had probably been wise to hide his identity on the road, for in the crowd at Leard's was Rube Newport, who had once had a run-in with him and wanted to take up the quarrel again that night. Harry Brown, one of Coker's group, asked Poliet Smith, a constable from Earlsboro Township to disarm Newport if he had a gun in order to prevent trouble. Others told Newport it was not the time to raise personal issues and also urged Smith to intervene, which he did. Coker and Bowlegs also recognized Mike Lawless, an Earlsboro saloonkeeper, but knew few others.[15] Living as they did in the northern part of the Seminole Nation, they did not recognize local members of the mob. The presence of those they recognized from Earlsboro indicates the distance that curiosity seekers had traveled to witness the proposed burning.

Coker's actions indicate that the Seminole authorities were ill informed about events at Leard's. At first, they probably thought, as they should have, that federal authorities would seek out the killer because the federal courts assumed jurisdiction in all criminal cases on January 1. Nelson Jones, the U.S. law enforcement officer of the district, was on the scene. Chief John Brown had left for Washington the day of the proposed burning, taking Thomas McGeisey with him. It is very likely that the mob leaders waited deliberately for the delegation to leave for the Capitol before making their move. It was only on Thursday that second chief Hulbutta Micco had become concerned that the crowd might harm their prisoners and asked J. Herman Patton, superintendent at Mekasukey Academy, to write Commissioner Walter T. Fears at Wewoka, requesting intervention by the Indian agent at Muskogee. Hulbutta Micco's message got to Fears the following day, but whether it went further is uncertain.[16] Coker and his party had no way of knowing that when they visited Leard's farm, they had prevented the burning of Lincoln McGeisey and John Washington by showing up unexpectedly that late at night.

They may, in fact, have contributed to a change in plans, which the mob leaders put into effect the next day: to find a victim who was not well known in the neighborhood and who they could claim was the killer. At about eight o'clock that morning, Thursday, January 6, Nelson Jones had an unexpected visitor at his house south of Passack Harjo's settlement. Thomas W. Martin stopped by on his way home to the Chickasaw Nation, where he was going because his wife was ill. Jones asked what was going on at Leard's. Martin said that they had not found the guilty man but that they had heard of a man named Sampson who was guilty and that they had an "Indian boy" to lead them to him. Jones told Martin that he believed Sampson was innocent but that, if they happened to capture him, he wanted him as a horse thief.[17]

This visit was unusual enough, but Jones became downright suspicious when Martin told him that, if he were inclined, he could have McGeisey and Washington. "He says to me this way," Jones said; "you could go over yet and get them fellows to-day, . . . and I says they took the responsibility to keep them there for me." Martin said that Leard and his father would not simply turn them loose. "What's the reason you can't go back that way and send them to me yet?" Jones responded. "You took them away." But Martin refused. Jones believed that the mob leaders were trying to trick him. If he took McGeisey and Washington, the mob would waylay him and take them away from him by force, he thought, thereby relieving Martin and Leard of their oath of responsibility to keep them safe. Martin urged Jones to send someone the next day because the mob had dispersed and the excitement had died down. Thus he told Martin that he would send his nephew Jim Jones either that evening or the next morning to get the prisoners for him; if Martin was telling the truth, Jones thought, the mob would release the prisoners to Jim Jones as readily as they would to him.[18]

Jones went to Violet Springs and directed Jim Jones to go to Leard's the next morning to pick up the prisoners. He did not have the authority to deputize his nephew, who was to go unofficially, but because Jim Jones had been about the Leard place, helping his uncle with his work and capturing Seminoles to be interrogated, the marshal believed that the mob would release the two with or without official paperwork if they intended to release them at all. He said, "If them fellows are satisfied that these boys are innocent, I want them and if they will turn them over to you, bring them." To be on the safe side, he instructed his nephew not to carry a gun and to avoid any trouble with the mob.[19]

Why was Jones so afraid to go to Leard's himself? There was a distinct possibility that he was a coward. Perhaps he believed that the mob would harm him if they overpowered him, as he believed they plotted to do, in order to take his prisoners away. Was he so naive as to think that the mob would not harm an innocent person? Or was he staying out of the way in order to keep his part of an "understanding" with Julius Leard that he would have business elsewhere if Leard found the murderer? Lack of definitive action had characterized Jones's behavior throughout the previous week.

Jones had done little to apprise other peace officers of events at the Leard farm. At no time did he attempt to inform his superior, Marshal Leo E. Bennett, at Muskogee. Every time he was at Leard's, he was within ten miles of the telegraph station at Earlsboro. Though he made the longer trip from Leard's to his home and back more than once, he made no effort to go the ten miles to Earlsboro to call for help. There was also Jacob Harrison (Unasey), a Seminole and an Indian policeman and deputy U.S. marshal who lived near Wewoka and was assigned to Marshal Bennett's jurisdiction. But Jones made no effort to reach Harrison. The court of Walter T. Fears, the U.S. commissioner, was in session at Wewoka throughout this time.

Thomas McGeisey had gone to him to swear out the warrants for Lincoln and George Harjo. Why had Fears, as an official of the federal court who knew of Thomas McGeisey's concerns about the mob, not looked into the matter and informed the marshal's office himself?[20] Had Jones given the impression that he had the matter under control? Early on, Jones had run into Dave Coker, who Leard claimed knew the identity of the murderer. Coker had offered to attend the dance at Passack Harjo's and seek out information, but Jones had not seen him again. Jones had also tried to reach Tom Coker and claimed to have tried to reach other lighthorsemen, but neither he nor his messengers found any of these men at home. He had asked Passack Harjo where they could be, and the old man said simply, "I do not know, I guess they are all gone."[21]

Now, in the wake of Martin's visit, Jones made a feeble attempt to reach Chief John Brown, who by that time was in Washington with the Seminole delegation. He loaded his trail outfit and, taking George Harjo as prisoner and William Poff, David Jones, George Moppin, and Jim Burgess as helpers, went to Sasakwa to use the telephone and to look for the fugitive Johnson brothers, whom he had used as an excuse when he left Leard's place. But when he got to Sasakwa, the wires were down. News that the mob had McGeisey and Washington had already reached there before communications stopped. The chief's son, Johnny, told Jones it probably would do no good even if he could get a call through. Jones asked Brown to call for him when the lines were repaired, and again Brown said that he believed it would do no good. There the matter dropped, and Jones withdrew from the affair. That night he and his men camped about four miles west of Sasakwa and a mile from the home of Lelia Johnson, where he hoped to capture her sons, whom he wanted for stealing cattle. He, Moppin, and Burgess captured Abe Johnson that night.[22]

Meanwhile, Julius Leard went after Palmer Sampson. Leard, Woodson Ballard, Chesley Guinn, H. Clay Roper, and Sam Pryor arrested Albert Washington, the "Indian boy" Martin had mentioned to Jones, and forced him to guide them to Palmer Sampson's house near Wewoka. In return for his services, they promised to release his brother, John Washington. When they arrived in Sampson's neighborhood, Washington did not lead them to the house but rode them around the area until dark, forcing them to spend the night in the woods.[23]

The next morning, Friday, January 7, 1898, Leard and his party forced Washington to lead them to Sampson. Washington said, "They told me if

I didn't go to that house and show them where that house was they would bring me back to Laird's house and kill me, so the next morning we went." They arrived a little after sunrise.[24] Mrs. Sukey Sampson (also called Sukey Natuksie and Sukey Cobuxey), her daughter Rhoda Natuksie (or Rhoda Fixico), and son Palmer were having breakfast when Pryor broke in the door with a fence post, and Leard and his companions ordered the family at gunpoint to put up their hands. While one of the men ransacked the house, the others hit Palmer over the head, tied his hands behind his back, put him on his horse, tied his feet under the horse's belly, and led him away. In an obvious attempt to cover their trail, they told Sampson's mother that they were taking him to Wewoka, where she immediately went. Both at the house and on the road back to Leard's, Washington had no idea what the men said to Sampson because they would allow the Seminoles to speak only English to each other. Sampson spoke it a little, but Washington did not.[25]

Palmer Sampson fit the general description of the killer except in one significant respect. He did not have the noticeable scar on his face.[26] Still, Leard and Pryor took Sampson to Oklahoma, ostensibly to have the children identify him, while the others returned to Leard's to give out the word that they had brought in a likely suspect.

Meanwhile, Jim Jones had arrived at the Leard farm to pick up McGeisey and Washington according to Nelson Jones's instructions. However, he apparently found the forty or fifty men there intimidating, for he did not say why he had come and did not ask for the prisoners. McGeisey and Washington were near the fire in the yard, chained together. Jones talked with them and, after an hour or two, decided to go back home. Ed Martin asked him to stay, saying that Leard had taken Palmer Sampson to Oklahoma for the children to look at.[27]

About sundown, Leard and Pryor arrived with Sampson. As they approached the house, they spurred their horses and came up on the run, firing their pistols in the air. The mob became excited and ran for cover, apparently thinking that the long-expected attack by the Seminoles had begun, and they were on the verge of returning fire when they realized it was Leard. While Leard was hitching his horse, he told Ed Martin that Sampson was guilty. Martin, extremely excited and barely able to control himself, announced to the crowd that they had found the killer, that the children had identified him, and that he had made a confession. At this point the crowd brought up Palmer Sampson with a chain locked around his neck.[28]

This dramatic turn of events, staged by Leard and Pryor for the crowd's benefit, was another major step toward giving the subsequent events the appearance of a mass mob action. They now began to ritualize the affair. The rituals of confession, prayer, and selection of the lynching site, such as those that Leard and Pryor would engage in during the next few hours, replicated those that had "underscored the legitimacy of the extralegal execution" and "provided a degree of order" in the New South, according to historian W. Fitzhugh Brundage.[29] These "stereotyped conventions" of mass lynchings, as Brundage calls them, would help legitimize what Leard and his relatives were about to do and help give the appearance of public sanction to their personal vengeance.

Sam Pryor began. "Be still," he told the crowd. "Bring Lincoln McGeisey down and chain them together and then I am going to have him make a statement in the presence of all." Jim Jones, who had the key to Nelson Jones's lock, took the chain off Lincoln's ankle, leaving John Washington locked to the other end. Pryor took the loose end of the chain that was around Palmer Sampson's neck and put it around Lincoln's neck, and Jones inserted the lock he had taken from Lincoln's ankle and snapped it. Washington was turned over to Jones, who gave the key to the lock on Lincoln's neck to Leard and told him to keep it until he came back for it.[30]

Then Leard told Sampson to tell how he had killed Mary Leard:

I heard him commence and say, Yes, I killed her. Julius Laird interpreted for him and says, Now commence at the first of it, where was you before you come up here to borrow the saddle? Palmer says, I was down at Tom McGeisey. He was questioned by Julius Laird and asked, Who was there with you? Answer, Lincoln. Did you and him start off from there together? Yes. Did you come up here to borrow the saddle? Yes. About what time in the day was it? He pointed to the sun about two hours high. Then what did you do? He says, I come here to borrow the saddle and she would not let me have it. Question, where was Lincoln all that time? He says he was down here on Salt Creek and waited for me where the road struck the bottom. What did you do when you went down there and told Lincoln that she would not let you have the saddle? Lincoln says let's go up and fuck her. No, go on and tell us about it, what time it was when you come up here that night. He says we come back after dark, hitched our horses on the back side of the lot there and come into the house from over there through the gate and Lincoln tells me to come, and Lincoln went into the house at the east door where the woman was. What did you hear while he was in there? All that I heard was I heard him say I want to fuck you. I heard the children crying and the woman scuffling and she come out of the south door of the side room of the little house. I was standing right at the big house and Lincoln says shoot her and I snapped at her and the gun would not fire, and she run out by the big house door over towards the gate and me after her and she turned in a circle towards the well making a circle north coming straight back to the east door of the kitchen and just before she got to the porch of the kitchen I struck her on the head with the gun. And then what did she do? Answer, she hollered. Question, did you hit her any more? Yes, I hit her twice. Then what did Lincoln do? Then he fucked her. Then what did you do? Then I took the gun and stuck it back into the house. Didn't you turn her over there and take the child and put it in the door? Yes. Then where did you go after you had done this? I went down to Possak Harjo's to the dance. How long did you stay there. Stayed probably until the middle of the night, then I went home from there. This was all of the statement.[31]

Most of the crowd had no way of knowing whether Leard's "interpretation" of Sampson's statement was accurate or whether he had given it freely. Many had no way of knowing that the story was a fabrication. But those close to Leard—Herschel Leard, Ed Martin, Sam Pryor, Bird Ivanhoe, Clay Roper, Jesse Guinn, for instance—certainly knew about young Frank's insistence from the start that there had been only one Indian on the premises, that his mother had been killed before dark, that she had been hit only once, that she had not been raped, and that Lincoln McGeisey was not the guilty person. From the start, Frank had told these facts consistently, relating them in the presence of a number of people outside his family's circle. These men, now fabricating this "confession," also knew that the killer had a distinctive scar on his face, a mark that neither McGeisey nor Sampson had. Despite that knowledge and the fact that Leard had gone around with Jones and verified McGeisey's alibi the previous day, Leard had held McGeisey. Leard had probably held him at first as a hostage to try to extort information from Passack Harjo's settlement, but it had been apparent for several days that McGeisey was one of Leard's intended victims. By the time word had gone out to Oklahoma on Wednesday that a burning would occur, it was a virtual certainty that Lincoln McGeisey would be burned. But by that time, too, it was apparent that there would be two victims. It appeared that John Washington was to be the second until Palmer Sampson's name came up. When that happened is uncertain, but it had happened by Thursday morning when Thomas W. Martin visited Jones in the southern part of the Seminole Nation.

Who named Palmer Sampson as a potential victim is also uncertain, but he was well-known to some members of the mob. This seventeen-year-old son of Sukey Natuksie and Sampson Walker had a criminal record. In his early teens he had pleaded guilty to stealing a horse from a white man in the Seminole Nation. The usual sentence for horse stealing, given in the federal courts at the time, was a year and a day. Whether he served any time for the early offense is not known. However, at the time he was captured by Leard, he had only recently returned to the Seminole Nation after nearly a year in the Kansas State Penitentiary at Lansing. A little over a year earlier, he had been charged with grand larceny for stealing a horse in Pottawatomie County. Authorities had captured him with two other Seminole juveniles, Billy Sarber and Johnson McKaye, aged sixteen and thirteen respectively, who had broken jail. On December 31, 1896, all received sentences of a year and a day, including time already served, Sampson for grand larceny and Sarber and McKaye for breaking jail. Oklahoma Territory had no territorial prison but had a contract with the State of Kansas to hold its prisoners. The boys arrived at Lansing on January 2, 1897, and were discharged the following November 27, little more than a month before Mary Leard's murder. Sampson was little known in Leard's neighborhood, and no one had seen him there before the killing.[32] Why had Leard, Pryor, Roper, and Martin, who had been intent on burning Lincoln McGeisey and John Washington two days earlier, now determined to burn McGeisey and Sampson instead? The answer may lie in Leard's obsession with Passack Harjo's settlement.

To anyone who knew the surrounding Seminole community well, it might have appeared that the whole affair was a vendetta by Leard, his family, and close friends against the extended family of Passack Harjo. Most of the Seminole Nation residents harassed by the mob or otherwise involved in the case were somehow connected to his settlement: his children, his relatives, men married to his relatives, renters, interpreters, hangers-on, frequent visitors, or near neighbors.[33] The familial relationships between these people and Passack Harjo were such that the whites would have understood. There were probably other less obvious relationships through band, clan, blood, intermarriage, or place of residence between others harassed by the mob and the Passack Harjo-McGeisey families. The strategic location of Passack Harjo's settlement near the border crossing at Violet Springs placed the old man and his people in a position to observe traffic across the border. Did they know something about Leard, who was well-known at Violet Springs, that he resented? Was he still following his former sideline business as an illegal whiskey dealer? After the fact, not only Seminole officials and U.S. authorities but some newspaper editors as well believed that the whiskey trade was at the bottom of the events at Leard's farm.

Though the exact cause of the mob's focusing attention on Passack Harjo's settlement may never be known, there are hints at other possible motives. It was generally understood at the time that some of the mob members held a grudge against Lincoln McGeisey. The Williams family, who rented from Thomas McGeisey's cousin Hettie Coker, were angry because of the theft of their property by Lincoln McGeisey and George Harjo. But what about Leard? Relations between Leard and his landlord had apparently been good before the murder. In the "confession" he attributed to Palmer Sampson, however, he had suggested that not only McGeisey's household but Passack Harjo's had been covering up the killer's identity all along. Had Leard become angry because McGeisey refused to come at once and help him search for the killer? Was part of his anger aimed at McGeisey when he swore vengeance against Seminoles at random if he did not find the killer? Was it that, or could it have been something as petty as an incident over a saddle? A story handed down in the Guinn family tells how Leard once loaned his fancy saddle to Lincoln, who had raked it with a spur, leaving a mark, and how Leard had sworn never to let him use it again. Or had the search for his wife's killer simply turned into an exercise in racial vengeance? The kind of smoldering racism implied in Leard's threat to exterminate the tribe was the kind often harbored by poor white renters against the Indians from whom they rented and whose economic control they resented.[34] For whatever reason, Leard was determined to burn Lincoln McGeisey, for he and the mob had been persistent in trying to get those they threatened and tortured to implicate McGeisey in the killing. When it became obvious that no evidence would implicate him, they made up some by having Palmer Sampson "confess."

General talk had it that some of the mob members also held a grudge against Palmer Sampson. Again, what it was is uncertain, but there are points for speculation. The grudge might have resulted from the horse-stealing episode that sent Sampson to prison. Among those subpoenaed as witnesses against him were Cap Guinn, J. A. (Jake) Guinn, and Mrs. Jake Guinn. The Guinn men, brothers-in-law of Herschel Leard, as well as their father, brothers, and brothers-in-law, had been active in the mob during the week following Mary Leard's murder. There was also a strong connection between Sampson's trial and Passack Harjo. Among the witnesses were also Peter Osanna, Passack Harjo's brother-in-law, whom the mob arrested; Parnoka, also arrested at Passack Harjo's; Duffie, Sam, and Anna Harjo, Passack Harjo's children. In addition, Billy Sarber and Johnson McKaye, sentenced to the Kansas State Penitentiary with Palmer Sampson, listed Passack Harjo as their father in the prison record. McKaye had also been among the prisoners picked up on the first day at Passack Harjo's house. His listing Passack Harjo in the prison record may have been an expression of clan relationship rather than lineage or simply a listing of an important leader in his band, a person to contact if need arose. Sampson, too, belonged to the same band as Passack Harjo, but nothing in his record connected him to the old man except the witnesses in his case. Although the "confession" Pryor and Leard claimed to have obtained from Sampson linked him and McGeisey, no one had seen him in Lincoln's company, nor had he been at the dance at Passack Harjo's as Leard claimed. Sepa Palmer, who had been at Passack Harjo's house the day of the killing and stayed that night for the dance, said, "Lincoln McGeisey came to Passack Harjo's about an hour and a half by sun; . . . I saw him there all evening and all night." He added, "Palmer Sampson did not come with him; Palmer Sampson was not at the dance at all."[35] Thus Sampson's "confession" appears to have been a deliberate attempt to connect the murder of Mary Leard to Passack Harjo's settlement and was certainly aimed at condemning Lincoln McGeisey.

If, in fact, Sampson made the "confession" that Leard "translated" to the crowd, how did Leard and Pryor get him to make statements that they had known all along were contrary to what Frank Leard had described as the circumstances of Mary Leard's murder? While they had him in custody, either at Dave Guinn's home, where the Leard children were staying, or elsewhere—"a lonely and secluded place," as one report said—Pryor and Leard resorted to the tactics they had used with other captives in an attempt to coerce a confession: physical torture and threats of death. Roper and others had strung up Lincoln McGeisey, but they had got only a confession about Joseph Williams's stolen property. They had told George Harjo that he would be killed if he did not confess and at one point piled hay around him and threatened to light it if he refused. But they had gotten nothing from him. Neither did they get any information from John Washington after stringing him up repeatedly. The mob leaders had led their victims to believe that if they confessed they would be taken before the federal courts for trial. Now, Palmer Sampson, after being strung up four times, apparently gave in to Pryor's and Leard's demands, admitted to their statements, and implicated Lincoln McGeisey, apparently hoping to save himself.[36]

True or false, coerced or freely given, the "confession" is perhaps the strongest indicator that Leard, Pryor, and the other mob leaders were intentionally creating the guise of mass mob action to cover their private motives. Lynchings by private mobs, W. Fitzhugh Brundage argues, "hardly represented the expressed sentiment of the local white community. More likely," he continues, "private mobs resorted to an improvised lynching in order to give their private grievances a patina of legitimacy that would have been absent had they simply murdered their victims in their jail cells or homes." Mass mobs, on the other hand, were ritualized affairs that reflected the sentiments of the local white community.[37] Though no such community existed in the Seminole Nation and had to be imported for the occasion, their numbers would provide Leard, Pryor, and Ed Martin their desired cover.

As they no doubt expected, Sampson's "confession" had the desired effect on the crowd assembled at Leard's farm that Thursday evening. After the "confession," the crowd was lively and in good spirits. Ed Martin announced, "Gentlemen, nothing will be done until three o'clock in the morning; the burning will take place promptly at three o'clock." It was then about six. That left enough time to recruit more people for the mob. Men started at once to notify Pottawatomie County citizens that a burning would occur. Guards took McGeisey and Sampson into the house and held them, and Jim Jones took John Washington away.[38]

News had spread in Pottawatomie County that guilty Indians were in custody, apparently well before Leard and Pryor took Sampson to the Leard farm, perhaps even before they took him to Oklahoma, so contrived was the affair. The news circulated first near Maud. From there, the story of Sampson's arrest and "confession" went northward to Earlsboro, where people talked openly about the burning and the need to protect white women from Indian ravishers.[39]

The plan was to burn McGeisey and Sampson at the Leard farm. In preparation, mob members trimmed trees to tie the victims to. Men began to arrive in large numbers after dark, well in advance of the three o'clock time set by Ed Martin. As the crowd gathered, there was an air of expectancy and a general understanding that, unlike what had happened on Wednesday night, the burning would take place this time without fail.[40]

There had been only halfhearted protests against the proposed burning at the time Martin announced it. One had come from Hiram Holt, the Baptist preacher and petty Pottawatomie County official who had apparently come with Roper's party from the northern part of the county and who had been in the mob for days, assisting in making arrests. He went into the house where McGeisey and Sampson were under guard and, with a Winchester across his knee, prayed so loudly that it attracted the attention of the crowd outside.[41]

Shortly before nine o'clock, the mob leaders sought to give the event an air of "legal" procedure and further ritualize the affair. They took McGeisey and Sampson to the fire in the yard, forcing the Indian teenagers to stand at one end, where they could talk to the crowd. They made Sampson repeat his "confession." This time Jamie Clower wrote it down. Someone called for a prayer. Some, when called on to offer the prayer, refused. Mont Ballard said that "such sons of bitches as them . . . didn't deserve no prayers." But J. W. Wilson, who had ridden with several of the squads, offered one anyway. These events, dramatic and staged, a part of the planned ritual, served to put a "moral" cast on the event and to justify the burning in the minds of those who had not previously heard Sampson's alleged "confession." Pryor, Roper, Leard, and Martin were achieving their goal of protecting themselves by obtaining what Brundage calls "communal participation" in the violence.[42]

To make certain that everything went as they planned, Leard, Pryor, and other mob leaders galvanized their control over the men. They prohibited anyone to talk to McGeisey or Sampson, probably to prevent them from denying the "confession" or telling how it was obtained. Mike Lawless, the saloonkeeper from Earlsboro, approached McGeisey as he stood by the fire. He had known Lincoln for four years and was familiar enough with him to say that he was sorry to see him in this predicament and that he hoped the mob would let him go. Lincoln shook his head and said, "No, there was too many—," and at that point the crowd became suspicious of Lawless. One of the leaders stepped forward and asked him what he was talking to McGeisey about and told McGeisey that if he had anything to say, he had better say it to the whole crowd. At about eleven o'clock, Sam Pryor lined the men up, military fashion, and counted them. There were sixty-four.[43]

By midnight, the mob had grown to about 125 men, nearly all of them armed, arriving by horseback or in buggies and surreys. About that time, Jim

Jones and Andy Morrison drove up in a buggy. After he had left earlier that evening, Jones had taken John Washington to Nelson Jones's house, left him confined and guarded, changed teams in his buggy, and gone by Morrison's store and saloon at Violet Springs, apparently to get whiskey, and invited him to go to the burning. When they drove up at Leard's, ten or twelve men crowded around their vehicle, guns drawn, apparently suspicious of anyone arriving at such a late hour. Jones got out of the buggy and went to the fire to warm his feet. He told Sam Pryor and other mob leaders that if they were going to do anything to McGeisey and Sampson, they should take them across the line into Oklahoma Territory. He left the impression that the message had come from Nelson Jones. It may well have, for Jones had made a round trip that day from Sasakwa to his home, but at the time these events were transpiring near Maud, he was back at his camp near Sasakwa.[44] Also, Jim Jones was only a lackey and during the previous days had demonstrated neither backbone nor a capability for original thought. To come up on his own with the idea of taking the burning outside Nelson Jones's jurisdiction was probably beyond him.

After about ten or fifteen minutes at the fire, Jones became afraid for his own safety because of the way the crowd was acting toward him. Julius Leard explained that a good number of them did not know him and believed that he had been sent by his uncle, perhaps to spy or to interfere. Also, some of the preachers in the crowd, particularly Jesse Guinn and James D. Hodges, were angry because Jones and Morrison had whiskey in the buggy. Burning two Indians at the stake was one thing; drinking whiskey was quite another. As Jones and Leard talked, men began to gather around them to hear what they were saying, so they moved off a little distance, only to have the crowd follow them. Jones decided that he had better leave, so he climbed back into the buggy with Morrison. Then some of the crowd moved as if to stop them. Leard told them, "Hold on men; don't hurt them fellows, they are all right." Now truly frightened, Jones appealed to Leard, "Don't leave me, don't leave me, Julius," as he started up his buggy. Leard said, "I won't," and walked beside the buggy about forty yards from the crowd, and Jones and Morrison made their getaway.[45]

After Jones and Morrison left, Pryor and others huddled and talked, apparently deciding whether to follow Jones's advice and, if so, where to take McGeisey and Sampson to burn them. It had been Jones's role as a federal peace officer that apparently caused Leard, Pryor, and the others to make the burning a public spectacle in order to escape prosecution. Apparently still wary of federal authority, they decided to follow Jim Jones's advice. The fact that they did so lends further proof that this was not the work of an enraged mob seeking extralegal "justice." Had it been, they would have been less concerned with their careful framing of Lincoln McGeisey or matters of criminal court jurisdiction and would have done their dirty work at Leard's, where they had first intended.

By two o'clock, they had made their decision. They took the prisoners to the fire and read the confession once more, apparently for the benefit of the newcomers in the mob. Pryor also reiterated his qualifications as leader by saying that "he had been out in Texas where a crowd had burned some niggers" and stated that Jones had advised him to take McGeisey and Sampson across the line before they did anything to them. The mob leaders put McGeisey and Sampson into a surrey, still chained together. Pryor ordered the men, who then numbered about 150, to line up. The procession of horses and vehicles started with Pryor in the lead. Next came the surry, carrying Ed Nix, a salesman; John C. Wellborn, a liveryman from Earlsboro; Ed Martin; and the prisoners. After the procession had strung out along the road, Pryor rode back to the rear, telling the men to go quietly and do no shooting or yelling.[46] The secretiveness reflected in this order provides still more evidence that the leaders were less concerned about seeking "justice" than about escaping punishment for the criminal acts they were committing.

Just as the procession moved away from the house, H. Clay Roper, Pryor's "lieutenant" and brother-in-law, kicked in the door of a side room, went across the yard, picked up a burning fence rail from the fire, took it back, and threw it into the house. Bird Ivanhoe, Pryor's half-brother, also carried fire to the house and yelled out that there was a trunk inside. It was the property of Thomas McGeisey, so someone in the crowd said, "Let the trunk and all go to hell." Once they had set the house ablaze, Roper mounted up and helped Pryor marshal the mob on the march to Oklahoma.[47]

Following Pryor's orders, the mob marched at a "good fast walk," westward along the road from Leard's toward Maud. The line of marchers was clearly visible; it was cold, and the moon was bright. When they came out of the woods onto the prairie east of the Seminole line, they stopped while Pryor conferred with a number of his men and those far back in the line watched and waited. Then the procession started again, went through the gate in the fence that the Seminoles had erected on the border, traveled a mile west and then to the south about half a mile to the edge of some timber to what the people in the neighborhood referred to as a Baptist "tabernacle."[48]

The "tabernacle" was in reality a brush arbor about half a mile south of the Maud post office and had been the site of camp meetings during the previous summer. The mob leaders selected it as the site of the burning, presumably because there, at a makeshift altar, Mary Leard had got on her knees, Baptist fashion, and confessed her sins before God and the community. They would take the two Seminoles there, they concluded, and "mingle their blood with her departed spirit."[49]

At the arbor, Sam Pryor remained in command. After the surrey pulled up, he took McGeisey and Sampson out and led them to a tree about nine or ten inches in diameter. On this blackjack oak near the altar of the tabernacle the Baptists had hung their lamp during their nighttime meetings. He directed McGeisey and Sampson to stand on opposite sides of the tree, east and west, facing south. Then he and Roper made them walk a semicircle in opposite directions so that the chain wrapped around the trunk. Thus they stood, about eight feet apart, facing the north, their arms and legs free, with about four feet of chain connecting each by the neck to the tree. Men pulled down the brush and poles from the tabernacle, well cured and dry after having stood since the summer, and piled them around the two victims so they could not move about. Perhaps as a way of stating his credentials as a burner once more, Pryor boasted to the crowd, which had been swelled by local residents from the neighborhood, that this was not his first experience but that he had helped burn a black at Paris, Texas, some years earlier.[50]

Then in the presence of more than two hundred men and a few women and children, the burning began. There were at least three preachers present: "Parson" A. E. Butterfield, James D. Hodges, and Jesse Guinn, the latter two of whom had left the Leard farm sometime earlier, presumably outraged because some of the men had brought whiskey, but perhaps, as some would later charge, because they were too cowardly to accompany the mob. Someone called on Hodges to pray, but he said that he could not do it. Then Andrew J. Mathis, who had joined the mob with Roper, was called on. He knelt by McGeisey and Sampson and prayed with his Colt .45 belted on the outside of his overcoat. Next, Pryor offered the victims a chance to pray, and McGeisey said something in his own language. Then, while Mathis was still on his knees, so he said later, he touched a match to the dry brush. As the flames caught, neither McGeisey nor Sampson moved. Not until the flesh began to drop from his right thigh and the flesh of his right arm began to burn did McGeisey move. When the flames touched his right ear, "his hand went up as though in the act of brushing off a fly." He groaned, bent over, "and taking one long inhalation of the fire, sank down on his knees and expired." From the time the flames reached him, Palmer Sampson fought with his arms and legs; he threw and kicked burning pieces of wood, some as far as twenty-five or thirty feet, but the crowd kept piling wood on the fire for some time until he, too, bent over and was still. After the burning, Pryor repeated his boast about burning the black in Texas. As a last pronouncement, he threatened vengeance against anyone who afterward divulged information about the burning.[51]

After the two victims were well burned, Bird Ivanhoe took a stick and cracked one of the skulls. As a result of the heat that had built up inside, the brains boiled out. Some men became sick and ran. Ivanhoe screamed "with exultation."[52]

By midmorning, the Seminoles had become aware that something had happened at the Leard farm the night before. John Palmer [Palmer Sarmonie], carried a message to Peter Osanna, the Seminole lighthorseman, from Kinda Palmer, who said that Thomas McGeisey's houses were burning. Osanna sent word back for Kinda, also a lighthorseman, to meet him at the fire. Osanna found his interpreter, John Davis, a black U.S. citizen who had lived long on Osanna's place, and went on to the McGeisey farm to investigate. When the two parties of Seminoles arrived about ten o'clock, the fire had destroyed the improvements except for a haystack and a corncrib, which were in danger. They were fighting the fire when fourteen men, riding hard from the direction of Maud, came into sight. In the group were Julius and Herschel Leard, Cap, Jesse, George, and Russell Guinn, George Pettifer, Mont Ballard, and Ed Martin. These men, some of whom had apparently been drinking, pointed their cocked Winchesters at the Seminole lawmen and their party. "They came up to us in a big rush," Osanna said, "all four of us, and they threw they guns down on us and said, 'Hold up your hands.'" Then Jesse Guinn and Mont Ballard rode up to them and, on Guinn's orders, Ballard disarmed them. Even though they knew Osanna was a lighthorseman, Guinn asked through Davis what business they had there. Osanna, unaware that the mob had burned McGeisey and Sampson and that these men had helped to do it, said that they had come to investigate the fire and to put it out. Ballard ordered them to stop fighting the fire, and Guinn, pretending innocence, asked who had started it, apparently in an attempt to find out if the Seminoles knew anything. Osanna said that they did not know but had come to find out. Then Julius Leard rode up and told the riders that he had known Osanna for years and ordered Guinn and Ballard to return the men's arms. He told Osanna and the others to drive in the cattle, leave his in the lot, and drive away Thomas McGeisey's cow that was in the herd. After that, he wanted them to leave, he said, for he did not want them there.[53]

Ostensibly these mob members had returned to the scene to get Leard's livestock, but the presence of the Seminoles afforded an opportunity to justify publicly what the mob had done the night before and to deliver further threats. Leard told them deliberate lies about what had happened. He told them that he had brought in Palmer Sampson, who had confronted McGeisey and charged him with helping Sampson kill Leard's wife. McGeisey then confessed, Leard said, and the confession was written down. Shortly after that, Leard said, one hundred men took McGeisey and Sampson away, but he claimed not to know what happened to them. Then he said, "You will see an account of it in the newspapers, you will then find out what became of them and what they said in their confession." Leard then told the Seminoles to tell all of their tribesmen that if they bothered "any more of the white folks," what had happened to McGeisey and Sampson was "no comparison" to what would follow. He said, "You know I have been good to all of these folks and them boys came up here and killed my wife." And as a parting threat, Leard said that if the Indians "bothered any more white folks . . . all Oklahoma would turn loose on them."[54]

Leard's statements indicate that the burning was a deliberate act of racial vengeance. He was not speaking as a distraught husband seeking justice for his wife but as a white man seeking retribution against Indians. His threats echoed Sam Pryor's earlier boasts that he had been involved in burning blacks in Texas with impunity, apparently because the local Texas community condoned it. Leard asserted that Oklahoma whites would condone not only the burning but any future mob action as well, so long as it was done in the name of race.

The Seminole burning, however, was different from lynchings in the South, like those Pryor bragged about, and Leard knew it. Here were no local demands for social, political, or economic control of one race by another at stake, to be reasserted in an act of racial violence committed in the name of "justice." The Seminoles were not a part of Oklahoma Territory society, and Oklahomans were not subject to Seminole law. They were, in fact, two societies, foreign to each other. But to cover the true nature of the burning—that is, an act of private vengeance against the Passack Harjo-McGeisey families—Leard, his relatives, the Martins, and the other mob leaders contrived to make it appear to be like those acts that typified mobs the public was accustomed to hearing about. Though they knew that both victims were innocent, they had contrived an alleged confession to make them appear guilty not only of the heinous crime of murder but of rape as well. By doing so, they could characterize the burning as an extralegal execution of the law, carried out in a fit of outrage at the horrible crime. They could appear to exhibit a passionate desire for justice for Mary Leard, though more than a week had passed since her murder.

The general public of Oklahoma, however, did not know that during that week, Leard, Martin, Pryor, Roper, Ivanhoe, and others had become frustrated at their failure to find the killer and had given in to Indian hating. Leard's statements to Osanna and the others in the early hours following the burning were simply the first step in a deliberate cover-up of the truth. The burning had been an act of vengeance not just against an extended Seminole family but against a tribe and a race. The leaders had managed to involve a large number of Pottawatomie County citizens in their personal vendetta, and they now intended to manipulate the public at large to validate the act and to hide their own roles in it.

While Leard was delivering his threats to Osanna, another large group of the burners, including the main leaders Pryor and Roper, had gone to Earlsboro on their way home north and west of there. Exhausted from several days' riding, Sam Pryor rode to Earlsboro in the surrey with Ed Nix, John C. Wellborn, and John O'Malley. Pryor was apparently on his way to the home of his brother-in-law Roper, who had borrowed O'Malley's horse. A. J. Mathis also stopped in Earlsboro, had breakfast and a few drinks, and rode on, reaching home about noon.[55]

Word of the burning spread through the Seminole Nation. When the news reached Wewoka about ten in the morning, Seminole authorities sent J. Herman Patton, superintendent of Mekasukey Academy, to investigate. With his principal R. P. Hokie, he reached Leard's place about eleven, where he found the buildings in ashes, whiskey bottles littering the ground, and a large group of armed men standing around. These were apparently Leard and the mob members who had just sent the Seminoles away. When Patton asked one of the men if there had been a lynching, he replied, "I suppose there has been." He told Patton that "a lot of fellows" took the Indians away and said, "I understand they deserved all they got; I understand they made a confession." Then one of the crowd asked, "Boys, why are we staying here?" They mounted and rode off toward Oklahoma. Patton examined the ashes to see if the victims had been burned with the buildings but found nothing.[56]

Dr. C. P. Linn, the national physician for the Seminoles, learned of the burning about 10:30 and went to Maud, where he found a little boy who took him to the burning site. The bodies were still held by the chain wrapped around the tree. Only their trunks remained; the hands, feet, arms, and legs had completely burned. Linn identified the larger one on the right as Lincoln McGeisey, who in life was larger than Palmer Sampson. Leaving the remains in place, he returned to Wewoka to inform the Seminole authorities, who made arrangements for retrieving the bodies for burial. Meanwhile, during the day, the curious came to gawk at the charred remains. That evening, Linn got word to Hulbutta Micco, the second chief, about what he had found.[57]

The chief asked Patton, Henry Taylor, and Peter Lincoln, a Seminole freedman, to go with him to recover the bodies. They also took a number of armed men because they feared an attack from the mob. It was difficult to find the site in the dark. After making inquiries they finally found a reluctant informant who directed them, and they reached the site about 4:00 a.m. Sunday. They chopped down the tree to remove the chain from around it, loaded what remained of the bodies, the chain still around the necks, in a wagon, took them to Taylor's farm, and buried them in a common grave.[58]

Meanwhile, Nelson Jones, who had conveniently absented himself from the scene the previous Wednesday, remained in the southern part of the Seminole Nation. Jim Jones had kept John Washington guarded and de-livered him to the marshal on Saturday. He told his uncle about the mob's capturing Palmer Sampson, his "confession" that he and Lincoln McGeisey were guilty of the murder, the crowd's releasing John Washington, and the burning. Jones went to Sasakwa, where Johnny Brown, the chief's son, told him that news of the burning had already come by telephone. Though Jones wanted to telegraph the chief, Johnny discouraged him, saying it would do no good and would just be a wasted expense. Jones decided to save the money.[59]

A ghoulish fascination with the burning gripped the Maud community. People made spurious claims to dramatic roles in the affair. The curious went to look at the scene. Stories circulated about "grease" having cooked out of the two Seminoles and soaked the ground around the spot and about pieces of Palmer Sampson's flesh found several feet from the charred tree, supposedly flung there as he kicked and threw pieces of burning wood. People took parts of the charred tree trunk as souvenirs, one enterprising man taking most of it to make souvenir pen holders.[60]

During the next few days, the reality of what had happened settled upon the Maud community. Those who had instigated the burning and were largely responsible for organizing it had returned to the northern part of the county, to the Chickasaw Nation, or to other places, leaving the local mob members, both those deeply involved and casual participants, to deal with the aftermath. Whether from fear of Sam Pryor's threats of reprisal, guilt, or the "code" common among lynchers, the participants quickly realized that they must close ranks. As news of the burning became widespread throughout the rest of the county and across Oklahoma Territory, they continued the effort Leard had begun with Osanna, seeking to garner support for their action and to create outrage among the general population by spreading false stories, either on purpose or from ignorance, to make Lincoln McGeisey and Palmer Sampson appear to be not only murderers and rapists but necrophiliacs as well.

SIX

Defense of Burning

To say that newspaper men in Oklahoma Territory during the 1890s suffered from frequent lapses in journalism ethics would be an understatement. In those days of yellow journalism, the story was the important thing; facts were not always relevant. The well-known ethnologist James Mooney, who had spent some time in the territory studying the Ghost-Dance movement among the Cheyennes and Arapahos, wrote in 1896 that "the newspaper liar has reached an abnormal development in Oklahoma."[1] By 1898, the three major political parties—Democratic, Republican, and Populist—published strong weekly newspapers at Tecumseh, the Pottawatomie County seat. Given the journalistic practices of the day and a civic pride wounded by implications that the county citizenry were lawless, the local press entered or abetted, either intentionally or unwittingly, a conspiracy of silence instigated by the mob leaders to protect themselves and editorially defended the burning of Lincoln McGeisey and Palmer Sampson.

The first newspaper report of the murder of Mary Leard appeared on January 7, the day before the burning. It was a garbled story about what had happened at the Leard house in the late afternoon of December 30, and it claimed that two men had been caught and lynched.[2] Creative journalism or not, the last statement, published before the burning, was probably the result of the mob leaders' intent two days earlier to burn McGeisey and Washington. More significantly, however, it reflected a propensity of white

Pottawatomie County editors to jump to ready conclusions about the assault on a white woman by anyone with dark skin. The story read like a common account of lynch law "justice," a statement of outrage against an alleged crime. But the local editor did not know that the burning of McGeisey and Sampson would be a deliberate, premeditated act of racial vengeance that would smack of settling personal grudges.

Because of the weekly newspapers' publishing schedules, nearly a week passed before Pottawatomie citizenry had another local account of the event. That communication lapse proved a boon for the burners, who needed time to fabricate, refine, and circulate the lies that would make their actions seem justified in the minds of the local population. Though Frank Leard had said again and again that Lincoln McGeisey had not killed his mother, the mob members insisted that McGeisey was involved. They had, after all, burned him, and now they must make it appear he deserved it. Though they knew from the start that there was only one Indian at the scene, they had created the story of a second and insisted that he was Palmer Sampson. And though they had known from the start that the killer had not raped Mary Leard, they now insisted that he had, in order to make his crime seem even more heinous and theirs less chilling and inhumane. It was the stuff that newspapers of the day thrived on. The more horrible the mob leaders could make Mary Leard's death appear to the public, the more outraged they could count on the public to be, and the more justified they would seem in the burning. Thus in those critical few days following the burning, the mob leaders and members took advantage of rumors, the only source of "news," to justify themselves.

Meanwhile, readers outside Pottawatomie County saw exaggerated accounts of the affair that reflected the lies the burners intentionally circulated. On the day after the burning the *Washington Post* reported the burning of McGeisey and "another Seminole half-breed," who had allegedly both murdered and outraged Mary Leard. The next day the *Post* reprinted a front-page story, which circulated widely through reprinting in Oklahoma Territory and Indian Territory.[3] It, like others, reflected little of the truth, reporting the burning as immediate outraged reaction to a crime. It did not account for the nine days that elapsed after the killing, the decision by mob leaders to burn someone from the start, and the deliberate selection of two people to burn in place of the killer.

Also, within twenty-four hours of the burning, rumors of a Seminole uprising began to circulate. The rumors may have started as a result of the armed force of Seminoles who went with Hulbutta Micco to retrieve the remains of McGeisey and Sampson. When he returned from inspecting and burying the remains, Dr. C. P. Linn reported a good bit of excitement among the Seminoles.[4] Rumors claimed that white men divided up the victims' bones for souvenirs and that one of the bones was on display in a newspaper office in Tecumseh. The Seminoles, "shocked over the awful tragedy," were now "greatly incensed over the reported use of the remains." The whites' lawlessness and the burning had, in fact, outraged the Seminoles, but there was apparently never any danger of their retaliating. In the absence of Chief John Brown, Hulbutta Micco kept matters under control by instructing all of the band chiefs to make certain that their members followed the law and did not attempt revenge. The chiefs, according to reports, carried out his instructions "to the letter." Hulbutta Micco may have taken this step anticipating Thomas McGeisey's return to the Seminole Nation, for Chief Brown and the commissioner of Indian affairs believed that his return might result in retaliation from the Seminoles. Thus, for the time being, they refused him permission to return home.[5]

Other Seminoles played down the idea of revenge. Peter Osanna, whom the mob had arrested, denied that the Seminoles sought revenge for the burnings. "There was nobody raising any disturbance," he said, "nor any attempt made or thought of by any of the Indians to revenge the murder of those boys; I was a light Horseman right in the country where this trouble occurred and if there had been any body arrested I would have heard of it."[6]

Still, the newspapers engaged in a phenomenon common in Indian history, the fabricated Indian uprising, transforming rumors or practical jokes into "fact." The local press on the borders of Indian country had consistently engaged in attempting to fan sparks of conflict into flames of Indian war because such events historically meant money in the pockets of local merchants through increased sales of supplies, firearms, and ammunition.

There was in this case, certainly, some genuine fear on the Oklahoma side of the line, but there was still more unfounded hysteria. People were afraid to stay in their homes and fled, terrified, to other neighborhoods or hid in the timber or fields, even spending the night. During the next three days, waves of panic hit Maud, Earlsboro, Tecumseh, and Shawnee in Oklahoma and Holdenville in the Creek Nation. On January 12, the *Muskogee Evening Times* reported that an official of the Union Indian Agency at Muskogee had returned from the scene, having found all quiet in the Seminole Nation.[7]

The whites in Pottawatomie County were probably truly afraid. Many of them understood firsthand the urge for lawless, vicious reprisal. A large number of them had recently given in to it after the murder of Mary Leard. Why should they not expect similar action from the Seminoles following the burning of their friends, relatives, and fellow tribesmen without due process of law? In reality, one official said, the Seminoles were acting "nobly and peacefully" under the circumstances. Henry L. Dawes, chairman of the Dawes Commission, who was concerned that the burning might put the recent Seminole allotment agreement in jeopardy, commended the Seminoles for showing self-control and confidence. And as it turned out, Dr. Linn's original report about excitement along the border originated from his concern not for the whites but for the Seminoles who might become victims of roving bands of trigger-happy Oklahomans. Indian Territory papers complained about the "fake news artist of the Indian Territory," one calling the story "the champion fake of the season." Said the editor of the *Muskogee Phoenix,* "Up in New England they are now devouring the startling news and implicitly believing it gospel truth."[8]

Though a mistake, the three or four days of excitement had worked for the burners' benefit. Some in Oklahoma believed that opponents of the Curtis bill had started the stories of uprising to influence the final vote on the legislation, which was then working its way through Congress, and others believed—with more reason—that mob members had started rumors, hoping "thereby to screen themselves from the law." Marshal Leo E. Bennett at Muskogee held the latter opinion, claiming the burners had started the rumors to create "a sentiment to shield the members of the mob."[9] Whatever their source, the stories had brought Indian hating into the open and raised it to a new level. Such feelings could only increase sympathy for the burners. The excitement took attention away from them and gave them time to get their story straight.

The story that appeared in the *Tecumseh Republican* on January 14, almost a week after the burning, was the first local, detailed report of events that led to the burning and is, without question, the one the burners told. It was the one that became fixed in the minds of Oklahomans and Indian Territory citizens who were not involved in the event or did not know the results of subsequent official investigations. It is, in fact, the falsified story that is still told, with variations, in Pottawatomie County after nearly a century.

This story of Mary Leard's murder, embellished with falsehoods and exaggerations, was clearly designed to justify the burning. It said that two

Indians came to the house and asked to borrow various articles. When she refused, they threw her to the ground, and each one held her while the other raped her. She broke free, grabbed her baby, and started to run. One of the Indians tried to shoot her, but the gun misfired. The other grabbed the gun from him and struck her over the head, breaking the gun barrel from the stock. Using a piece of the gun as a club, he hit her several times more. The two then left but returned about half an hour later and sexually violated the corpse. Suspicion fell on Lincoln McGeisey. Though he denied his guilt, white Oklahomans strung him up until he implicated Sampson. When they went for Sampson, his home was barricaded, and they had to force their way in to capture him. On the way back to the Leard place, he allegedly confessed, implicating McGeisey. Once confronted with Sampson's confession, McGeisey also confessed, and both signed a written statement. In addition, the Leard children allegedly identified both as the killers. Exactly how "justice was meted" the *Republican* did not know. "No one," the story said, "seems to know any particulars except the story of the awful fate which two charred remains, of once living beings, conveys to the imagination."[10] This was the story Julius Leard had promised the Seminoles the morning after the burning that they could read in the newspapers.

The story would have gone unchallenged had it not been for the false reports of an impending Seminole uprising. On January 12, Secretary of the Interior C. N. Bliss asked Governor Cassius M. Barnes of Oklahoma for a full account of affairs on the border. Though doubting the rumors of Seminole outbreak, Bliss asked the secretary of war to dispatch troops to Wewoka as a precaution. Indian agent Dew M. Wisdom at Muskogee had doubted the rumors from the start, but sent his son and clerk, J. Fentress Wisdom, to investigate. Also in the field were Walter T. Fears, the U.S. commissioner who had been holding court at Wewoka; Luman F. Parker Jr., assistant U.S. attorney for the northern district of the Indian Territory; and U.S. Marshal Leo E. Bennett and his deputy James F. (Bud) Ledbetter, assigned to the recently established northern district court of the Indian Territory at Muskogee. These U.S. officials from the Indian Territory debunked the stories of an outbreak, and military officials quickly realized that troops were not necessary.[11] Once highly placed Washington officials became involved, however, federal authorities in Oklahoma Territory could not let the event remain a local affair for Pottawatomie County officials to handle.

On the day before Bliss's inquiry, Governor Barnes had taken preliminary steps to find out what had happened. It had taken him a day or two to learn that the burning had occurred in Oklahoma rather than in Indian Territory. Assured by Pottawatomie County officials that every effort would be made to bring the mob participants to justice, the governor issued a proclamation of reward, calling the episode "acts of lawlessness and barbarism" and condemning the "inhuman torture" of the Seminoles as an act "in which humanity and civilization was outraged." Though stressing his confidence in Pottawatomie officials to see justice done, Barnes believed the "enormity" of the crime "and the peculiar conditions surrounding" it called for territorial assistance. Thus he offered one thousand dollars—the largest amount permitted by Oklahoma territorial law—for the arrest and conviction of the mob members.[12]

Unlike Barnes, others were not so certain that Pottawatomie County officials would seek justice. In Washington, Seminole Chief John F. Brown called for prosecution of the perpetrators, though he doubted it would happen because several of them were well-known and influential. His appeal led to a resolution on January 14, offered by Senator Matthew Quay of Pennsylvania through the senate committee on Indian affairs, for a $25,000 appropriation to prosecute and convict the mob.[13]

Governor Barnes's confidence in Pottawatomie officials was, in fact, misplaced. The citizens they served were well aware of the attention territorial and federal officials were bringing to focus on them. The *Tecumseh Republican* said, "Every effort possible is being made by the local authorities, but owing to the circumstances surrounding the affair and the condition of things in that part of the county it is very doubtful if the real perpetrators are ever apprehended."[14] If the citizens of Pottawatomie County had anything to do with it, they would not be, despite the *Republican*'s assertion that local officials were doing everything possible.

Although the Department of the Interior, through Governor Barnes, had taken immediate action by offering a reward, Justice Department officials in Oklahoma were slow to become mobilized. Apparently uncertain or unaware they had jurisdiction, they lost nearly two weeks of valuable time, which allowed the burners to close ranks and solidify their unity. On January 20, however, Congress forced action by a Senate resolution directing both the secretary of the interior and the United States attorney general to report what steps they had taken to find the facts regarding both the murder and the burning and their intended steps to punish the offenders.[15]

The next day, the attorney general's office began to press the case. Attorney General Joseph McKenna asked U.S. Attorney Caleb R. Brooks at Guthrie the same questions the Senate had asked him. Brooks had already directed the marshal to send deputies to Pottawatomie County and had sent Assistant U.S. Attorney Thomas F. McMechan of Oklahoma City to determine whether Oklahoma officials had jurisdiction in the case. McKenna, feeling the Senate's pressure, did not want to hear that Brooks was awaiting a report; because of the "great importance" the burning case had assumed through Senator Quay's interest, he wanted Brooks's "prompt personal attention." U.S. Attorney Pliny Soper at Vinita, Indian Territory, already had testimony in hand. McKenna directed Brooks to consult Soper and let nothing stand in the way of prompt action.[16]

By then, resistance to the federal officials was beginning to rise in Pottawatomie County. Unlike Governor Barnes, Brooks was convinced the mob could not be tried successfully in their home community. When, near the end of January, he believed erroneously that there might be as many as three hundred conspirators, he warned that the process would be costly because the marshal could "not expect to get any assistance from any citizen of that county, but must take men there with him."[17] All of this early posturing and presupposition of action was based on an erroneous belief that the mob and its leaders had been exclusively Pottawatomie County citizens from the immediate vicinity of the burning.

Local resistance to federal investigators was organized and firm. Assistant Attorney McMechan had faced a stone wall in his search for information: "The people of Pottawatomie County are very much in sympathy with the persons who burned these Indians. It is a very hard matter for one to get information. . . . I was informed that it would not be well for me or any other person to go into the neighborhood in which the burning took place if it was known that the object was to discover parties who participated in the burning." Thus McMechan had learned only accounts told in the community, that is, the mob's "official" account of events surrounding the killing of Mary Leard, the determination of the "guilt" of McGeisey and Sampson, and the burning. However, his preliminary evidence showed that if the United States decided to prosecute on the charge of conspiracy, he could easily learn the names of some who participated in the burning.[18]

The task would prove more difficult than McMechan perceived. On January 26, Brooks wrote, "The people in the community of the burning and in the county of Pottawatomie are all very much in favor of the conspirators and aid them in every way possible, and condemn any officer or other person who they suspect of desiring information of the guilty parties. The conspirators are banded together for the purpose of resisting arrest or interference of the officers, all of which has made it very difficult for us to get anything like authentic information." The legal process was also in the burners' favor. When arrested, they would appear before the U.S. commissioner in Pottawatomie County for preliminary hearing, a grand jury in that county would then investigate, and any trials held would take place there. Most unsettling of all was that the United States could not prosecute them for murder but for conspiracy, which carried a maximum sentence of only six years. "I think," Brooks said, "if the conspirators knew that we can only hold them here on a limited penitentiary charge, they might surrender and waive a preliminary hearing, but they fear that we will hold them for the Indian Territory authorities." Brooks had determined to swear out warrants for conspiracy but wanted to know if they could not be tried for murder and conspiracy in Indian Territory even though the burning occurred in Oklahoma, because the United States had full authority there.[19]

After he had completed a preliminary investigation, Canada H. Thompson, U.S. marshal for Oklahoma Territory, concluded that it would be not only difficult but expensive to get evidence and to arrest the burners. With an estimated two to three hundred to be arrested, he faced a manpower shortage. Of twelve deputies in the entire territory, only six were available for field duty. If the burners did not resist, he might make the arrests with his present force, but if they did, they could wipe out his men. He decided simply to let circumstances lead him concerning raising a posse and to work with two office and three field deputies, realizing that if the burners fought as they had announced they would, he would need a posse of at least fifty men.[20]

Meanwhile, Thompson put a plan in operation. Success in making arrests would depend on quick action and an element of surprise so that the marshal could do his work before public sentiment could rise against him and his deputies, who included the veteran lawmen William Fossett, Heck Thomas, and William M. (Bill) Tilghman. Thompson also hired seven possemen, persons who lived in the vicinity or whom he called "proven men" to assist them, including George W. Berry, who had lived in the Seminole Nation most of the time since 1881 and was fluent in the Muskogee language; Thompson Brown, a Seminole, their translator, whom the mob had harassed; and Neal Brown, an old friend of Bill Tilghman from his Dodge City days and his posseman in recent years. Their job was to help locate suspects and witnesses and collect evidence. Canada

Thompson, the leader of this effort, was a seasoned investigator. He had worked as a confidential investigator for the Rock Island Railroad Company, investigating and gathering evidence in a number of important cases.[21] As events would demonstrate, Thompson's persistence and thoroughness in the burning cases were invaluable.

Their first task was to pacify the Seminoles. When Berry began work in the Seminole Nation on January 21, sentiment was so high against prosecution in Pottawatomie County that the Indians at first refused to tell what they knew. The deputies met with Seminole leaders, who sent runners out to bring in those who supposedly had information. The deputies and their assistants fanned out, traveling by horseback, wagon, and buggy over the Seminole Nation, parts of the Creek Nation, and southern Pottawatomie County, interviewing witnesses and taking depositions, securing as much information as possible. There were practical obstacles to getting that information. Many of the Seminoles either did not speak or understand English or did so with difficulty, and the work of interviewing had to be done through Thompson Brown. It was difficult to recreate the sequence of events in early January because the Seminoles did not tell time by the clock but by the position of the sun. And some did not reckon days. For example, when asked what day the mob had captured him, Sam Harjo replied through Brown, "I do not know, I do not notice days." And determining distances was also a problem. The Seminole Nation had no section lines, and travel routes consisted of a tangle of trails and wagon roads.[22]

Open resistance to prosecution by Pottawatomie County citizens as well as white renters in the Seminole Nation added danger to the difficulty of Marshal Thompson's investigation. The white community had become so unified in opposition that for a time the investigators could not obtain hay and grain for their horses, a necessity in the winter when graze was not available. They received warnings not to camp in one section of the Seminole Nation where they had gone to question witnesses. One night, as George Berry was on his way to an interview, about twenty armed men, presumably burners, surrounded him, held him up, and forced him to chew up and swallow the depositions he had taken earlier that day. They searched him but failed to find other papers he had. Had they found them, Marshal Thompson believed, the burners would have "undoubtedly killed him." In summing up his men's work in the Seminole Nation, Thompson said that it "was done rapidly, efficiently and thoroughly and with loaded guns." Their work was "dangerous in the extreme"; one false move would have resulted in "a small war." Though he believed he had enough evidence to make arrests after he had taken depositions from the Indians, Thompson wanted evidence from the whites, who he knew would be reluctant to give it. Thus he had his men who were unknown in the region pose as cattlemen and was able thereby to get some evidence. After the first two or three whites talked, then started what Thompson called a "chain." By early February, Thompson believed not only that he could identify the burners but that the courts could convict them of conspiracy.[23]

Part of Thompson's difficulties stemmed from the congressional demands for a full-scale investigation and prosecution, after which the whites of Pottawatomie County began to close ranks. S. J. Scott, a well-known Tecumseh groceries and furniture merchant, touted locally as "an old Indian Trader and friendly to Indian people," drafted letters to Congressman John S. Little and Senator James K. Jones, both from Arkansas and members of the congressional committees on Indian Affairs. His letter, published for local consumption in the *Tecumseh Republican*, aimed to help counter the Senate's proposed resolution to appropriate $25,000 for capturing and prosecuting the burners. Scott presented what he called "the facts" as he learned them. The story he told was basically the one that had been printed in the *Republican* a week earlier, but with certain changes in "facts" and refinements aimed at enhancing the sense of outrage on the part of local whites. In this refined version, Mary Leard was knocked on the head before she was raped: "Then, while writhing in the agonies of death, one of the Indians held her head between his knees while the other Indian ravished her. Then the Indian who ravished Mrs. Leard held her head in like manner until his companion ravished her also." They left and returned and, when she was "about dead, both again ravished the woman." According to those who laid out the body, Scott said, "she was dead when they last violated her person." The remainder of Scott's version followed the general lines of the story previously told.[24]

Scott defended the action of the burners. Apparently anticipating accusations that here was another instance of southern mob action, Scott said that the county's population consisted of people from nearly every state. Throughout this cross-section of humanity, he had heard no one who said that "burning was the proper thing to do"; but, he said, "I have heard a great many say that they should have been killed outright, without judge or jury."[25] These statements, of course, were based on such versions of the story as Scott told.

Scott sought to inflame racist passions in his readers. "Think," he said, "of the mutilated form of that woman, think of the innocent little boy, who, in the dark hours of that darkest of all nights, ran off the hogs from his murdered mother at the door, the distracted father who came back in time to help bury his wife, of the white men neighbors who came and looked on and traced out the murderers, would you cover up the awful crime committed by the brutal beasts? Will money voted by congress to prosecute a mob make more secure womanhood? Will it insure protection to virtuous, inoffensive, weak mothers, sisters and wives of hard-toiling workingmen?" These hardworking folk did not approve of the burning, nor did they approve of prosecution of the burners, Scott argued. Then, like most bigots who believe in the innate inferiority of darker races, he claimed "many friends" among the Indians, but his friendship, he said, was "not for fiends like these." Like other whites in Pottawatomie County, Scott claimed that he did not know any of the burners, nor did he care to.[26] The conspiracy of silence was in place. And Scott's language clearly shows the public believed that race was at the bottom of the affair.

Newspaper editors throughout Oklahoma Territory generally supported the racist views and mood of resistance displayed by Pottawatomie County. They accepted as fact the story circulated by the burners. One Guthrie paper, for example, said: "While deploring the incident there comes a feeling of satisfaction that the manhood and chivalry of Oklahoma's adopted sons is in prime condition just now, and that neither Seminole nor Senegambian can outrage a white woman in this territory and not die."[27] Pottawatomie County editors reprinted such editorial comments from outside the county to boost local support for the burners.

The editor of the *Tecumseh Republican* supported the burners by attacking the Oklahoma City *Times-Journal*, which claimed to be the only newspaper in the Territory to condemn the burnings. The Oklahoma City *Oklahoman* also attacked the *Times-Journal* editor, stating sarcastically that the Seminole Council had introduced legislation to adopt him, with annuity privileges, into the tribe as a reward for his work on behalf of the two rapists and murderers. The *Republican* reprinted that item and added in its best racist form: "The bill has been supplemented by a proffer of the fattest squaw in the tribe and a ready-made pappoose [sic]."[28]

Given the prevailing attitude in Pottawatomie County, Marshal Thompson had rightly concluded early on that officials there would never prosecute or convict the burners for murder, in which the county had jurisdiction.

By the end of January, most federal officials agreed with Thompson and decided to build cases solely on the charge of conspiracy, under federal jurisdiction.[29]

As a result of Thompson's and McMechan's preliminary investigations, the U.S. court at Guthrie issued more than seventy warrants, which Thompson began to serve the first week in February. With six office and field deputies and the possemen he had used in his investigation, Thompson scoured the countryside. The work was slow because local sympathy for the burners remained strong. The suspects were scattered or in hiding, and after three days, only fifteen were under arrest, including W. H. Vansickle, Jesse Guinn, Mont Ballard, and George Pettifer, but none of the mob leaders. Thompson expected to arrest fifty more, though it was reported that many who were implicated in the burning were leaving the territory. The men in custody—most from Maud and Earlsboro—were described as "a sturdy honest looking set of men, most of them are farmers, one minister of the gospel, and another a blacksmith. One of them, Hardy Williams, is only 15 years old." Observers noted that both Thompson and McMechan treated the prisoners "with the utmost kindness" and seemed "to have no desire to harass them unnecessarily." A kind of party mood prevailed at the jail in Tecumseh. The local sheriff made jokes with the prisoners, and the saloons sent beer to them.[30]

After two weeks, the marshals had arrested nearly seventy and taken them before U.S. commissioners at Shawnee, Tecumseh, or Oklahoma City, all charged with conspiracy and released under bonds of $800 to $1,500 to appear at the next term of the district court at Guthrie. Local officials apparently were not discriminating when it came to those who signed the bonds, taking the signatures of anyone, even renters. All pleaded not guilty and waived preliminary hearings, except Poliet Smith, Edward Nix, and W. H. Davis, apparently to avoid giving testimony. In the preliminary hearing, however, after two witnesses, these three changed their minds and waived further examination. Whether intimidation caused this sudden change of plan is uncertain. Sam Pryor, the organizer of the burning, had threatened retaliation against any of the mob members who divulged information, and federal officials found evidence that there was an organized effort among the members to intimidate witnesses, threaten officers, and prevent the leaking of information.[31]

During these proceedings, Thomas McGeisey was in Shawnee and Tecumseh, monitoring the process. When asked his opinion regarding the guilt or innocence of those arrested, he refused comment, saying it was improper for him to do so while the investigation was going on. He wanted the law to take its course, and to observers, he seemed to be searching for the facts rather than seeking revenge. The truth was that McGeisey was probably more involved in pushing the investigation forward than it appeared. He had known that his son was innocent of Mrs. Leard's murder before he left for Washington, D.C. While at the capital, he was with the Seminole delegation that prevailed upon officials to intervene in the case. Upon his return to the Seminole Nation, he had undertaken his own investigation and was convinced that Palmer Sampson as well as his son was innocent. He would later write the commissioner of Indian affairs, "I have fully investigate whether the boys were guilty or not for murdering of Mrs. Leard. I am now satisfied both of these boys were wholly innocent, especially for my son, I can prove by more than a dozen witnesses all prominent people, that he was innocent, but he was put to death by fearful outrage, just to get the revenging, that was all—for I am satisfied that they knew he was innocent." Thus he urged the commissioner of Indian affairs to prosecute them to the fullest extent of the law.[32]

With McGeisey at Tecumseh and Shawnee in early February were a number of Seminoles and others, summoned as potential witnesses in the preliminary hearings. Among them were George Harjo, Peter Osanna, Kinda Palmer, John Palmer, John Davis, Sam Ela, John Washington, Sam Harjo, and Thompson Brown, their interpreter. A number of them borrowed advances from deputy marshal W. D. Fossett and McMechan against their fees as witnesses. Some apparently used the cash to go out on the town and, as Marshal Thompson put it, "were decoyed to Shawnee and into the back room of a saloon and brutally beaten and on trying to escape, were fired at."[33]

After the initial excitement caused by the arrests and preliminary hearings, Pottawatomie County citizens regained some of their confidence. The mob members still believed that Pottawatomie County courts would never convict them, and fears of being taken to the Indian Territory for trial began to subside. The editor of the *Leader* even complimented Thompson for his handling of the arrests, as did Foster of the *County Democrat*. Editor C. A. Stauber of the *Republican* expressed a kind of sick humor about the arrest of W. H. Davis, editor of the Earlsboro *Plain People:* "Just because a man murders the English language occasionally is no reason for suspecting him of mob violence." Stauber also tried to make it appear that those who were wanted were cooperating with the marshal's forces by coming in voluntarily.[34] But cooperative spirit was not exactly the image conveyed by other sources, which reported that many of those implicated were leaving the country to avoid arrest. Though officers were not pursuing these men and were treating the arrested with "all consideration," public resistance to the arrests continued. McMechan claimed that the sentiment at Maud was with the mob and "that it would not be well for him or any other person to go into that neighborhood if the object was to locate conspirators."[35] One newspaper tied that resistance to the assertion that those arrested were "all prominent in this county in political and church circles and have friends in all parts of Oklahoma Territory, who are coming to their assistance."[36] That statement was only partially true. Some were not so prominent.

In the wake of the arrests, the ubiquitous S. J. Scott appealed in the burners' behalf to both Marshal Thompson and U.S. Attorney Brooks. While admitting that the burning should not have occurred, he wanted them to consider the character of those whose information had brought charges against certain men. Four or five, for instance, had been arrested after statements made by J. M. Johnson. Johnson, whom Scott called "a tramp" that had never been in the neighborhood of the burning, had just completed a ninety-day sentence in the county jail for stealing. Johnson could not name anyone who was in the mob, according to Scott. Scott gave testimonials for some of the burners, including the Reverend J. D. Hodges, whom Scott did not know very well but who bore "the name of a man who strictly attends to his own business & could not have been connected with the burners." And finally, Scott protested any information filed by Nelson, David, or James Jones, who were themselves arrested and under bond. "Much consideration should be given to the character of the individuals swearing out the papers," Scott said.[37] Whether Scott was simply ill informed or lying is uncertain, for the men whose character he defended had been in the mob.

Despite the arrests, editor Stauber of the *Tecumseh Republican* and others took heart in the report of preliminary investigation that McMechan had filed with the attorney general of the United States in January. While emphasizing the circumstantial quality of the evidence against McGeisey and Sampson, the report basically reaffirmed earlier reports, including the assumptions of two killers, the defiling of Mary Leard's body, and the alleged confessions of McGeisey and Sampson. McMechan's report, relayed by the attorney general to the Senate on February 4, became public and, printed widely, gave a kind of "official" status to the version of events told by the burners. The information that McMechan had obtained had been gained grudgingly and was seriously in error as his own subsequent investigations would show. Editor Stauber argued that McMechan's report verified the one Scott sent earlier to the Arkansas congressional members in support of the burners.[38] Stauber had no way of knowing, probably, that both Scott's and McMechan's versions had come from the same source—Julius Leard and his cohorts.

By the third week of February, the marshals had arrested most of the the known mob participants, and the accused had secured bonds and were awaiting the action of a grand jury. The public had only the burners' word that Sampson had confessed and implicated McGeisey. Investigators in the field, however, who had gravely doubted McGeisey's guilt from the start, had begun to hear rumors that McGeisey was innocent and that Sampson may have been forty miles away at the time of the murder. As soon as word of the burning reached the Seminole delegation in Washington, Chief John Brown publicly raised questions about their guilt. After the initial investigation had gotten well under way, Governor Barnes asserted McGeisey's innocence and Marshal Heck Thomas the innocence of both. Investigation had shown that no one had seen Sampson in Leard's neighborhood prior to the murder, and during the interrogation of Mary Leard's father and brothers, they had never indicated that there had been more than one killer or that Mary Leard had been raped.[39]

Public statements from "high officials" about the Seminoles' innocence annoyed local newspapermen. J. E. Doom of the *Tecumseh Leader,* said such statements were meant "to prejudice the public against our countrymen, leaving the impression that our people are a reckless and lawless people." Much of the distrust and fear that had gripped the community since the burning, he said, had resulted from stories of Indian uprising and rumors that federal authorities would take the burners to Muskogee and jail them to await trial. The press, he said, was duty-bound to protect the public from "those sensational newsmongers."[40] The Pottawatomie County press corps, presumably, were not among the mongers. Thus with local editors and citizenry assuming that the story that the burners had told was true, they prepared for what they predicted to be a difficult struggle against the money and power of the federal government. Part of that defense was a campaign to justify the burning as a means of meting out justice, even if the two Indians proved innocent.

The type of lynching they defended was that which prevailed in the South. Though practiced in America since colonial times, lynching by 1898 had become prevalent within the lifetime of adult Americans. By the late 1890s, certain mythologies concerning lynching had become fixed in the public mind. One was that the most common cause of lynching was rape, though rape was not alleged in more than 80 percent of all lynchings. Another was that only members of the lowest level of society engaged in lynching, while, in reality, legislators, jurists, professional people, merchants—in fact, members from all levels of society—took part. And underpinning the practice was a deep-seated belief that the judicial system was defective; it worked slowly, and legal maneuvering sometimes denied justice. Thus there was the popular belief that lynching had a positive effect by helping to maintain law and order.[41]

That it was necessary to defend lynching at all must have been somewhat disconcerting to local editors, given the climate of public opinion regarding lynch law at the time. The prevalence of lynching as an extralegal mode of obtaining "justice" caused legal scholars to give it close scrutiny in the waning years of the nineteenth century. They tended to agree with the general public regarding the matter of law and order, concluding that lynchers and vigilantes responded to "an unsatisfactory American legal system." In the minds of lawyers, judges, and legal scholars, "devotion to the strict letter of the law . . . gave way to their primary desire for order." They viewed lynching as a means of repressing crime, though there was no evidence that it did. As historian Richard Maxwell Brown has written, "To them the law rigorously applied seemed to hamper justice while lynch law enhanced it. It is this that explains why some founders of state bar associations could be unashamed participants in lynch law. They saw no contradiction."[42]

Though Oklahoma Territory did not have a lynching record to match that of some states, it had its share of mob action during its short history. Groups that historian W. Fitzhugh Brundage labels terrorist mobs early on had attempted to intimidate black settlers who had come into the territory in such large numbers that whites began to fear what they called "negro domination." Generally labeled "white caps," these mobs in Oklahoma Territory had warned blacks to leave Downs in 1890, Norman in 1893 and 1896, and Blackwell in 1897. After the Cherokee Strip opened in 1893, white caps and vigilance committees also intimidated sooners and claim jumpers, cattle and horse thieves, and politicians. They put sooners and claim jumpers on notice at Cross, Kremlin, and Round Pond; they ordered a townsite officer and the mayor of Round Pond out of town; and a vigilance committee organized at Enid to fight cattle and horse thieves. When there was an attempt to suppress vigilante activities near Round Pond, the reaction was predictable because, said the *Watonga Republican*, "there are many protective associations in the strip." Elsewhere in Oklahoma, reports of vigilance committee activities came from Choctaw City in 1894, Edmond in 1895, and Perry in 1896.[43]

When territorial governor Cassius M. Barnes reported that the Seminole burning was the first lynching in Oklahoma, he either was ignorant of the territory's history, was glossing it, or had an unusual definition of lynching. Oklahoma Territory had experienced its first lynching on the day after the land rush opened the territory in 1889. From then until 1898 there were at least nine other reported lynchings involving eighteen victims. The most striking statistics regard the race of the victims: two whites, two Mexicans, five blacks, and ten Indians. In 1897, the national press set the number of lynchings in Oklahoma Territory at six in 1896 alone. The number, not substantiated by the local press, seems high in light of documented cases and Governor Barnes's statement.[44] Barnes may have had in mind only mass mobs such as the newspapers depicted the one at Maud to be, for the documented lynchings in Oklahoma had not been that type but had been the work of small, private mobs. Regardless of the type or size of the mobs, Oklahoma editors throughout this violent era of territorial history, like their counterparts in the South and elsewhere, embraced myths regarding lynching and the concept of lynching as a social corrective and an extralegal means of meting out "justice." Through the years, only the *Langston City Herald*, published at the all-black town of Langston, had consistently printed editorials against lynching and supported Anti-Lynch League organization.[45]

The citizens of Pottawatomie County differed little from other territorial residents in their attitudes toward vigilantism and lynch law. Their propensity for vigilantism had revealed itself in recent times in the organization of local Law and Order Leagues in 1895 and late 1897 and white capper activities in 1896. Pottawatomie County residents also tended to view lynching and mob law as a social corrective. In early January 1896, someone murdered and robbed two elderly bachelor brothers named Mountz. Evidence indicated that four men were involved, and circumstantial evidence led to the arrest of Israel C. McGlothlin.[46] While he was in jail at Tecumseh, six masked men overpowered the jailer, broke open the cell door, and took McGlothlin to the city park, where they strung him up three times, nearly killing him in an effort to make him reveal his accomplices. The local newspaper lauded their efforts: "While nearly every body condemns mob law yet in this case the perpetrators were merely trying to bring the evidence out so the law could get hold of the murderers."[47] Despite the frequent activities of small terrorist mobs and the editorial support for lynching, Pottawatomie County and the territory had not experienced lynching by a mass mob like that at Maud appeared to be.

Given the climate of opinion, though, county residents would have expected little else than an editorial defense of the burning of Lincoln McGeisey and Palmer Sampson. J. E. Doom of the *Tecumseh Leader* justified it by making the timeworn what-if-it-had-been-your-wife/daughter/niece question. He asked his readers to think of the mother with the nursing babe, her alleged violation by the two "fiends," and the hogs devouring her corpse. The action of the mob, he argued, had its origins in the "nobler feelings of outrage."[48] Of course, Doom failed to point out a major difference between the burning and most mass lynchings: the lapse of time between the murder and the burning. Doom failed to mention that it took more than a week for those "nobler feelings," as he called them, to find their way to the surface and transform themselves into mob action. But Doom did not know that the lynching was not spontaneous; that Leard, Martin, Pryor, Roper, and others had had to recruit numbers by sending out news of a planned burning; that most who responded to the call went out of curiosity, not out of a desire to see "justice" done.

To build his case for the nobility of burning, Doom published what purported to be a signed confession by McGeisey and Sampson, which he copied from the *Shawnee Quill*. It read:

> I came here on Thursday to Okffsto: I saw his wife; I came then to George Wolf's, I saw him and one man and one woman go to Eurka Sile. I saw one woman, she came out and talked to me then to Cayitolar. From there to McGeesy, from there to Salt Creek. I met with Lincoln McGeesy. I asked him for money, he asked me what I wanted with it. I told him I wanted to get some whiskey, he said he had some whiskey. He said to me: "Lets go to Jules Laird." I asked him what for, he said, "to borrow his saddle." We came up in about 300 yards of the house. I asked the woman where the man was and she said he had gone to the store. I said to her I wanted to borrow saddle she said there was saddle there but it was not Mr. Laird's.

I told her I wanted a drink of water. I went and got a drink and warm by the fire. Then I went back to where Lincoln was; he asked me what the woman said, I told him she said the man had gone to the store; Lets go down to the house and ravish woman, may be she got money. We went, climbed over fence. Lincoln told me to go in the house and get the gun; I went and got it and went to kitchen. I snapped the gun at her. She went out of the house at the other door; I followed her out. Lincoln said "give me the gun." He knocked her down with the gun. She fell on her face. He gave me the gun and I put it in the house Lincoln turned her over and committed rape on her. Then Lincoln McGeesy said "Lets go." When we got off half a mile he said me go to my house and he would go to his home. I went home—I don't know where Lincoln went.[49]

Of course, Doom's readers did not know, as investigators did, that numerous witnesses had placed Lincoln McGeisey elsewhere at the time of the killing and strongly believed that Sampson had been elsewhere as well. Neither could the readers have known that the "confession" was at odds in many details with the "confession" that Julius Leard allegedly "translated" to the mob on the evening before the burning, and even more at odds with the description of the crime that Frank Leard had repeated over and over. Authenticity of the document, of course, is out of the question. It does not agree with what most of the subsequent investigation showed about events at the Leard home. It came to Doom secondhand, and a copy of the original was never produced.

By the middle of March, there was no sign that support for the burners had flagged. At a rally on March 6 at Remus, resolutions passed "embracing" those charged with the burnings and presenting the accused as poor and unable to defend themselves against the "unlimited resources" of the federal government. Joseph McColgan, a local rancher, and others appealed to newspapermen to exert their influence in behalf of the burners and to collect donations. Chairman of the meeting was Hiram Holt, the Baptist preacher who had prayed loudly over McGeisey and Sampson the evening before the mob burned them. Secretary was A. J. Vinson, who, like Holt, was a mob member out of jail on bond. The committee to represent the people in collecting and distributing funds and assisting with their advice were W. R. Foyil, Elias Riddle, "Elder" T. H. Day, Jeff Howard, D. T. Queen, and McColgan. The committee went to work, holding public fund-raising meetings at Tecumseh and Shawnee on March 12 and 14. In this committee, the mob members had perfected their organized resistance to prosecution.

Only Foyil, a physician, had been involved with the mob and was out on bond. As a voice for the mob, they put out only the information that the burners wanted the public to know.[50]

Editor Doom of the *Tecumseh Leader* urged the citizenry to listen to the committee's appeals "in behalf of those persecuted people." Federal officials were posturing, he said, basing their case on testimony by disreputable people, while much of the press presupposed guilt. If they took the accused, who were mostly poor men, to Muskogee or elsewhere in Indian Territory for trial, their trial would cost thousands of dollars. Thus Doom appealed for funds to help them get a fair trial.[51]

As stories concerning McGeisey's and Sampson's innocence continued in newspapers in Oklahoma, Indian Territory, and the states, supporters of the burners argued that federal officials were misdirecting their efforts. Like others, the editor of the Guthrie *Capital*, for example, questioned the amount of money and effort the United States was spending to bring the burners to trial. Why did not the governor and U.S. officials exert effort to capture the real offenders, who were supposedly still at large, instead of going after the burners? Mobs lynched blacks in the South "almost monthly," he argued, but the government seemed unconcerned. "But when a couple of odorous, ignorant, bestial Indian rapers are summarily 'done up,'" he wrote, "then the great government heart gets exercized [sic] because the people deal out the law! When did a sciofulous [sic] brutal Indian become more to the government than a southern negro?" The government should change its direction: "Does it not seem rediculous [sic], as well as the height of injustice, to be pursuing those farmers who are supposed to have assisted in the burning of these Indians, and forget all about the real criminals, the atrocious beasts uncaught? If the Indians burned were innocent, has there been anything done to capture those who are guilty?"[52]

To help rally support locally, C. A. Stauber of the *Tecumseh Republican* challenged Governor Barnes's authority "in offering a reward for criminals whose crimes were committed outside the borders of Oklahoma."[53] Whether he knew it or not, Stauber had indirectly focused on the Achilles heel of Pottawatomie County citizens' conspiracy of silence. Settlement of jurisdictional issues between the two territories would ultimately destroy the citizenry's unity. Other county newspapers such as the *Shawnee News*, the *Tecumseh Leader*, and the *County Democrat* contained editorial comments in a vein similar to Stauber's.[54]

Events in Pottawatomie County made it difficult for county editors to maintain a sense of righteous indignation and assert that the county was a law-abiding community. During the period of the investigation and arrests, several killings, shootings, and stabbings occurred. Whiskey trade with the Creeks and Seminoles continued, particularly at Earlsboro. Stauber blamed several of the recent murders on the county's "drinking dives." Saloon owners from Earlsboro, Violet Springs, and elsewhere had been prominent in the mob, and reporters had assumed from the start that the killer of Mary Leard had been drunk although Frank Leard denied it. Perhaps taking their cue from Chief John Brown and Indian agent Dew M. Wisdom, who publicly blamed the burning on the whiskey trade, newspaper publishers frequently mentioned whiskey as a contributing factor when they reported on the affair.[55] Ironically, however, they mentioned it in reference to the Indians, while the evidence showed that it had been the mob members who were drinking heavily. Also, the whiskey trade may have been at the heart of Julius Leard's vendetta against Passack Harjo's settlement.

In editorially supporting the burners, Doom had capitalized on the political mood of the county. The populists had wielded strong political power from the early days of the territory but had seen their power begin to slip in the election of 1896. The McKinley administration had taken office in early 1897, and while the Republican president had appointed Governor Cassius M. Barnes and other territorial officials, he and his attorney general, Joseph McKenna, had outraged territorial Republicans by not making a clean sweep of the Justice Department officials. They retained U.S. attorney Caleb R. Brooks and his Democratic assistants and allowed federal judges appointed by the Cleveland administration to serve out their four-year terms. Two of those judgeships became vacant in early 1898. In the midst of the investigation of the burning, McKenna left office, and his successor, John W. Griggs, asked for the resignation of not only Brooks but assistant attorneys Roy Hoffman and McMechan, who was deeply involved in investigating the burning, effective in late February. John W. Scothorn of Guthrie replaced Hoffman immediately, but McKenna asked McMechan to remain long enough to finish the investigative work that he had begun in the burning case.[56] Doom the populist could use his readers' distrust of Republicans to argue successfully that the incoming officials would likely use the case to make their reputations.

Other Oklahoma editors thought they, too, spied the specter of politics behind federal attempts to prosecute the burners. Evan McMaster of the

Oklahoma City Sunday Globe blamed the prosecution on "Cleveland's barbarism," calling it "territorial oppression" that resulted from Democratic policy. McMaster also wrote "that Oklahoma has no friend in its federal officials." A Republican who had apparently backed Reed of Maine instead of McKinley, McMaster called Governor Barnes a "carpetbagger," who had defamed the territory at every turn regarding the burning. "The prosecutions," McMaster wrote, "are carried on under a statute as foreign to the present offence as the English laws against witchcraft. Fee grabbing is the object sought."[57] The McKinley administration offered McMaster a little hope, however, that "the incoming crop of judges" might not "make a specialty of prosecuting homesteaders for perjury."[58]

The Democrats, on the other hand, blamed the Republicans for the prosecution. It was a Republican-controlled Congress that had appropriated the twenty-five thousand dollars at Senator Quay's request. The congressmen who voted for the legislation were "ignorant of the suffering and annoyance that people have to bear living on the border of an Indian country," wrote A. T. Foster, editor of the *County Democrat*. "There is probably not one of their members that ever saw an Indian," he said. In his view, Congress had coddled the Indian for fifty years, and the present prosecution of the burners continued its protection of what he called its Indian "pets." That was particularly true of the Republican Party, he argued, which placed the Indians' interest first. Preserving the Indians created "fat jobs for party tools." The party valued blacks second because it could be sure of their Republican votes and placed the white man last because he was "free born," "free thinking," and "law abiding."[59]

Their paranoia and Indian hating aside, the Oklahoma editors raised a good question: why Senator Quay's special interest in the Seminole burnings? Though it may have appeared to some that Quay was "petting" the Indians, in reality he had no more love for American Indians than did most politicians in Washington at the time. He had long supported efforts to close out the affairs of the Five Civilized Tribes and to open their lands to non-Indian settlement, and he had been an advocate for establishing a territorial government over Indian Territory. The burning put much of these efforts at risk. The Seminoles were the only one of the five tribes to have reached agreement with the Dawes Commission. A final agreement had been worked out on December 16, and the Seminole council had ratified the agreement on December 29, the day before the murder of Mary Leard. Secretary C. N. Bliss referred the agreement to the Senate on January 12, when reports of the Seminole "uprising" were at their height. By that time, opposition to the agreement had become organized in the Seminole Nation, and a protest against it reached the Senate ten days later. Also, working its way through Congress in the spring of 1898 was legislation aimed at closing out the affairs of the tribes with or without tribal consent. Quay did not want the Seminole burning to jeopardize either the Seminole agreement or the Curtis bill, and he used what influence he had with the powerful Senate Committee on Indian Affairs to ensure that it did not.[60]

Whatever Quay's motives for taking a personal interest in the burning cases, his public interference in what had been a local concern focused attention on what the *Stillwater Gazette* had called "county liability" for lynchings. In a rare editorial only a year before the burnings, the editor had argued that those charged with law enforcement were powerless to prevent "mob murder" or vigilantism and that it was absurd to say that lynching was justified because the judicial system was too slow or because of fear of acquittal or pardon. "The fault is not with the sheriffs, the prosecuting officers, the judges, or the governors, but the people. County liability makes 'the best citizens,' who are now interested only in excusing lynchings, vitally interested in preventing them."[61] Of course, the editor was talking about lynching in the South. When it came to Oklahoma, it was quite another matter. In the wake of the Seminole burnings, he joined Pottawatomie County editors, who attempted to relieve the citizens of the county of their liability by running through the usual list of justifications for lynching: to protect womanhood, to obtain immediate "justice" and save the taxpayers' money, and to ensure that the accused did not escape punishment in the slow legal process.

By the second week in March, the sensationalism surrounding the arrests had subsided. Marshals had arrested sixty-seven for conspiracy, but about twenty of the mob ringleaders remained at large, hiding, officials believed, somewhere near Maud, despite protests by the local press that none of those involved sought to evade capture.[62] The truth was that they were hiding in the Choctaw and Chickasaw nations and elsewhere.

The editorial defense of burning during the first three months of 1898 made it clear that the editors did not have the facts in the case. The mob leaders had been successful in making the public believe that this lynching was like those common in the South, where public approval, with only few exceptions, had prevented local prosecution of mob members. It is not surprising that editors were baffled by the interest federal officials had taken in this case and could conclude only that it was wanton persecution. They might have taken heart if they had known that federal authorities were concerned about the effect editorial image polishing would have on the grand jury investigation of the burners, scheduled to begin when the district court convened at Tecumseh in April. U.S. Attorney Brooks doubted that a local grand jury would indict, but he was willing to go forward with the case. His successors in the McKinley administration, who would complete his work, faced the same doubts. And, as if to underscore their doubts, the court had difficulty finding jurors to serve on the regularly scheduled grand jury because of the burning cases.[63]

Thus while they were awaiting the grand jury investigation, the burners had reason to be confident. The newspapers had readily accepted the story of events relayed by the mob leaders. The news focus on mob participants from Maud and Earlsboro unwittingly deflected attention from the leaders and organizers such as Sam Pryor and H. Clay Roper, who had come from neither of those areas. The mob leaders had prevented investigators from getting at the truth concerning the event, and, shielded by the support for mob members in Pottawatomie County, they would remain undetected for months.

SEVEN

A Matter of Jurisdiction

During the district court's April session at Tecumseh, Assistant U.S. Attorney John W. Scothorn urged the attorney general to seek indictments of the burners in the federal courts of Indian Territory as well as those in Oklahoma. Uncertain whether the Tecumseh grand jury would indict them on conspiracy, and convinced that the county attorney would not prosecute them on other charges, Scothorn offered to take the evidence Oklahoma authorities had amassed to an Indian Territory grand jury if authorized to do so.[1] He knew that the two territories differed in their general public attitudes toward lynching. Unlike Oklahoma, where the people condoned lynch law and the newspapers justified it as a form of social corrective, the Indian Territory had no history of lynching, though there had been murders and other crimes as heinous as those allegedly committed against Mary Leard. Instead of defending lynching, newspaper editors in Indian Territory defended justice through the court system. Meanwhile, federal officials in both territories sought a means to prosecute the burners of McGeisey and Sampson, although building their cases would not be easy, given the prevailing attitudes on both sides of the line and the conflicting jurisdictions of the two territories.

Editorial statements and exchanges brought many of the differences between the two territories into focus. Though the national press had claimed that four lynchings had occurred in Indian Territory in 1896, the record was not substantiated. In fact, the territory was relatively free of lynching history. In 1880 a mob of Cherokees and others had crossed the line into the Creek Nation near Fort Gibson and taken two Creek freedmen, alleged to be horse thieves, back into the Cherokee Nation and hanged them. A mob of Creeks and U.S. citizens had threatened to lynch the Buck Gang after their capture at McDermott, Creek Nation, in 1895, but authorities spirited the outlaws off to jail at Fort Smith. As the white population grew in Indian Territory, tensions between them and blacks increased, but the local press had reported no lynchings. From the time the story of the Seminole burning broke, most newspaper editors in the northern district of the Indian Territory emphasized the differences in the territories' lynching histories and condemned the burning. To the editor of the *Muskogee Phoenix*, it was "a sad commentary upon the state of advancement and civilization of the people living on the Seminole boundary." Though he accepted published reports of the alleged guilt of the two Seminoles and the atrocity of their crime, he condemned their torture: "Those who participated in this exhibition of bloody barbarism are guilty as the guiltiest murderers and brutal themselves as the unfortunate, ignorant brutes they tortured with fiendish ingenuity."2

Like the *Phoenix* editor, Waddie Hudson of the *Tahlequah Arrow* did not at first question the Seminoles' guilt. However, he knew, as did many east of the Oklahoma line, that the mob leaders had taken their time in choosing their victims. "That it should be possible in these civilized times, of such an enlightened country," he wrote, "for a posse of citizens, to contemplate calmly a burning at the stake, is shocking and disheartening. The question of guilt or justice aside, it was simply an inhuman and revolting act." It could leave a "lasting stigma" on the respectable segment of the population: "But when a body of citizens in a spirit of revenge, commit a crime that makes deliberate murder seem a mercy, there is no escaping the curse it will throw upon a community in which the crime was committed." The only route to justice, he argued, was an official investigation and a speedy trial of the burners, with the meting out of "punishment merited those guilty of such atrocious crimes."3

Hudson argued further that the burning would "stand as a monumental and lasting disgrace" upon the territory should the rumors of McGeisey's and Sampson's innocence prove true. He wrote: "One cannot approve of the hasty actions taken by people in the heat of passion, especially when demonstrations for the thirst of blood was displayed by a class of citizens who have shown themselves to be of bad morals, deserving the light of circumspection thrown upon them that justice be carried out regarding their actions. No one will sanction such barbarism, no matter for what end it was carried out, as the laws of nature and providence have placed within the power of the people the weapons through which justice should be carried out, and none can ask more than it be merited through these channels."[4]

Though Hudson and others in the northern district had faith in the new federal courts in the Indian Territory, Oklahomans doubted that whites could obtain justice because of the special status of the Indians. A. T. Foster, the U.S. commissioner and editor of the Tecumseh *County Democrat*, acknowledging the burning as "a blot and stain on a civilized and christian community," justified it because "the apathy shown by legal authorities in bringing the Indians to justice left every woman on the border in danger of a fate similar to Mrs. Leard's." Foster continued, "The men of Pottawatomie county are peaceable, law-abiding citizens, brave honorable men who are ever ready to sacrifice their lives to uphold the honor of womanhood and avenge her dishonor, regardless of whether the skin of her destroyer be white, black or copper colored."[5]

Despite Foster's statement that his fellow countians would lynch equally, regardless of race, he, like other Oklahoma editors, had brought race into the debate over the burning by calling the Indians the government's "dusky pets," "treacherous savages," and "red devils." Such language underscored the reality that the line between Pottawatomie County and the Seminole Nation separated not only different governmental and judicial systems but societies with different racial dynamics as well. History had taken a strange turn on their common border in early 1898. Whites in Oklahoma used timeworn rhetoric to label the Indians savages in order to justify the burning, while to those living east of the dividing line, it was the whites who were savages.

The racial implications of the burning had not escaped the Seminoles or Indians elsewhere in Indian Territory. To Chuller Fixico, a Creek, for example, the event signaled the need for members of the Five Civilized Tribes to consider emigration to another country, perhaps Mexico. Talk of emigration was not new. As congressional action and federal policy eroded tribal autonomy and sovereignty during the 1890s, discontent had grown among the segments of Indian nation societies most resistant to change, particularly the Cherokee Keetoowahs and the Creek, Seminole, and Choctaw Snakes. For years, small groups had considered the option of removing to Mexico or South America.[6]

To Chuller Fixico, there was a connection between the burning and the Seminole agreement with the Dawes Commission. As the Indians' jurisdiction over their own affairs and the authority of their laws eroded, they had become like beasts ready for slaughter; and "as they stand looking to the western part of the Indian Territory," Chuller Fixico wrote, "they think that they are nothing else but fitting subjects of the U.S. penitentiaries and to be chained to-gether and burnt to the stake." The United States had undertaken change in the Indian Territory, mainly through the efforts of the Dawes Commission, ostensibly to extend the "strong arm of U.S. protection" over the Indians. But "we learn," Chuller Fixico said, "that just as soon as this was done the thourough [sic] bred U.S. citizen commenced catching these Indians and chaining them together and burning them to the stake, and where do these dusky skins look for protection for they cannot find any civilized people or christian government to protect them on this continent." He urged the Indians of the five tribes to emigrate; it was their only possible salvation. They should go, even if they should "die on the road searching for more light in freedom and liberty."[7]

Arguments that the peoples of the two territories could not happily merge supported arguments for separate statehood for Indian Territory, which had gained wide acceptance there but strong opposition in Oklahoma. To the editor of the *El Reno Evening Star*, the burning simply pointed up inadequacies of the law that resulted from the existence of two territories side by side. He argued that a majority of the mob were "whiskey peddlers, and other individuals of a lawless character who would not exist but for the opportunity offered, by an inadequate law, for plying their various illegitimate trades and practices" along the border. Settling the affairs of the Five Civilized Tribes and combining the two territories in a single state would solve the problem.[8] To the editor of the *Purcell Register*, published in the Chickasaw Nation on its border with Oklahoma, the burning was the commission of a crime of outrage in an attempt to "blot out" a crime of passion. He attacked Indian Territory editors with "holier-than-thou" attitudes. The territory had, after all, furnished the "two foul fiends," as he called McGeisey and Sampson. He expressed outrage at editors who used the burning to argue for separate statehood for Indian Territory, which Indian leaders—except in the Chickasaw Nation—were then proposing.[9] Suspicions resulting from the existence of the two territories side by side and from the great social, political, economic, and judicial gulf between them would have to be overcome or put aside for the government to be successful in prosecuting the burners.

Though it appeared to Pottawatomie County citizens and other Oklahomans that federal officials were united and single-minded in their pursuit of the burners, such was not the case, at least not during the first few weeks following the burning. Finally spurred by the Senate's request for action, Oklahoma's federal authorities had begun investigating and acquiring evidence that they hoped would lead to indictments. Meanwhile, three separate federal investigations had occurred in the Indian Territory, sometimes going on simultaneously and at times at cross-purposes.

Leo E. Bennett, U.S. marshal for the northern district, had ordered one investigation following the reports of a Seminole uprising. Bennett sent deputies ahead of him to the Seminole Nation; before he could get there, they had determined that the story was a hoax. As part of his investigation, Bennett had also ordered the retrieval of the chain and locks used in the burning. On January 10, Dr. C. P. Linn, Dew M. Wisdom of the Union Indian Agency, and Commissioner W. T. Fears went to Henry Taylor's home to exhume the bodies of McGeisey and Sampson.[10] Meanwhile, Bennett's deputies gathered much information, and the report that Bennett filed with the attorney general on January 20, though inaccurate, was the most accurate account of the events at the Leard farm filed in the first weeks following the burning.[11]

The Office of Indian Affairs undertook another investigation as a result of pressure from the Seminole delegation in Washington. On January 19, Chief John Brown pointed out to the secretary of the interior a provision in the 1856 treaty with the Seminoles and Creeks that "promised protection and guaranteed indemnity for all injuries resulting from invasion or aggression" and asked for an investigation of the murder of the two Seminoles, the "inhuman torture" suffered by the others, and the value of property destroyed. Though Secretary C. N. Bliss ordered the investigation in late January, investigators from the Union Agency at Muskogee did not get into the field until late March, when they met with the Seminoles at the Council House at Wewoka and took detailed statements from most of the Seminoles, Creeks, and blacks the mob had harassed or detained as well as from Thomas McGeisey and Mrs. Sukey Sampson. As a result of their findings, Agent Wisdom forwarded a report to the commissioner of Indian affairs, recommending indemnities be paid to McGeisey and Mrs. Sampson for loss of their property and children, and to the others for indignities and maltreatment by the mob.[12]

The prosecutor's office for the northern district of Indian Territory conducted a third investigation in preparation for a grand jury impaneled on January 17 during a session of the court at Vinita. U.S. Attorney Pliny Leland Soper directed the investigation. A native of Kansas and a graduate of the Columbia Law School, Soper was an experienced attorney, having been assistant U.S. attorney for Kansas from 1889 to 1894 and attorney in the Indian Territory for the Atchison, Topeka, and Santa Fe Railroad from 1894 to 1897, when he became U.S. attorney for the northern district. Luman F. Parker Jr., his assistant, was at South McAlester, Choctaw Nation, when the alleged uprising occurred and had gone to the Seminole Nation at Marshal Bennett's request to assist the deputies in their investigation. Soper sent Parker back to the Seminole Nation to take testimony and line up witnesses for the grand jury. Parker returned to Vinita with an extremely inaccurate version of what had taken place during the first week of January, part of it apparently obtained from Nelson Jones and James Jones, but Soper believed he had enough evidence to indict and convict twenty people for crimes committed in the Indian Territory. So confident was he, in fact, that he assured the attorney general that the pending Quay appropriation resolution was unnecessary. Concerned that he could indict on only three offenses—arson, kidnapping, and assault with intent to kill—he offered whatever testimony he could obtain during the grand jury's work to the U.S. attorney for Oklahoma Territory to use in indicting the burners for murder.[13]

The grand jury at Vinita was the first step in unraveling the burners' version of events leading to the burning and in breaking their conspiracy of silence. Judge John R. Thomas took care in charging the jury, stressing their duty in the context of the new federal judicial system that had assumed authority in all criminal cases in the Indian Territory on January 1, when the tribal court jurisdictions ceased to exist. Everyone, he said—Indian, white, black—was indictable for violation of federal law; distinctions could not be made on the basis of nationality. The jury called as witnesses not only Nelson and James Jones but most of the Seminoles and Creeks the mob had harassed. The most revealing testimony came from Nelson Jones and John Washington, who gave outsiders for the first time a picture of what had really transpired at the Leard farm. Now the public began to understand that the burning had not been an act of passion generated by a sense of outrage but had been, instead, the culmination of a cold, methodical, weeklong process of selecting victims. The grand jury returned two indictments involving forty-four men: *United States vs. One Cash, et al.*, for kidnapping and *United States vs. One Cash, et al.*, for arson in the burning of McGeisey's improvements.[14]

Soper's report of these matters to the attorney general opened the first door to cooperation between federal officials in the two territories. Until then, there had been no communication between them. Both groups pursued separate investigations and prepared for prosecution in their own ways, learning what the others were doing through communication with the attorney general or reports in the newspapers. There were uncertainties about jurisdictional matters on both sides of the territorial line. Soper had mistakenly believed that U.S. Attorney Caleb Brooks in Oklahoma had jurisdiction in murder cases. Brooks had been uncertain from the start about jurisdictional and statutory matters in the case. Soper's letter offering to share his evidence in prosecuting for murder, opened the door to communication in early February. Soper now proposed that they cooperate in prosecuting the burners on other charges. Soper had seen a news report regarding Brooks's inquiry to the attorney general about matters of jurisdiction, and newspapers in Oklahoma carried reports that the burners might even escape prosecution because Brooks was uncertain about what statute to try them under. Soper became alarmed that they might indeed escape. His indictments against them were strong, he believed, and he begged Brooks not to hold them in Oklahoma on minor charges for which they could receive only short sentences. He offered copies of his indictments and asked Brooks to proceed under Section 1014 of the U.S. Revised Statutes to have those charged and arrested sent to Indian Territory for trial. The grand jury scheduled to convene on March 8 at Wagoner, Creek Nation, would consider the case again. Meanwhile, there was a man, Soper claimed, who wanted to turn state's evidence and whom Soper intended to bring forth. He was confident of convictions for kidnapping and arson if Brooks would help him.[15]

Soper's appeal worked. Now convinced that convictions would bring much longer sentences in Indian Territory, Brooks argued that the Oklahoma authorities should gather evidence and send the accused to Indian Territory. With Brooks now willing, the attorney general directed him and Soper to cooperate in bringing the offenders to trial quickly "in a locality, if possible, unaffected by prejudice or other undue influence."[16] Brooks met some resistance from Marshal Canada H. Thompson, who urged him to try the burners in Oklahoma before sending them to the Indian Territory. Brooks once more became indecisive and left the decision to the attorney general. Meanwhile, he asked Soper to hold his evidence, and when the preliminary hearings then going on in Shawnee were over, Brooks would send a copy of the proceedings to Soper to help build his cases.[17]

With authorization from the attorney general, Soper sent his assistant attorney, Luman F. Parker, to Shawnee, where a conflict arose between him and Thomas F. McMechan. Parker had conducted the examination before the Vinita grand jury and knew the evidence. Soper believed he could help McMechan, who was in Shawnee to conduct his investigation while a large number of the accused were there for preliminary hearings. McMechan was far ahead of Parker in gathering evidence. One of the first investigators in the field, he had firsthand knowledge of the evolving evidence in the cases. He arrived in Shawnee for the preliminary hearings on February 6, but as it happened, only Poliet Smith, Edward Nix, and W. H. Davis refused to waive preliminary hearings. Only two witnesses were heard in their cases. Harry Brown testified about his trip with Thomas Coker and Younger Bowlegs to the Leard farm on Wednesday night before the burning, and J. M. Gloer testified that burning Seminoles was openly discussed on the street in Earlsboro two or three days before Palmer Sampson became a suspect. After these witnesses, the three accused abruptly waived further examination, and the court set bond.[18]

Besides obtaining this testimony, McMechan worked quietly and privately with his stenographer, interviewing witnesses and taking evidence for later grand jury hearings. He realized the errors in his earlier reports, for he now learned for the first time the details concerning events at the Leard farm between January 1 and January 8. He now knew that the mob had sent out parties, arrested Seminoles, and brought them to the Leard farm for questioning, where they held them prisoners, some for days, judged them guilty or innocent, and then turned them loose or held them as they chose. Their work was deliberate: "They did nothing in a hurry; when they would arrest an Indian they would question him about his whereabouts upon the day and evening of the murder and then they would ride out and bring in other parties and examine them to determine whether or not the defendant which they had on trial was guilty." McMechan learned for the first time of the physical torture, intimidation, and threats that the Indians had endured.[19]

To McMechan, the most revealing information came from Nelson Jones. When Marshal Bill Tilghman brought Jones in, Jones asked for an interview with McMechan and voluntarily gave a long, rambling statement about events during the week preceding the burning. In his earlier reports, McMechan had assumed that Mary Leard had been raped and her corpse defiled, but now he learned that neither had occurred. McMechan had believed from the start that Lincoln McGeisey was not guilty, but now he became certain of it and began to have doubts about the guilt of Palmer Sampson. He learned that Frank Leard had insisted that there was only one Indian and had categorically denied that Lincoln McGeisey was his mother's killer, and that a number of witnesses that Julius Leard himself had interviewed had corroborated McGeisey's story concerning his whereabouts at the time of the murder. Finally, McMechan learned in detail the role that Jones had played in the affair.[20] Jones's statement was clearly self-incriminating. Why he gave it is uncertain, for it would have been to his advantage to insist that McGeisey and Sampson were guilty. He may have believed simply that the courts would not convict him.

As a result of his investigation, McMechan became optimistic about the prospects of prosecuting the burners. He believed that he and the marshals could "weave a web around the defendants" from which they could not escape. He also thought he noted a change in "public sentiment," saying, "I believe that there will be no trouble to get a Grand Jury in Pottawatomie County to indict them, provided we have jurisdiction in the crime; and I have confidence enough in the people of Pottawatomie County to believe that a Petit Jury can be secured who will see that the laws of the country are fully vindicated."[21]

It is not surprising, with his belief that he was building such a strong case, that McMechan was not as forthcoming with information as Soper expected. Parker claimed that when he arrived in Shawnee with his notes, McMechan refused to give him any information. Soper complained, questioning McMechan's motives, and reported to the attorney general that McMechan had told Parker that the latter had no business in Shawnee, that he would pass his information to the U.S. attorney in Oklahoma, and that Parker could seek his information there.[22] Soper's report to the attorney general was only partially true and reflected the cross-purposes at which officials from the two territories worked at times.

Soper accused McMechan of taking advantage of the information Parker had obtained and of refusing to give any in return. In reality, McMechan said, Parker had no information that he and the marshals in Oklahoma had not already obtained, except a statement by Nelson Jones, whom the marshals had a warrant for at the time and whom McMechan later interviewed. Parker had shorthand notes of testimony by Seminoles, which McMechan could not read, but McMechan had the same witnesses whom he intended to examine himself. Parker had a chain that was allegedly around the Indians' necks, but McMechan believed the evidence had been compromised and rendered useless because one of the U.S. commissioners in the Indian Territory had taken a part of the chain and kept it. Parker offered a list of the mob members the Vinita grand jury had indicted, but McMechan had those and more. Thus, McMechan argued, there was no way he could have taken advantage of Parker because he had already obtained, or could easily obtain, the same evidence Parker had.[23]

McMechan also denied Parker's charge that he had been discourteous in refusing to give him any information. On the eve of leaving Shawnee, Parker had asked for the names of all witnesses that Oklahoma officials had subpoenaed, all the people they intended to arrest, and all of the testimony McMechan had. McMechan claimed that Parker had asked the impossible. He did not know the number or the names on the warrants, nor did he know all the witnesses. He had instructed the marshals to subpoena anyone they found to have information about the burning. The only testimony he had taken at the time was from the Indians that had been before the Vinita grand jury and the two witnesses in the Davis, Smith, and Nix preliminary hearing, which Parker had attended. As an assistant attorney, McMechan believed it his duty to forward what information he had to his superior, first, and let him decide what information to give Soper.[24]

McMechan was especially stung by Soper's intimation that he was seeking personal "credit" for his work. He had not wanted to take on this case but had done it as part of his duties as an assistant attorney. Because of Brooks's belief that stronger sentences could be obtained in Indian Territory, Brooks had hesitated to act until pushed by the attorney general. With so many men already arrested in Oklahoma, McMechan believed that Oklahoma officials should follow the legal process through before they turned the accused over to Indian Territory officials. McMechan was particularly stung that Soper had questioned his motives after they had known each other professionally for fifteen years.[25]

McMechan's testiness was understandable. After difficult work, he was finally getting somewhere with his investigation. Why should he risk jeopardizing that progress by the intrusion of an interloper, especially from another jurisdiction? The burners had resisted investigators because of their nagging fear that Oklahoma authorities would send them to Indian Territory. Interference by officials from the northern district at a critical time in the investigation would not make McMechan's job any easier. McMechan also probably had some doubts about Parker's competence. Like Soper, McMechan was an experienced attorney. He had practiced as a criminal lawyer in Illinois and Kansas before going to Oklahoma in 1889 and had served as the attorney for Oklahoma County before becoming assistant U.S. attorney. Parker, on the other hand, had been a stenographer before becoming Soper's assistant and appears to have received his appointment through the influence of the railroad industry, his father serving as a high-ranking attorney for the Frisco system. McMechan believed he had extended all the professional courtesies due someone like Parker from outside his jurisdiction. By requesting information from him, Parker had asked McMechan to usurp the authority of his superiors, who were the ones to decide such matters as sharing evidence.[26]

Despite Soper's alienation of McMechan, Brooks continued his cooperation. He sent Soper testimony taken in the preliminary hearings of Smith, Davis, and Nix, and affidavits acquired from Nelson Jones. Soper, in turn, sent Brooks a copy of the Vinita grand jury testimony. In an effort to remove the potential for further conflict, Soper and Brooks agreed that when their separate investigations ended, they would place the matter before the attorney general to decide which territory would try the accused first.[27]

Another issue, however, stood in the way of full cooperation: antagonism between the marshals of the two territories. According to Soper, deputy U.S. marshals in Oklahoma Territory harbored bad feelings toward Leo E. Bennett and his deputies because Judge John R. Thomas of the northern district court had refused to turn members of the Jennings gang over to the Oklahoma marshal's office. Had he complied with Parker's request, McMechan would have aggravated the strain in relations, he believed, by handing over information that Oklahoma marshals had gathered, even before that information went to their superiors. Soper wanted desperately to have a personal interview with Marshal Thompson and Brooks to attempt to lessen tensions between them, for he wanted to go to trial with evidence as fully developed as possible. Despite Soper's and Brooks's agreement that stiffer penalties were certain in Indian Territory, Thompson continued to argue for trial first in Oklahoma. Whether the Jennings case was a factor or not, Thompson did not want to give the accused up until Oklahoma had tried them, arguing with confidence that the Oklahoma courts would convict the burners of conspiracy.[28]

Some loose ends and critical questions nagged at Soper. At Shawnee, Parker had met a Tecumseh attorney, W. H. Melton, who claimed to know two witnesses who could identify the mob members who kidnapped McGeisey and Sampson and those who burned them. Because of bitter feeling in Pottawatomie County and fear of losing business for cooperating, he wanted to sell his information. Not having authority to make such a deal, Parker suggested Melton go to Thomas McGeisey or to John F. Brown, the Seminole chief. Soper was much interested in following this lead, however. Testimony that Soper had obtained indicated that Frank Leard had refused to identify McGeisey as his mother's killer. Only the mob members claimed that he had identified McGeisey. Testimony had well established McGeisey's whereabouts on the day Mary Leard was killed. Soper believed that McGeisey was innocent and that if Frank Leard had charged McGeisey at a late date, he must have done so after "threats, influence or persuasion." Soper wanted to know which, and only the burners could tell.[29]

It was at this point in the case that the change in personnel occurred in the U.S. attorney's office in Oklahoma. John W. Griggs had succeeded Joseph McKenna as U.S. attorney general. On February 12, the solicitor general had called for the resignation of McMechan and Assistant Attorney Roy V. Hoffman to become effective February 21. The department, however, temporarily retained McMechan, who was at a critical point in his investigation of the burning cases, and asked him to stay on to continue his work until the grand jury convened at Tecumseh. This latter decision may have been at the insistence of Senator Quay, who asked McMechan to report to him personally, especially on what Frank Leard had said and whether rape had occurred. Brooks wanted McMechan to stay on through the grand jury session, but he did not, although he was responsible for having witnesses subpoenaed and worked practically to the day the jury convened in early April.[30] Brooks, too, was scheduled to leave office, but paperwork on his successor, S. L. Overstreet, had not cleared channels by the time the grand jury convened. Thus Brooks stayed on and with John W. Scothorn did the initial work with the grand jury until Overstreet arrived a few days later.

Despite McMechan's optimism as he left office, federal officials still doubted the outcome as the grand jury proceedings began at Tecumseh.

They expected difficulties in the impaneling process because the popular cause of the burners would disqualify many. Brooks, who left office convinced that the cases should have been tried first in Indian Territory, had grave doubts whether they could make convictions stick, even if they could get a jury to indict.[31] Brooks had expressed his concerns to Attorney General Griggs in late February. Griggs believed everyone "who took part in the perpetration of this crime is guilty of murder." He wanted to know why Brooks did not think indictments could be brought against them in Pottawatomie County. Was it just the local sympathy for the burners, or was it something else? Griggs seemed willing to investigate the courts in Pottawatomie County if necessary and told Brooks to report to him on how the courts made up jury lists, who prepared them, how names were drawn, whether grand and petit juries came from the same lists, and who summoned the jurists.[32]

As it turned out, the results of the grand jury investigation were somewhat surprising. Overstreet and Scothorn presented what they believed to be evidence "more than ample" to indict thirty to forty of the sixty-one on charges of conspiracy. Overstreet found it difficult to find witnesses who would testify and to find the facts. "Many," he said, "who would otherwise willingly and voluntarily tell the truth are afraid in this instance, and threats have been made." Thus he planned to ask for a special venue for impaneling a new grand jury should this one fail to indict. Perhaps to Overstreet and Scothorn's surprise, the jury returned indictments against nineteen on five counts of conspiracy, and the court set bonds at $3000. The court also bound over for the next grand jury sixteen whom this jury refused to indict and set their bonds at $2000. The list of the indicted reflected just how far federal officials were from getting to the bottom of the affair. The indictments named some who were among the mob leaders, such as Julius Leard and Edward and Stoke Martin, and others who were deeply involved in hunting Indians, such as Jesse Guinn, Joseph Williams, George Pettifer, Herschel Leard, Mont Ballard, and Nelson and James Jones. Others named were little more than onlookers. Conspicuously absent from the list were the names of Pryor, Roper, and Ivanhoe. To Overstreet, however, any indictment was a success, which he attributed to the "rigid examination" done by Brooks and Scothorn in impaneling, which had been "a difficult task, on account of the strong, sympathetic feeling of almost the entire county for those who were engaged in the conspiracy and murder."[33]

This surprising turn of events also resulted in part from the investigation that the Office of Indian Affairs had conducted during March, working through the Union Agency at Muskogee. Investigators had taken evidence carefully. Some of it had appeared in print just before the district court convened at Tecumseh. The *Guthrie Daily Capital*, which had been a supporter of the burners, now said that as the investigation continued, the more horrible the burning became: "Truth almost staggers the mind when it is confronted with the indignities and cruelties practiced by this senseless mob of human beings, and the acts of those men will be handed down as one of the darkest plots in the history of the southwest."[34]

The details the *Capital* revealed caused an erosion of sympathy for the burners. The story recounted the treatment that the Indians had received, especially John Washington and George P. Harjo, and presented the leaders of the burners as ruthless rather than law-abiding. It told how the mob held Harjo for three days, despite Frank Leard's failure to identify him, in an attempt to get him to confess or implicate someone else, how they had asked him whether he preferred to be shot or burned, how they had brought hay into the room where they kept him and told him to prepare to die, and how they had told him that McGeisey had implicated him. The news article also told how they strung Washington up, kicked him, punched him with Winchesters, and threatened him with death by fire. The public had known from the start that the mob had taken McGeisey and Sampson across the line into Oklahoma in order to avoid prosecution. Now, the public surfacing of facts concerning the ruthless and deliberate way they had gone about selecting their victims and the nonprovocative manner in which U.S. officials had handled the suspects in the case had caused public sympathy for the burners to abate somewhat. This shift in public opinion no doubt had an impact on the outcome of the grand jury investigation. Besides revealing the viciousness of the mob leaders, evidence continued to point to the innocence of McGeisey and perhaps that of Sampson. By mid-April, there were also reports that a suspect in the murder of Mary Leard was under surveillance.[35]

Though the public image of the burners as honest farmers and law-abiding citizens had tarnished, the burners still garnered support. Shortly before the grand jury, petitions had circulated in east Texas, and presumably elsewhere, where lynching was a popular pastime, asking the attorney general to transfer jurisdiction from the United States to local authorities in Oklahoma Territory. On seeing a notice of the petition at Denton, one outraged Texan urged the attorney general to remain firm. To transfer the cases would defeat justice and assure acquittal, he wrote, "as these fiends would be tried by a jury of their own stripe, a class of people who have no sense of honor or justice. A collection of the fugitives from justice and the off-scourings of the western states. A collection of criminals and cut throats who would not hesitate to burn every Indian in the Territory at five dollars a burn." He believed these cases were an opportunity for the United States to make an example, to open the eyes of the public to the outrage of lynching, which occurred all too frequently.[36] On the local front, mob members and their friends continued to raise money through the newspapers and to hold mass meetings to make appeals for funds to help defeat prosecution.

While the grand jury was in session, Congress deliberated legislation to pay indemnities to the Seminoles for their harassment and loss of property. Outraged, A. T. Foster of the *County Democrat* said Quay and his fellow Indian lovers were "willing and anxious to sacrifice the lives of any number of white men, destroy numberless homes, rob wives of their husbands, mothers of their sons and leave children fatherless and friendless merely to show the world their pseudo humanity and christian love for their poor red brothers." But Foster argued, "the life of one wife and mother, like Mrs. Laird [sic], is worth more than the lives of a thousand of such red devils as those who outraged and murdered her, in fact, their death is a priceless blessing to civilization instead of a loss."[37] Foster also argued that the three-thousand-dollar bond set after the indictments was excessive, simply a continuation of an unjust vendetta by the federal government against Pottawatomie County. Foster was the U.S. commissioner before whom several of the accused had appeared for preliminary hearing in February. He had set low bonds and believed a third of the current bond would have ensured their appearance in court.[38] But it was getting more difficult to maintain the image of those indicted as law-abiding, honest farmers in light of the evidence presented to the grand jury.

At the close of the grand jury, future action in the cases seemed uncertain. Only three days remained in the regular term of the court. The burning cases had so overcrowded the docket that, with other court business, there was no time left to arraign those indicted or to have them enter a plea. It would be some time before the court could get to those matters. The Oklahoma Supreme Court would not even set a date for the next session of court in Pottawatomie County until its June term.[39]

Pottawatomie Countians took advantage of the hiatus to bolster their image and protect the burners. The mob members engaged in intimidation. Dr. C. P. Linn, who had examined the remains of McGeisey and Sampson and had exhumed them to retrieve the locks and chain as evidence, resigned as physician for the Seminole Nation "because of threats against him by members of the mob."[40] The county press continued to insist, despite mounting evidence to the contrary, that there had been two killers and that Lincoln McGeisey and Palmer Sampson had raped Mary Leard and defiled her corpse. When the U.S. marshals arrested a suspect in the killing in late May, the county press took a skeptical view. A twenty-year-old Seminole named Keno, alias Keno Harjo and Keno Condulee, had allegedly confessed to the crime in a letter to his sister, a student at Emahaka Mission school. He claimed he had killed Mrs. Leard and then fled. His sister divulged not only the contents of the letter but also her brother's whereabouts. After a twenty-two-day chase, marshals captured him in the Chickasaw Nation and took him to the jail at Guthrie. Keno had supposedly ridden from Violet Springs, where he had bought whiskey, to a relative's house not far from the Leard home on the day of the murder. Witnesses had also seen his distinctive pony—a bay pacer with a roached mane—in the vicinity of the home.[41]

The *Tecumseh Leader* argued that the arrest of Keno was staged to make the Indians burned at Maud look innocent. The editor wrote of the case against Keno: "We don't believe there is a word of truth in it. The letter is not published so far as we have seen. It is an easy matter to get someone to 'confess' now in order to make the case against the citizens arrested as strong as possible. Let us see if the U.S. authorities push the prosecution of Harjo as energetically as they have accused the burners."[42] The editor's Indian-hating sentiments surfaced in his reaction to the reports that Keno's sister had turned him in. "Devotion to the eternal principles of justice don't affect the average dusky maiden of the forest that way, even though she may have attended Emma Hockey's mission school."[43] These sentiments were echoed in the *Republican*: "Mrs. Laird's brutal and heathenish murderers have paid the penalty of their crime and while the U.S. authorities may think they have the guilty party under arrest, they will probably be fooled by their informants."[44]

In the wake of these developments, the Oklahoma City *Times-Journal* editor renewed his attacks upon the burners, implying that they had deliberately burned McGeisey and Sampson and then hid behind "the public sentiment of Pottawatomie county to save them from the gallows."[45] The editor had accurately read the accumulating evidence. However, Pottawatomie County editors continued to attest to the version of the story that the burners had circulated, arguing that witnesses had fabricated the case against them. The editor of the *Tecumseh Leader* wrote, "The prosecution begins to look more like persecution than an honest effort to subserve the best interests of either the whites or the Indians."[46]

The Tecumseh editors felt publicly vindicated later that summer when Oklahoma officials released Keno. Though Abe Johnson, then in the Leavenworth prison, supposedly had relevant information, the preliminary hearing in early August failed to produce evidence to connect Keno to the case.[47] Other Seminoles had evidence against him but were reluctant to talk in the wake of the mob's action. But local editors were not privy to that information. Said the editor of the *Leader*, "This is what we predicted when he was arrested. The mob got the right Indians, and they held them nearly a week before executing them. If the marshals wanted to protect the Indians, why didn't they do it then?"[48] And the editor of the *Republican* wrote of Keno's release: "That is about what every one unprejudiced thought at the time of his arrest, but a few criminal-worshipping fanatics seemed to desire his conviction in order to 'prove' the innocence of the Indians burned at the stake and strengthen the case against the burners." It was with that in mind that the marshals had taken him to Guthrie rather than to the nearest U.S. commissioner. "The officers will probably come to the conclusion some day," the editor predicted, "that private individuals meted out justice for the Leard outrage and murder, and that they did it with dispatch and very small expense to the county."[49]

The editors were wrong. Federal investigators would never waiver in their belief that Keno was the murderer of Mary Leard. Even Nelson Jones may have thought him the killer before Palmer Sampson became a "suspect." When he left the Leard farm the last time, Jones went to track down Abe Johnson and his brother. Also, James Jones told George Harjo that he, Jones, knew who the killer was but would not tell.[50] Jones was a braggart, and his statement to Harjo may have been posturing. But, like his uncle, he may have known that Keno was the likely suspect, as may have Abe Johnson, whom local investigators considered a key witness in the summer of 1898. For some reason, government officials at Washington refused to authorize his return from Leavenworth to Guthrie to testify. Still, local officials believed the evidence against Keno was strong. The persisting belief that he or someone else, certainly someone other than McGeisey or Sampson, was the killer would add to the zeal of federal prosecutors in Oklahoma and Indian Territory as they worked to bring the burners to trial.

EIGHT

Horace Speed, Special Prosecutor

On April 11, 1898, while the grand jury was still in session at Tecumseh, McKinley's new attorney general, John W. Griggs, asked U.S. Attorney S. L. Overstreet if he would like a special assistant to work on the Seminole burning cases. He put Overstreet on the spot, asking for an immediate answer, but Overstreet could not say. Though at the time uncertain of the outcome of the grand jury, he was confident that he and his assistant had presented ample evidence to indict thirty or forty for conspiracy. Nevertheless, within two weeks he had a special attorney, whether he wanted him or not.[1] The special counsel was Horace Speed, a determined and able investigator who would not only get at the truth surrounding the burning but lay the groundwork for the successful prosecution of some of the mob.

Speed received the appointment by virtue of a long career in government service and strong connections to the Republican Party. Born in Kentucky in 1852, he had studied law at Indianapolis in the offices of Harrison, Haines and Miller, was admitted to the bar, and entered private practice. Through his connections to the law firm of Benjamin Harrison, elected president in 1888, Speed became a member of the Cherokee Commission, which negotiated the government's purchase of the Cherokee Outlet and worked out land allotment agreements with various western tribes. He sought the office of governor after the creation of Oklahoma Territory in 1890. Failing that, he took an appointment as U.S. attorney for the territory. Allegedly, no one in Oklahoma was closer to President Harrison than he, and by 1898 he was perhaps the most influential Republican in the territory. Speed, who lost his position after Grover Cleveland became president in 1893, had entered private law practice in Guthrie.[2]

Speed's appointment as special prosecutor came at the behest of Senator Matthew Quay. When Quay approached him in early April, Speed decided to undertake the task if the pay was adequate for what he accurately predicted would be the hard work and risk involved. They agreed to a long-term commitment, a year or two perhaps, with the aim of convicting four to ten of the burners as examples for the rest. When Quay and Speed presented their idea to Attorney General Griggs, Quay agreed to pay the expenses from his own pocket: one thousand dollars per conviction for as many as five to ten. Griggs agreed if Overstreet and Soper, who were in charge of the cases, did not object. Griggs, who felt put upon, made it clear to Overstreet that Speed had been "urged" upon him. To Speed's credit, he agreed to get letters from Overstreet and Soper to make certain they did not object to his assistance.[3]

As Speed expected, there were no objections, at least voiced publicly, because the interference came from such a high level of government. In fact, Overstreet welcomed the appointment. Speed quickly developed a personal sense of mission regarding the cases. Thus when Pliny Soper also opened the door to his assistance in seeking indictments and convictions in Indian Territory, he was understandably well pleased.[4]

Speed convinced Soper that they held a common ground in their determination to convict the burners. Speed did not want to meddle, replace one of Soper's assistants, or receive any pay, he said. He wanted simply what Soper wanted: to bring the burners to justice. But he had concerns about the extent and sufficiency of evidence. Thus, thinking as others before him that the mob leadership was centered at Maud, he proposed to visit Maud to gather facts. Speed believed it imperative that an attorney take the evidence in such a way that it could go unchallenged. He proposed to spend the summer in the field, developing the evidence, and working out points of law and questions of admissibility. He clearly had a plan but insisted he would not go to the Seminole Nation, which was in Soper's jurisdiction, without Soper's approval. Once he obtained the evidence, he wanted to assist Soper if the cases went to trial in Muskogee, again, only with Soper's "free consent and good will."[5]

Soper, who had wanted the cases tried in Indian Territory from the start, welcomed Speed's offer. He realized that he had a better chance of getting a conviction if he tried the burners on additional charges in the Indian Territory than if they were tried only in Pottawatomie County. He asked the attorney general to appoint Speed as his special assistant under the conditions Speed had outlined to him. He said, "I do not look at these cases as a personal credit to myself or office." What he wanted was a conviction.[6]

Securing indictments and successfully prosecuting the cases depended on their concerted effort. As summer began in 1898, they had no eyewitnesses to the burning because participants refused to talk. Specific identity of the burners was necessary. Thus at Guthrie in July, Soper, Speed, and Overstreet shared what evidence they had. Later that month Overstreet and Scothorn agreed that the cases should be tried in Indian Territory. Speed and Soper met in Muskogee and reviewed the evidence. After the meetings at Guthrie and Muskogee, Speed realized that the evidence pointed to certain mob leaders, men who came from outside the region where the burning occurred and whose names investigators had not yet learned. Thus he and Soper decided that Speed should go to the Seminole Nation and Pottawatomie County, as he had wished, to try to identify the kidnappers of McGeisey and Sampson, for they believed that kidnapping would be their best charge. Also, realizing that he and Soper would have to rely on the testimony of some men they considered "toughs," Speed wanted to corroborate their stories through as many "less guilty" people as possible.[7]

Soper planned strategy concerning the trial site. The court for the northern district of Indian Territory convened on set dates at Muskogee, Vinita, Miami, Tahlequah, and Wagoner. He wanted to begin the trials in the Cherokee Nation at the Vinita session in early October rather than at Muskogee, in the Creek Nation, for he anticipated a request for a change of venue on the grounds of prejudice because the Creeks and Seminoles, as he said, were "practically allied Nations."[8] However, Soper was overly optimistic. It soon became obvious that obstacles were in the way of preparing for such an early trial date.

First, some of those under indictment in Indian Territory had fled from Pottawatomie County. In August, the attorney general sought to ensure cooperation between the territories and among the districts of Indian Territory in locating them. In preparation for a grand jury that would convene at Muskogee in December, he instructed Overstreet to have the defendants in Oklahoma Territory arrested and placed under sufficient bail to ensure their appearance whenever required. He sent similar instructions to the U.S. attorney for the southern district of the Indian Territory.[9]

Second, Attorney General Griggs waited until August to approve the investigation Speed had sought to conduct. Soper had requested special assistance for Speed because of the danger involved. The burners who were in Pottawatomie County remained tightly organized. Two men allegedly had been killed and one severely whipped there because the burners suspected them of giving evidence. Soper thought it unsafe for Speed to go into that region alone to conduct an investigation. Thus Griggs gave official status to Speed as Soper's special assistant and, for his protection, authorized a posse, headed by W. D. Fossett of Oklahoma, Marshal Thompson's office deputy who was well acquainted with the accused and the evidence. Before going out, Speed compared all of the existing evidence, determined where the gaps were, and planned his work to fill them. On September 12, Speed and his men outfitted at Shawnee, where he interviewed a number of those under indictment and their friends. During the next ten days, Speed and his party went to Earlsboro, Maud, Remus, Romulus, Violet Springs, Young's Crossing, Sacred Heart, and Wewoka.[10]

Speed began his tour with confidence high. Among the men he interviewed at Shawnee were a number who had been at Leard's house, had helped arrest Indians, and had been at the burning. Speed's plan was to split the mob and break their conspiracy of silence. Though in reality he had a great deal to learn, he told these men that he knew what the facts were, and his purpose on this trip was to determine the best witnesses to testify to them. A number of those under indictment, he said, had been law-abiding before their involvement in the mob. They had abetted the crime by being present and sympathizing with the mob activity. But the most guilty were those mob leaders who at the time lived in the Seminole Nation or until recent times had lived there or in other Indian nations. Here, he apparently referred to Leard and the Martins, among others. In addition, he told them, at least nine of the mob members had engaged in selling whiskey to the Indians. Speed deliberately distinguished between such men and the eastern Pottawatomie County citizens that he interviewed in an effort to get the latter to cooperate. He wanted to prosecute the violent ones and the habitual criminals, he told them, and the evidence he obtained on this trip would determine which ones those would be. During his meeting with the mob members at Shawnee, Speed learned that a group of men at Earlsboro, who had no stake in the Maud community, were willing to talk in return for exclusion from prosecution.[11]

With this new lead, Speed began his investigation at Earlsboro. So tight-lipped had been the mob participants at Maud that federal officials to this point did not know about Pryor, Roper, Ivanhoe, Mathis, and other mob leaders. Because they were outsiders, some Maud mob members may not have known who they were, but others, such as the Guinns and Herschel Leard, knew exactly who they were. At Earlsboro, Speed now learned about these other mob leaders—mainly Leard's relatives and their cohorts from northern Pottawatomie County—that previous investigations had not identified. In return for this vital testimony, he promised not to prosecute several men. By this action, he "inserted a wedge to split the combination of the defendants," as he said. He wrote his wife on a postal card for any prying eye that might have access to read: "Have arranged with several so they will not be prosecuted—the better class of men—and hope, in fact am sure, there will be a general turn in that direction, so we need try only the toughs and those who are still fighting." Those he promised not to prosecute included two who could testify to the burning and one who promised to get the testimony of the man who drove the surrey that carried McGeisey and Sampson into Oklahoma. The first two were probably Mike Lawless and P. B. Staggs, who had gone to Leard's together on the night of the burning; the latter was probably Ed Nix, who had gone to the burning in the surrey with John C. Wellborn, who was apparently the driver and who, after the burning, had moved to Weatherford, Oklahoma. Speed also found other informants, though not mob members, who knew much about the mob's activities, including A. W. Anderson and Eugene Arnett, storekeepers at Earlsboro, and Mrs. F. B. Malven, who lived northwest of there. From them Speed first learned about H. Clay Roper, the Lewis family, A. J. Mathis, and others who had passed through Earlsboro on their way to Leard's and again on their way from the burning.[12] These informants, especially Arnett, would continue to prove extremely valuable to Speed.

At Maud, the effect of the "wedge" Speed had "inserted" at Earlsboro created "shock" among the burners that "was so severe that they began at once to hold councils at night and ride all day," he said; "they are not delighted now but frightened and are getting ready to beg for terms." And from Wewoka he wrote Mrs. Speed, "There is no danger. The men so far are delighted to make terms and are all trying to be friendly. The four of us are not a set they want to tackle anyhow."[13]

Speed now had a better understanding of what had happened during the first week of January. Until then, outsiders had thought that the mob was simply a group of farmers from Maud who committed the act in a state of excited anger over Mrs. Leard's murder. Now Speed knew that mob organizers from outside the Maud community had gone there determined to burn someone. Sam Pryor, he learned, had gone to Leard's several days before the burning to direct the killing of *some* Indians. A number, including Clay Roper, had come from northern Pottawatomie County. Five others had gone to Leard's a day or two before the burning, he learned, leaving home before the mob had heard of Palmer Sampson. Speed now had eyewitnesses to every step in the mob's action, including the burning of the two teenagers and the torching of McGeisey's house, and additional evidence that cinched the case against Nelson Jones for his role in the affair. In summary Speed said, "An examination of the record of the men active in the crime shows nine whiskey men, five preachers, and over twenty—the most active and lawless—old Reservation habitues."[14] This latter description certainly fit the Martins and mob members from the Lewis family to which the Leards belonged. Despite his new knowledge, however, there is no indication that Speed knew the Lewis family connections among Pryor, Roper, the Leards, and others in the mob. That knowledge would have made his work easier in the succeeding months.

After his investigation, Speed gave a newspaper interview in which he touted the success of his mission, claiming to have amassed enough evidence from the less culpable to "prosecute only the habitual criminals and more violent members of the mob." It was simply a question now of determining who would be used as government witnesses. Speed gave the newspaper a factual account of what had happened at the Leard farm and of the burning and asserted the innocence of McGeisey and Sampson. He claimed that the leaders of the mob knew who the real killer was and had the means to prove it but would not because to do so would be to admit they had burned two innocent people. The description of the killer, Speed asserted, fit Keno, whom the authorities had had in custody that summer. His purpose in relating the story, he said, was "to break the combination of the defendants," by turning them against one another.[15]

The information Speed had gathered convinced him and Soper to seek new indictments before the grand jury at Muskogee in December. Only two indictments had come out of the January grand jury at Vinita: *United States vs. One Cash, et al.*, charged with kidnapping and *United States vs. One Cash et al.*, charged with arson. Soper wanted additional indictments to prevent the defendants from taking severances, to which the law entitled them. If all of the fifty-four named in the existing indictments did so, the cases would run on for three months. Soper wanted the advantage of determining the first to be tried. "If a new indictment is filed against a few men," he said, "so that a conviction is sure against each and every one of them and that case is called for trial first, I think it will have a great tendency to weaken the defense and the other parties, or a great many of them will plead guilty." Speed harbored no hope they could convict Leard or Ed Martin but believed they could convict eight men who were not related to Mary Leard as fast as they could be tried, especially Nelson and James Jones, whom he considered "morally the most guilty men in the whole transaction." How many to try involved "a question of policy," he said. "It may be thought that many certain convictions promptly had, of ringleaders, will have greater effect for good than a larger number convicted, with some acquittals in the trials." Speed and Soper found a friend in Judge John R. Thomas, who, in charging the grand jury, stressed that "the perpetrators of the burnings should be made to suffer."[16]

Speed and Soper presented strong evidence. They brought forth a parade of witnesses, including John Washington, Billy Thlocco, John Palmer, Kinda Palmer, George Harjo, Sam Harjo, Sever, Parnoka, and Albert Washington—all of whom the mob had harassed—and the men from Earlsboro, whose stories had broken the case for Speed. The jury indicted forty-five for kidnapping and forty-nine for arson, named in five cases: *United States vs. Julius Leard, et al.*, for kidnapping; *United States vs. Texas Ranger, et al.*, for kidnapping; *United States vs. Nelson Jones, et al.*, for kidnapping; *United States vs. Texas Ranger, et al.*, for arson; and *United States vs. Julius Leard, et al.*, for arson. That late in the investigation, Speed still did not have the given names of Pryor, Roper, and other mob leaders. With writs issued immediately and trials expected in the spring, Speed fought off overconfidence about the certainty of conviction, but he believed that he and Soper had finally broken the unity of the mob members.[17]

The arrests following the new indictments were easy enough in Pottawatomie County. Oklahoma officials issued thirty-one writs, mainly for residents near Violet Springs, Earlsboro, and Maud, where the deputy U.S. marshals met no resistance. Bill Tilghman, for instance, simply stopped by the home of Mont Ballard near Maud one day and told him that a deputy would be by for him the next, and when the deputy came for Ballard, he was waiting, despite being angry at being arrested. Tilghman and his posse gathered up the men and moved about, holding them in camps on the way to Tecumseh. Of those arrested, only A. E. Butterfield, Hiram Holt, and J. D. Hodges, all preachers, could make the combined bonds of four thousand dollars on the kidnapping and arson charges when they appeared before the U.S. commissioner at Shawnee. The deputies took those who could not make bond to the U.S. jail at Guthrie to await transfer to Muskogee.[18]

Arrests elsewhere were difficult. Many of the most active members of the mob, including all of the leaders, had scattered. Others who had not been so active left Pottawatomie County to avoid prosecution or to avoid retribution for telling what they knew. By early February, 1899, only twenty-three of the forty-nine were under arrest. Twenty-three for whom there were warrants had gone into the southern district of the Indian Territory, where Speed reported only "grudging compliance" regarding two and "nothing done as to the rest." These included the Lewis family. Leard by now must have realized his mistake in letting Pryor assume leadership of the burning. From Texas, Pryor probably did not understand matters of jurisdiction in Indian Territory as well as Leard did. He apparently feared federal authorities there, but, by taking the Seminoles into Oklahoma, he had committed his crime in a jurisdiction in which his and Leard's relatives lived, making them more vulnerable to prosecution. It would have been far better for the Lewis clan if he had done his dirty work in the Seminole Nation, for only Leard and one cousin lived there. Thus when it became clear that the federal government would pursue the cases, members of the Lewis clan abandoned their farms in Pottawatomie County and fled. The Lewis and Early families and H. C. Roper settled at Beebe, Chickasaw Nation, near other of Leard's relatives. Also settling near there were Herschel Leard and his brothers-in-law Russell Guinn and Joe Dodson. Julius Leard went to Mannsville, Chickasaw Nation, where Ed Martin kept a store. The McKibbon family settled near the family of Sam Pryor and other members of the Lewis family near Stuart, Choctaw Nation. Pryor and Ivanhoe went to Texas as did other members of the mob, and James Jones went to New Mexico. Deputy marshals Tilghman and Heck Thomas of Oklahoma, who sought those who had gone to the Choctaw and Chickasaw nations, had difficulty in locating them because, like other federal officials, they apparently did not know the extent to which many of the fugitives were related. To assist them in their search, Speed requested special deputy status for them in the southern district so they might help make the twenty-three arrests.[19]

The burners apparently had a great deal of sympathy among the white residents of the Chickasaw Nation. Most of the thousands of white noncitizens in the Chickasaw and Choctaw nations had gone there from the southern states, bringing with them extreme racial biases. There were individual conflicts, blacks were ordered out of neighborhoods, and newspaper editors supported the idea of lynch law as a social corrective. However, no lynchings had occurred. It is not surprising that when a deputy marshal brought in Julius Leard and Edward L. Martin, people at Ardmore quickly made their bond of eight thousand dollars to prevent their transfer to Muskogee. "The readiness with which these bonds were made shows the standing of the two men," the *Ardmoreite* said.[20] The statement said more about the character of the general white population in the Chickasaw Nation than it did about Leard and Martin.

In Oklahoma, the Tecumseh papers again raised their old chorus in the wake of the highly publicized arrests. Now giving some credibility to the belief that McGeisey and Sampson were innocent, the editor of the *Republican* asked, "Why can't we hear of the government spending time and money to ferret out the perpetrators of the brutal, hellish murder of that lone woman?" At about this time notices appeared, announcing payments of damages to the Seminoles as a result of the burning. To these the editor responded, "Now how much does the government propose to make the Indian nation pay the family of the outraged and murdered woman? The whole Seminole nation would not compensate for that crime and its consequent injuries."[21] Consternation among Pottawatomie County citizens grew as time passed, and some prisoners who could not make bond remained in the Guthrie jail or were transferred to Muskogee.

In the Muskogee jail, tension was high in the cell block. Mob members harbored bitter feelings against Nelson Jones, David Jones, and George Moppin, whom they blamed for their plight. Jailers had to keep the three in a different cell for their own safety.[22]

By the spring of 1899, arrests of the remaining fugitives had practically ceased. Deputies brought in Herschel Leard and Ed King in March. With so many still out, in early April, Soper became concerned because the trials were set to begin in May. Most still out were apparently in Marshal John S. Hammer's jurisdiction in the Chickasaw Nation. Thus Soper endorsed Speed's earlier request for the deputization of Tilghman and Thomas to assist Hammer because they were familiar with the fugitives. Later that month, deputies delivered Andrew J. Mathis and James Jones to the Muskogee jail. Jones, also under indictment for grand larceny in Pottawatomie County, had made bond on charges related to the burning by the signature of a man named Eicholson at Tecumseh. When Jones jumped bail and went to New Mexico, Eicholson went after him, captured him, and delivered him to the court at Tecumseh. Thus as the trial date approached, about two thirds of the accused were in jail at Muskogee or free on bail, and a few others were still in jail at Guthrie.[23] The remainder, including the three main leaders of the mob—Samuel V. Pryor, H. Clay Roper, and George Bird Ivanhoe—and others were still at large.

Horace Speed went to Muskogee on May 1 to help prepare the prosecution and to clarify his objectives in the trials. To him, the people involved in the crimes fell into five classes, according to evidence indicating degrees of culpability. By categorizing the accused this way, Speed made his decisions about whom to prosecute.

First was the Indian who killed Mary Leard. "I have not been able to satisfy myself who the guilty Indian was," he wrote, "although I have tried hard to identify him. The Seminoles give me no help on this matter. The defendants are convinced that Palmer Sampson did the murder. I expect to learn the facts after these trials are ended. If the guilty Indian was not Palmer Sampson he must be hunted down, convicted and executed."[24] Speed would later reaffirm his earlier conclusion that Sampson was innocent and the killer was, indeed, Keno, who was still on the loose.

Second were the relatives of Mary Leard. Speed wrote, "It has not seemed to me wise to attempt to punish these while the murderer of the woman is not punished or even identified."[25] Though he did not say it, public sympathy would probably have stood in the way of convicting Ed Martin, the victim's father, and Julius Leard, who had lost not only his wife but his daughter Cora, who died of her injuries in April following the murder.

Third were former deputy U.S. marshal Nelson M. Jones and his nephew, James Jones, who to Speed were the guiltiest of all those indicted: "They could have protected those prisoners if they had tried; they talked lynch law and burning; suggested and directed the torture of John Washington and other suspected Indian prisoners to force confessions, knew the burning was to take place, encouraged it, and expressed satisfaction when talking of it the day after the burning."[26]

Fourth were men who were not Mary Leard's relatives but "who took an active part in burning the Indians, apparently delighting in the cruelty." Here, Speed included the leader of the mob, Sam Pryor, alias Texas Ranger, and his associates H. Clay Roper, Jesse McFarland, and Bird Ivanhoe, who were still uncaught; A. J. Mathis, who prayed for the Indians at the arbor and later boasted that while he was still on his knees he lighted the fire; Mont Ballard, who had been very active in arresting and holding the Indians, had attended the burning, talked of fighting the law enforcement officers, and allegedly told arresting officers, "There were no Indians burned there but there was a barbecue in the hollow." He also allegedly said "he saw there chunks of roast beef big enough to feed a dog," and told the marshals, "You G———D——— fellows have come too late." Speed also included in this group Hiram Holt, one of the most influential men in the mob, a preacher who helped arrest and guard Indians, prayed for the Indians after Ed Martin announced the burning, "and then left the place evidently as a matter of rascally prudence"; and Jesse Guinn, a preacher, who was more active than Holt in arresting and guarding Indians and left the Leard place with Holt a few hours before the crowd did. There were six or eight more who Speed thought were "of about the degree of guilt with Guinn."[27] In the fifth class, Speed placed mob members in general, "who were aiders and abettors by their voluntary presence and by different acts of assistance or approval."[28] In establishing his categories of defendants, Speed was still apparently ignorant of the family connections between Leard and Pryor and Roper, and perhaps of the connection of Herschel Leard to the Guinn family.

The task before the prosecutors was monumental. Of the forty-seven indicted, one had died, seventeen were in jail at Muskogee, eleven were out on bail, three were still not fully identified, and fifteen were fugitives. Speed and Soper knew, too, the names of several others not named in indictments who had left the country.[29]

Speed and Soper hoped to reduce the task before them by demoralizing the burners and breaking whatever unity remained among them. They would start with those that Speed had singled out as the most guilty. "If the first two are convicted," Speed thought, "it will be a victory. If the first five are convicted I shall feel that the mob spirit will be cowed. If the first seven or nine are convicted and all the others made to go on the stand as witnesses for the prosecution and tell all the facts so far as each knows them the effect will be salutary beyond description."[30]

Speed's confidence was a result, in part, of the broad spectrum of potential witnesses from whom he had acquired evidence. Though he had lost an important Seminole witness in the death of John Washington in January

1899, he had others that could testify about Washington's experience at Leard's farm. Speed had a number of reliable informants at Earlsboro, and earlier that spring, he had met in Tecumseh with about twenty of the accused from Maud in an effort to persuade them to turn state's evidence. They included George Cash, Hiram Holt, Cap Guinn, George Guinn, Dave Guinn, Charley Woodard, and W. H. Vansickle, though some did not talk with Speed but went simply because they had heard that others were meeting him.[31] Of this group, Cash would prove an important witness.

Speed placed a good deal of significance on the trials for their anticipated effect in suppressing mob activity. It would be the first time he was aware of that lynchers were punished in the Southwest. But if the trials were to have that effect, it was "of the utmost importance that no slip, misstep or failure shall occur." Thus, he believed every trial must end in conviction, for "the moral effect and the lasting results" would diminish if they tried them all, convicted most, and acquitted some. Acquittal, he said, "would practically mean a drawn battle—a partial success on each side." If he could reach his goal, he believed "the next time a mob is proposed in that section, people invited to join will refuse, saying that mobs are followed by trials, the members become witnesses against the leaders, convictions follow, and it is best to let the law officers punish crime." Success rested on his assumption that after one or two went to trial, those defendants not named as government witnesses would "throw up their hands, plead guilty and beg mercy."[32]

The approaching trials attracted considerable public attention. Because the case had created such public interest both at home and abroad, hundreds of spectators from Oklahoma and Indian Territory made their way to Muskogee for the event, as did reporters from major newspapers in the Midwest and East. The court process itself was enough to create attention, with nearly fifty people indicted for kidnapping, nearly fifty indicted for arson, and more than a hundred subpoenaed as witnesses. Added to that was the story, which, said the *Vinita Daily Chieftain*, had "in it the element of murder, lynching by burning, the death of alleged guiltless persons, an alleged attempt at an uprising of the Seminole Indians and a conspiracy, the latter involving several hundred persons."[33] To the press, part of the sensationalism derived from the fact that the defendants included what it called some of "the well-to-do and respectable element" of Pottawatomie County, whom Congress had appropriated funds to prosecute. There was an air of expectancy as the prosecution team of Soper, Speed, and Assistant

U.S. Attorney Orlando J. Wilcox prepared to take on attorneys such as J. Warren Reed and James M. Givens of Muskogee, who had been retained by the defendants.[34]

For some in the local press, a kind of vindication for the Indian Territory was at hand. The United States press had made much in recent years of the lawlessness in the Indian Territory. The burning of McGeisey and Sampson had demonstrated that the Americans in Oklahoma Territory, too, could be lawless. The approaching trials gave opportunity for one Muskogee editor to write: "Glad, indeed, are we as a people that this crime cannot be laid at the Territory's door. Already in too many instances has the Territory been made a scape-goat for the sins of others. For forty years the Indian Territory has been given the credit of furnishing an abiding-place for every desperado captured or executed between Mason and Dixon's line and the Gulf of Mexico."[35] While there was some obvious satisfaction gained from the indictment and prosecution of the burners, there would be even more if the prosecution should prove successful.

NINE

The Trials

Judge John R. Thomas, a native of Illinois and former member of the U.S. House of Representatives, had become judge in the northern district in 1897. He grew impatient with attorneys who belabored points and who attempted, through legal maneuvering, to delay court processes. During court proceedings, he often drew cartoons of courtroom action and wrote personal letters. He was openly opinionated and had expressed his views on the burning shortly after it occurred, calling it "one of the greatest outrages" ever committed in the region. Like most people, he at first assumed McGeisey and Sampson were guilty, but they would have been apprehended and convicted, he argued, had the mob let the law take its course. Defending the recently expanded federal court system in the territory, he asserted that there had been no miscarriage of justice since it had gone into effect in 1896. "Indian Territory has shown that it can take care of its criminals and will continue to do so," Judge Thomas said.[1] Thomas had kept current with the progress of the cases, for he had impaneled the grand juries at Vinita and Muskogee in 1898. Now he would hear the cases. Although Speed and Soper had built strong cases against the accused, they found an ally in Thomas, who would significantly help to shape the outcome of the trials.

Speed and Soper were seasoned prosecutors, but their opposition in the first trial, that of Nelson Jones, promised to test their skill. J. Warren Reed, the senior member of the defense team, had earned the title "That Lawyer Who Always Wins His Cases" before he left his native West Virginia and settled in Fort Smith, Arkansas, in 1889. He made a specialty of defense, and during his first seven years before the Court for the Western District of Arkansas, he won more acquittals than any other attorney practicing before the court at the time. In 1897, after the court system was expanded in the Indian Territory, Reed moved his law offices to Muskogee. When the case of the burners was called, Reed and his assistant, J. H. Koogler, immediately moved for a severance and separate trial, as Speed and Soper had anticipated. Judge Thomas revealed the unyielding stand he had taken regarding the cases when he said, "You do this to kill time, I suppose. . . . The defendants have a right to a separate trial if they demand it, but if you do that, I will take you the most rapid, or liveliest, gait that you ever traveled in your life."[2]

Speed and Soper had a good case against Jones, who laid the groundwork for his own conviction. He had conducted himself no better in the wake of the burning than he had the week preceding it. Apparently assuming that no prosecutions would follow the burning, he had at first publicly claimed the locks and chain found on the remains of McGeisey and Sampson. He had also told the press that he had had McGeisey in custody but that the mob had overpowered him and taken his prisoner away, ostensibly only to use him to help secure evidence against Sampson. But at the Vinita grand jury hearings in January 1898, Jones's confidence began to waver. He denied that the chain and locks entered in evidence were his. Jones's earlier statements had probably been a part of his continued bragging, for a member of the Guinn family had apparently supplied the chain attached to Sampson and used at the burning.[3]

Jones realized that testimony at Vinita had incriminated him. The Seminoles had placed him at the scene of their torture and illegal confinement, making it obvious that he had been derelict in his duty. He began to try to improve his position after the hearings by charging federal officials of the northern district with corruption and attempting to create a jurisdictional dispute between the territories. When that ploy led nowhere, Jones asked Marshal Bill Tilghman to set up an interview with T. F. McMechan, to whom he gave a voluntarily statement, saying that he wanted those "who have done this deed to be caught."[4]

Once he began to cooperate with investigators, Jones's own statements practically guaranteed his conviction. He admitted his failure to take

Lincoln McGeisey away from the Leard farm when he had him in custody. His defense, however, was that fifteen to twenty armed men had faced him down, and he had left the Seminole prisoners with the mob, even after Ed Martin had said that he and Leard could not guarantee their safety. But Leard and Martin testified that the mob did not force Jones away and that he could have taken the prisoners if he had wanted them. In addition, Leard, Martin, and Martin's two sons claimed that Jones encouraged the burning, suggested the hanging of John Washington, indicated that he would look the other way if the mob wanted to deal with the guilty Indian, and was drinking much of the time he was at the Leard farm, as were the men who were with him. The drinking may have accounted for his alleged inflammatory statements and for his leaving the impression with Leard and others that he had the authority to "deputize" them to search for suspects.[5]

But perhaps most damaging to Jones's case was his admission that at no time during the week before the burning did he attempt to notify the federal authorities about what was going on. When asked why he did not gather a number of Seminole lighthorse policemen to arrest the men who had prevented him from taking his prisoners, Jones said, "The light horsemen knew just as much about it as I did," and explained that he had been unable to find those he had tried to reach. Jones presented himself as working alone, without help. There were deputies stationed at Wewoka and Holdenville but "they did not come out at all," he said. "I might have made a little mistake in the way I handled myself," he admitted; "if I did, I am very sorry."[6]

Jones had maintained all along that he never believed McGeisey and John Washington were guilty, that he knew nothing about Sampson, and that he had heard no talk of mob activity. "I never believed they would mob an innocent man, I could not believe it," he said, after he heard the news. He said of Lincoln McGeisey, "I never believed there would be an innocent man suffer at all, because we did not think we had the guilty man; they said it was not the man, the little child said the man was innocent; that is where I got my information."[7]

During the seven days of Jones's trial on the charge of kidnapping Lincoln McGeisey, the jury listened to a number of witnesses. The most damaging testimony about how Jones had conducted himself, however, came from members of the mob. Thomas Welt Martin testified that Jones and his men had brought whiskey to the Leard farm, one claiming that it was "as free as the water that runs." Stoke Martin and Julius Leard told how Jones had instigated the hanging of John Washington in an attempt to find if he knew anything about the killing. Jim Dickerson testified that as early as the night after the murder, members of the crowd that had gathered, apparently Pryor and Roper, were saying that the killer ought to be burned. Others testified that Jones abetted and promoted the lynching. Stoke Martin and Julius Leard testified that Jones had said that if the killer were found, he would remove himself from the scene and let the mob do what they wanted. Leard and others testified that when Jim Jones and Andy Morrison came to the Leard farm the night before the burning, Jones told Leard that Nelson Jones sent word that if the mob intended to do anything to McGeisey and Sampson, they should take them across the line into Oklahoma. Halock Harjo, a Creek who was in Jones's camp near Sasakwa the morning of January 8, swore he heard conversation between Jim Jones and Nelson Jones that indicated Jones had anticipated the burning. The burners who testified were pleased to help convict Jones, for they, like Pottawatomie County citizens, believed that the Joneses "worked up the feeling of the mob to burn the Indians, then sneaked out of all participation in the deed, and became vigorous in hunting down white men who were in the mob." The prosecution had built a strong case against Jones, showing that he was not only derelict in his duty by failing to take the Seminoles and protect them but that he had encouraged the mob.[8]

Jones's defense was that he was in camp near Sasakwa when the mob took Lincoln McGeisey to Oklahoma and burned him. His defense attorneys attempted to define kidnapping literally as the transporting of McGeisey against his will to Oklahoma. Judge Thomas, however, defined the crime much more broadly in his rulings. By all accounts, Reed staged a brilliant defense, challenging the credibility of witnesses, particularly Julius Leard, who had given some of the most damaging evidence against Jones. At times, it appeared to spectators that he outmatched Speed.[9]

Judge Thomas sent the case to the jury with a forceful charge concerning their duty. At one point during the trial, he had let his opinion of Jones be known: "If ever there was a case, on this mortal earth where a man did encourage and incite a crime which has been a blot on civilization, and the age, the defendant has proven to be that man."[10] This tone carried over into his charge. Perhaps because the federal court with its extended jurisdiction was a relatively new institution in the northern district, Thomas carefully defined terms for the jurors. He explained the two counts of the indictment, charging Jones as a principal and an accessory before the fact,

and the concepts of burden of proof and reasonable doubt. He explained the
"chain of evidence" requirement for conviction on circumstantial evidence
and the concept of conspiracy, stressing that conspirators are bound by each
of the conspirators, whether present or not at an unlawful act. Thomas
explained that one who took part in the arrest, detention, and carrying of
a person into another jurisdiction was guilty of kidnapping as a principal,
and one who, though not present, counseled or abetted it before the act was
guilty as an accessory before the fact. He urged the jurors to consider Jones's
role in the affair. An officer, he said, who intentionally left the scene of a
contemplated crime and deliberately stayed away so that the crime could
take place was a principal. It was not material, he said, whether McGeisey
was guilty of Mary Leard's murder. As to Jones's lack of action—his failure
to take McGeisey away, to notify his superiors, or call for help—Thomas
said, "A failure to speak or act in the law, as in ordinary life, may be the
most convincing evidence which could exist." It took the jury less than four
hours to return the verdict of guilty of kidnapping.[11]

During Jones's trial, which ended on May 18, the public learned for the
first time the truth about what happened at the Leard farm and at Maud
during the early days of January 1898. The preponderance of evidence
presented against Jones was clear and revealed a great deal about the mob
in general. In commenting on the testimony, a local newspaper said that
it showed "that the horrible crime with which the mob is charged was
without mitigating circumstances of any kind and the perpetrators of the
deed, especially the ring leaders who incited the mob to the act, will merit
the full legal punishment for their participation in the crime."[12]

The Jones verdict came as a relief to Speed, who did not want to try
any more cases than necessary. If he and Soper could convict four of the
burners this session and continue the others until next term, perhaps Pryor
and Roper would be in custody by then. After their trials, Speed wanted "to
quit the cases entirely." The whole affair was nerve-wracking: "Each one is
a risk and the strain of anxiety is intense: as exhausting as any I have gone
through with any time."[13]

The second case, called on May 19, was *United States vs. Andrew J.
"Buck" Mathis* on the charge of kidnapping Lincoln McGeisey. With Jones
convicted, Speed and Soper wanted to convict one of the mob leaders. Speed
would have preferred to try Pryor, Roper, or Ivanhoe, but he had to settle
for Mathis, a braggart who had a disreputable character. Before the trial,
Speed offered to show Mathis's attorneys his evidence against their client,

hoping he would plead guilty, but he refused. Speed, Soper, and Orlando
Wilcox faced attorneys James M. Givens and William M. Cravens. Givens
had practiced in Muskogee only a few years, and Cravens, an associate of
J. Warren Reed, had practiced in Fort Smith before moving to Muskogee.[14]

In a trial that lasted five days, testimony showed Mathis's deep involvement in the crime. He had been in the mob every day except two from
the day following the murder until the burning. Mathis, who prayed over
McGeisey and Sampson and then boasted that he lighted the fire while he
was still on his knees, was one of the mob leaders that forcibly transported
the boys to Oklahoma. Cravens and Givens apparently had little character
in Mathis to support their defense. Speed presented him as a man without
a conscience, getting him to admit during the trial that while he was on his
knees, praying with his Colt .45 strapped on the outside of his overcoat, he
felt no pity in his heart for the two Seminole teenagers.[15] Judge Thomas
cared little for him, either. As was his habit, while the attorneys were
summing up the case, he was writing a personal letter in which he said,
"I am now trying one of the men who burned the Seminole Indians at
the stake—his name is Mathis and he is the wretch who lighted the fire
around the poor victims. Col. Cravens is now addressing the jury in behalf
of the defendant, but if one may judge from the manner and expressions of
countenance of the jurors he will—as he ought to be—convicted."[16] And
he was. On May 23, it took the jury only a short time to bring in a verdict
of guilty.[17]

It looked as if Speed's strategy was paying off. The editor of the *Muskogee
Phoenix* realized the significance of this second guilty verdict, saying that
the convictions would "have a salutary effect upon the hot-headed and
frenzied individual who insists upon taking the law in his own hands
whenever a favorable opportunity presents itself."[18] The Pottawatomie
County press, however, justified the county population's support of the
burners by insisting, despite the evidence, that McGeisey and Sampson had
killed Mary Leard and then violated her corpse, intimating that the burners
would have likely gone to trial for murder in Pottawatomie County, and
claiming that the citizens' clear and unanimous sympathy for the burners
was the reason the United States was trying them at Muskogee "on a much
smaller charge than they would have stood trial for in Oklahoma."[19] But as
the federal officials had maintained all along, if the matter had been left to
the local Oklahoma courts, the burners would probably have not gone to
trial at all.

The prosecution's momentum halted with the third trial, *United States vs. James Jones*, which began on May 24. Jones was without doubt one of the most unprincipled members of the mob. Before the grand jury at Vinita, he had magnified his role of "assisting" his uncle Nelson Jones. At the same time, he played down his role in arresting Seminoles and in other mob activities, of hauling whiskey and supplies, and inciting the mob. In an attempt to ameliorate his and his uncle's roles in the affair, he tried to make a case for the guilt of McGeisey and Sampson. He alleged that when Julius Leard came in late on the Tuesday night before the burning, Leard claimed to have found enough evidence that day to prevent Nelson Jones from taking McGeisey away and threatened to use force to keep him. The following morning, the mob allegedly prevented Marshal Jones from taking the prisoners. Jim Jones claimed a major confrontation took place, with gunplay. Nelson Jones, however, had refuted his nephew's account of events, many crucial points of which were not corroborated by any other evidence. Nelson Jones also swore more than once that the line of men he confronted had numbered only about fifteen. And the confrontation had occurred late in the afternoon, not in the morning. He said that his nephew had gone home at noon that day and was not there when the confrontation with the mob took place. Also, Nelson Jones insisted throughout the investigation that Leard had always claimed to believe that Lincoln McGeisey was innocent.[20]

Nelson Jones had nothing to gain and everything to lose in his own case by refuting his nephew's account of events at the Leard farm. Sympathy for the defendants would have been much higher if they could have proved McGeisey and Sampson guilty than it was because they were apparently innocent. That mitigating circumstance, in turn, might have had a strong impact on the jury.

Because of the unsavory character of James Jones and evidence of his role in the mob's action, the prosecution expected conviction. After he rested his case, Speed believed "that it was the strongest of the three." Jones's defense was basically that he had been chased away by the mob and was at Violet Springs when they took McGeisey and Sampson across the line. To the court's and the prosecutors' surprise, on May 27 the jury returned a verdict of not guilty.[21]

What had gone wrong? Part of the fault may have rested with Judge Thomas. He had not given as forceful charge to the jury as he had in the other cases. He told them that if Jones returned to the Leard farm with the intention of participating in the kidnapping or if he delivered a message from Nelson Jones, urging the mob to take McGeisey across the line, he was an accessory before the fact. However, Thomas said, "If evidence be equally balanced and susceptible of two meanings antagonistic to each other, the one pointing to the guilt of the defendant and the other to his innocence, you should give to such evidence that interpretation which is most favorable to the defendant."[22] Soper believed the not guilty verdict resulted from "the fact that the mob, which contained some eight or nine preachers, drove Jim Jones away at the time of the abduction because he had whiskey in his buggy." Speed blamed the jury, which he called a "pick up" jury, and promised to "have a better one sent for" to hear the next trial. He could find some consolation, however, in the fact that Jones remained in jail under two other indictments related to the burning as well as another indictment in Oklahoma for cattle rustling. It appeared that he was facing a number of years in the penitentiary, despite his acquittal in Muskogee.[23]

The last case to be called during the May court session was *United States vs. Mont Ballard*, which began on May 31 and which Speed likewise expected to win, as he said, "if the jury is not crooked."[24] Having convicted Jones and Mathis, Speed and Soper felt it was necessary to convict someone from the Maud community, which they could not allow to escape punishment. Leard would have been their first choice, but public sympathy would be too strong in his favor. Speed would probably have liked to try Jesse Guinn, whom he particularly despised, but there had been so many Guinns in the mob at various times that it was difficult for witnesses, especially Indians who spoke through interpreters, to separate them.

Still, he might have selected Guinn or one or two others had Ballard simply kept his mouth shut. Ballard was thirty-eight years old, a native of West Virginia, who had lived in the Seminole Nation before he obtained land in Pottawatomie County, where he and his wife built their farm. By 1898, Ballard had a good farm, immediately northeast of the Maud post office. Speed knew that Ballard, a good friend of Julius Leard, had been a very active mob member, but not a leader, and that he had expected the guilty Indians, if found, to be hanged. When he heard that the mob leaders intended to burn them, Ballard allegedly said, "My God. They are going to burn them Indians. Hanging is bad enough without burning them." It was not lynching Ballard objected to, but the type of lynching. He attended the burning nevertheless, and in the aftermath made offhand and nonchalant remarks about it and angry and defiant statements that urged resistance to federal authorities. These statements caused Speed to select Ballard to prosecute. He offered Ballard's attorneys the evidence he had against their client, hoping he would plead guilty, but he refused.[25]

In presenting their case, Speed, Soper, and Wilcox called eighteen witnesses. They established Ballard's presence at Leard's farm most days following the murder, his part in squads sent to round up Indians, his presence when the mob leaders strung up Lincoln McGeisey and when the mob took McGeisey and Palmer Sampson into Oklahoma, and his presence at the burning.[26] Through their testimony those who had been mob members reflected a cross section of Pottawatomie County society and provided insights into the mob mentality.

Some witnesses were Mont Ballard's neighbors, friends, and longtime acquaintances. James Alfred Smallwood, about twenty-two, lived two miles northwest of Maud. He had gone to Leard's farm out of curiosity on Sunday and stayed three days. He had returned to Leard's, again out of curiosity, the night the mob took the boys across the line. About ten days after the burning he had run away to Kansas and stayed until word came that it was safe to return; thus he had escaped being arrested or indicted.[27] A. J. Vinson [called Vincent], who was forty-two at the time of the burning, farmed about six miles southwest of Maud and had known Ballard since 1892. He admitted on the stand that he believed in "speedy" execution of the guilty. He had gone to Leard's on Sunday and had returned on that last Friday "to see the fun." He said of the burning: "I didn't call that fire funny, but I went over there as a prospector like the rest of them." Afterwards, Vinson had hid out in the Chickasaw Nation.[28] Bert Catron had farmed about three miles southwest of Maud for three years when the burning occurred. One of the first to arrive on the murder scene, he had gone back to Leard's twice more out of curiosity, including the nights the mob strung up McGeisey and took him and Sampson across the line. He had also witnessed the burning. On the stand, he said that he had not gone to hunt down Indians, but, he said, "I thought if it was necessary I could do it."[29]

Prosecution witnesses George Brown, Ward Chievers, and George Cash told similar stories. George Cash and his brother-in-law Philip H. Cooper, who had also been in the mob, were the founders of Maud. They built the first store, where the post office was established in 1896. Cash had rented from Mont Ballard for three or four years. He had been at Leard's four days, including the last, when he had gone, he said, because "the general supposition was there would be something done with them, and I had a desire to see it."[30]

The most forthcoming prosecution witnesses were Mike Lawless and George Pettifer. In 1898 Lawless lived at Earlsboro, where he farmed. For seven or eight years before that he had been in the saloon business. Though many of the witnesses had denied talk or even a general understanding that a lynching would occur, Lawless swore the news had gone abroad on both Wednesday and Friday. He had gone to Leard's both times because he claimed to have known Lincoln McGeisey—no doubt in his capacity as a saloonkeeper—for four years. He had gone to the burning out of curiosity but had left as it began. "About as quick as that fire started," he said, "I told [P. B.] Staggs I have got enough of this, and I am going away from here."[31] Pettifer, who was from Maud, had been at Leard's four days, had been active in hunting Seminoles, and had attended the burning. He went further than any other witness in attributing statements that encouraged violence to Mont Ballard. Once, he said, Ballard stated that if the guilty were found, "they ought to be killed and let the hogs eat them clean up." And, he said, on the last night at Leard's, when someone called for a prayer, "Mont Ballard said such sons of bitches as them they was no prayers deserved, they didn't deserve no prayers."[32]

Perhaps the most reluctant prosecution witness was John Stankewitz. He had moved onto Mont Ballard's farm in November of 1897 and was helping Ballard build a rental house on the property about a mile south of Ballard's home. He had gone to Leard's three times out of curiosity, first "just to see the woman" and the last to see the Indians. He went the last night with Ballard. Though they remained with the crowd and attended the burning, he claimed not to remember anyone, except Ed Martin, involved in putting the Indians into the surrey, he claimed not to know anyone in the procession because he and Ballard were about 150 to 200 yards back in line, and he could not identify anyone at the burning and claimed not to know who piled the brush around the Indians or lit the fire. Yet he could give a detailed account of Ballard's whereabouts during the daytime hours of that last Friday and could swear that Ballard made no statements and took no active part in taking the Indians across the line and burning them because he, like Stankewitz, simply went along and remained well back in the crowd. When Soper asked him if there was not a rumor that the mob would burn the Indians, Stankewitz said no and supposed that his memory had failed in two years. But, retorted Soper sarcastically, it had not failed regarding Mont Ballard.[33]

The prosecutors had the same problem with other of their witnesses that they had with Stankewitz: failed memory. A frustrated Pliny Soper asked A. J. Vinson: "Could any man of common ordinary intelligence, . . . have been in that crowd, or been around the Laird house on Friday or on Saturday or on Sunday night, and on days subsequent, and up to and including Friday night, and not have known what they intended to do with the Indians if they found that they were the guilty Indians?"[34] Those who admitted that there had been talk of lynching claimed to have gone to Leard's not knowing if they *really* expected anything to happen or *particularly* what it might be. Neither could the witnesses name leaders or those directly involved in the burning except outsiders: Ed Martin, Sam Pryor, and Bird Ivanhoe. Even then, they claimed not to know who gave the order to start to Oklahoma, who was in line, and who was in charge of the burning.[35]

The reluctance of the witnesses to be forthcoming with information came from three sources. First, some obviously hesitated to testify against their neighbor Mont Ballard and were quick to say good things about his reputation. Testifying against an outsider like Jones or Mathis was different from testifying against one of their own. Second, there was a fear of self-incrimination. Third, the prosecutors believed other mob members had intimidated the witnesses. James Alfred Smallwood denied the existence of a group of mob members "banded together and oath bound" to prevent others from giving evidence.[36] A. J. Vinson denied that there had been threats against mob members except the one that Pryor had made the night of the burning. "Is there not an organization called the Committee of Safety," Soper asked, "which has come up since the government began to investigate these cases, where there are different parties that are members that have organized for mutual protection, and for giving of all information?" When Vinson replied not so, to his knowledge, Soper accused him of lying.[37] Soper was referring to the committee, in which Vinson was an officer, established ostensibly to raise defense funds for the accused.

Despite the reluctance of some witnesses, the prosecution sought to establish Mont Ballard's involvement in a conspiracy to kidnap McGeisey and Sampson. They got support from the bench. Judge Thomas overruled Givens's objections to testimony by Thomas McGeisey, George Harjo, Louis Graham, and George Cash about the general atmosphere at the Leard farm or statements about violent acts against the Indian captives. He allowed testimony that tended to establish a conspiracy to do harm. Statements of one or all bound the conspirators together, Thomas ruled. The defense also tried to exclude testimony regarding the burning. When Givens objected to Bert Catron's testimony about the burning, Judge Thomas admitted it, saying that it showed the purpose of the kidnapping. And in response to the defense attorney's objections to testimony about Pryor's activities and the burning of the Leard farmstead, Judge Thomas ruled that the testimony helped to determine the spirit of the mob.[38]

Givens and Cravens made a strong effort to appeal to the emotions of the audience in order to mitigate the evidence of Ballard's actions. They tried to get testimony into the record that might build a case for Lincoln McGeisey's guilt. If they could establish the commission of a murder, they argued, then there could be legal grounds for Ballard to have gone armed to Leard's place to assist in arresting or guarding the suspects. But Judge Thomas ruled not so, if he came from another state: "It is not for him to come to the Indian Territory to enforce the laws; if he came he came as a trespasser."[39] Givens inserted into many of his questions the idea that Mary Leard had been raped. Speed objected vociferously each time because he knew, as Leard and the mob leaders knew, that she had not. Judge Thomas put it to rest by saying to Speed, "Let it go. So far as this case is concerned it is not the least particle of difference whether she was murdered or not murdered, or whether she was outraged or not outraged, but for the purpose of fixing the time."[40]

The defense attorneys also tried by various means to impeach the credibility of some of the prosecution's witnesses. They emphasized, for instance, that George Harjo had been arrested by Jones for larceny and that some of the stolen goods had been found at Thomas McGeisey's house. They tried to show that Louis Graham was simply seeking revenge because of the mob's arresting him, and they intimated that he was a horse thief. They accused some of the witnesses under indictment of trading testimony for immunity. They hinted that George Brown had a grudge against Ballard, who had once accused him of stealing cotton. They also accused David Jones of holding a grudge against Leard and the Martins for refusing to help him arrange bond. They played up Mike Lawless's rather unsavory reputation as an Earlsboro saloonkeeper and owner of a gambling house and raised questions about his court appearances for illegal activities in the whiskey trade.[41]

The defense tried especially hard to impeach the testimony of Albert Washington. Like most of the Seminoles involved, he did not speak English, and translation had been a problem throughout the investigation and trials. Washington did not know the days of the week very well and indicated time of day by using his hands to show the height of the sun. Givens tried to confuse him about the days on which certain events happened and accused him of lying. Washington testified, for instance, that Ballard and Jesse Guinn had gone with Leard to capture Palmer Sampson and that Ballard had ridden a yellow horse all that week, but, in reality, neither man had gone after Sampson. It became clear later that Washington had confused Mont Ballard with his brother Woodson and Jesse Guinn with Chesley R. (Chess) Guinn. Givens also claimed that Washington had a criminal record, but Washington said that he had once been exonerated on a charge of stealing a saddle. Finally, Givens accused him of having supplied Palmer Sampson's name and having volunteered his services to lead Leard to him. That accusation, of course, Washington denied.[42]

The defense did not, however, challenge the credibility of William Tilghman, the venerable U.S. marshal, or the highly respected posseman Neal Brown. Tilghman told how he had Ballard and several others under arrest in camp near a big log fire to keep them warm. "Ballard made the remark," Tilghman said, "that that would be a good fire to roast Indians by, and went on to state that he had been down by where the Indian boys were burned, and was there the next morning, and said he was satisfied that somebody had been burned there, that there were chunks of meat there big enough for a back log, that they had been burning Indians or niggers or somebody else." About Ballard's arrest the second time, Tilghman said, "He seemed to be mad about it, and I told him not to blame the local authorities, the authorities at Washington had ordered it, and he said g———d d———n the authorities at Washington, if they listened to me they would have given them a touch of high life."[43] While Brown had Ballard in custody at Shawnee, the burning came up. Brown said, "I spoke up and said, it must have been a horrible way to die, to be burned, and Mr. Ballard spoke up and said, no, it was not, he said it was an easy death, and I says, how do you know . . . he laughed and said, I have been told so."[44] Ballard's hostility toward federal officials and his propensity for making nonchalant statements about the burning probably explain in part why the defense attorneys did not put him on the stand in his own behalf. Having his statements placed in the record by the prosecution did not help his case.

When its turn came, the defense called only seven witnesses. The attorneys sought with these witnesses to challenge the accuracy of earlier

testimony—especially that of Albert Washington—to mitigate the circumstances of the mob's actions, and to establish Ballard's character and good
reputation in his community. As part of the defense, Givens and Cravens
argued that in three instances when prosecution witnesses claimed Ballard
was involved in mob activities, he was elsewhere: helping to dig Mary
Leard's grave, working at home and traveling to Tecumseh, and building
a house.[45] Though Judge Thomas had ruled emphatically and repeatedly during the prosecution's presentation that the Oklahomans had no
authority in the Indian Territory, the defense attempted to demonstrate
that Leard and those who helped him, including Ballard, thought they
had been deputized by Nelson Jones. Julius Leard had claimed from the
start that on his arrival at the Leard farm, Jones "authorized" Leard "to
arrest any suspicious characters" he might find and "to take all the help" he
might need. Similar statements had been obtained from others during the
investigation. On the stand, Leard stuck by his story.[46] As a final effort in
the defense, Ballard's attorneys managed to enter testimony supporting his
good character, some even from defense witnesses, but all from members
of the mob.[47]

The defense witnesses, like the prosecution witnesses who had been in
the mob, exhibited selective memories. Jesse Guinn claimed he could not
remember how many of his own brothers had been at Leard's place. "Some"
were there he had "heard," he said. As far as he knew, no one hindered Jim
Jones from taking Lincoln McGeisey away that Friday, and he did not know
why they held the Indians.[48] Julius Leard simply lied, claiming he had no
idea who had strung up McGeisey and therefore did not know if Ballard
was one of them. Though he said, "I was in favor of having them done away
with as soon as possible," he had heard no talk about lynching and denied
there was an understanding what would happen to the Indians. Ballard was
there the night the mob took the Indians to Oklahoma, but he had simply
gone along, said Leard, and taken no active part. Leard also had no idea
who had taken charge of McGeisey and Sampson, claiming to have gone to
get his horse when the procession started.[49]

Speed and Soper were convinced that these witnesses knew about the
organized efforts to intimidate others and had tried to get them to admit
it. They had questioned some defense witnesses about it, including David
Jones, who testified that intimidation had gone on up to the time of the trials.
While he was being held in jail with Ballard in early February, he swore,
Ballard had said, "that any man that testified in this case or told anything

about this here case that they would treat him just like they treated the Indians." Ballard had also said, Jones testified, that the men were afraid to turn state's evidence because "they knowed better."[50]

Speed, Soper, and Wilcox seemed convinced that Jesse Guinn particularly was deeply involved in the intimidation. In cross-examination, Wilcox asked, "Is there not a detective association in Oklahoma among the people accused of this burning for their protection against the law?" "Not that I know of," replied Guinn. Was there not a Committee of Safety established two or three years earlier to take care of horse thieves and was not its president named Day? Guinn did not know, but he knew a preacher named Day. Again, was there an association formed to protect the accused from the law and for "putting out threats against anyone who should testify"? Guinn did not know. Had not two or three men been killed in Pottawatomie County for their involvement in the burning? Guinn had not heard of it.[51] Speed, who particularly despised Guinn, could not help but be sarcastic and asked Guinn's wife, Mary, "Was there any Baptist preachers around that country who were not in the kidnapping of those Indians?" "I don't know" was the response.[52]

Testimony in the Ballard trial ended by noon on June 3, and Judge Thomas charged the jury.[53] As in the earlier trials, Thomas carefully defined critical terms, making certain the jury understood that one who was present and consented to the action was a principal in the crime of kidnapping. If the evidence indicated that Ballard was at Leard's house while the Indians were held, assisted in or knew of violent acts against them, and made statements that they should be done away with, the jury should convict him. If they found that Ballard believed the crowd intended to commit a felony and voluntarily associated himself with them, he was guilty. As in earlier cases, Thomas cautioned the jury that it was immaterial whether McGeisey had killed Mary Leard. Thomas went to greater lengths in these instructions than in the earlier cases to define *conspiracy* and the requirements for determining whether Ballard conspired to kidnap McGeisey. "A conspiracy," he said, "is a breathing or acting together. It means that there was a common purpose, supported by concerted action. That each conspirator had the intent to do it, and that each understood the others as having that purpose." Thomas also blunted the defense argument that the mob members had made citizens' arrests. People could make such arrests upon reasonable grounds for believing a felony had been committed but not people of one country, territory, or state acting inside the jurisdiction of another. Citizens from other jurisdictions could make arrests in Indian Territory only with legal warrants.[54]

Thomas left little room for the jury to consider acquittal. Near the end of his lengthy instructions he said, "Although you may believe from the evidence that Lincoln McGeisey was lawfully and properly arrested in the Indian Territory, yet if you further believe that after he was so lawfully arrested in Indian Territory, he was unlawfully and forcibly carried out of the Indian Territory into Oklahoma, against his will, the parties kidnapping would be as guilty as though he had never been lawfully arrested."[55] The case went to the jury; the following morning, Sunday, June 4, it returned a verdict of guilty.[56]

To some observers in the crowded courtroom, the verdict could have just as well gone the other way. The defense attorneys had fought hard, they believed, and might have made their case if Judge Thomas's "instructions to the jury had not been so strong and clear."[57] The testimony had showed that others were more deeply involved than Ballard: Pryor, Roper, Ivanhoe, Mathis, the Martins, and other leaders, who were for the most part related to Leard and were from outside the Maud community. Among the mob members from eastern Pottawatomie County, were some who had been as active as Ballard: George Pettifer, W. H. Vansickle, Joseph Williams, Chesley R. Guinn, and a number of the Guinns from Maud. Wilcox might not have known how pertinent a question he had asked Jesse Guinn, who claimed no kinship to Chesley: How many Guinns were "around that outfit" at Leard's during the week? Jesse Guinn, who had been in the mob most days, claimed that he did not know.[58] Though Ballard was guiltier than some, he was no more so than others who escaped prosecution.

Ballard's trial was the last before the court session closed, requiring a disposition or continuation of the remaining cases and the sentencing of those convicted. On June 5, the court entered a *nolle prosequi* for defendants George Moppin, George Cash, A. E. Butterfield, James Hodges, William Poff, David Jones, and Ed King. It continued the others until November 13, the defendants being released on their own recognizance or one thousand dollars bail. Perhaps to keep the mob members from resting well or from scattering further, Soper asked to continue the cases of arson against some for whom he had asked to enter a *nolle prosequi* on the kidnapping charge. The court sentenced Nelson Jones to twenty-one years at hard labor in the Missouri State Penitentiary at Jefferson City. Andrew J. Mathis received ten years in Jefferson City but was later transferred to the federal prison at Leavenworth, Kansas. Mont Ballard received a ten-year sentence at Leavenworth. Attorneys for the three filed motions for new trials on the basis of practically every objection they had made during the trials as well as on many points in Judge Thomas's instructions to the jury.[59] All motions were denied.

While Soper and Speed congratulated themselves and each other, Oklahomans did not receive the news of the convictions warmly. They had no sympathy for Nelson Jones, but the conviction of Mathis and Ballard was another matter. The newspapers continued to print stories of rape and corpse violation, despite the evidence to the contrary. They continued to insist on the guilt of McGeisey and Sampson, though evidence was conclusive regarding McGeisey's innocence and had cast considerable doubt on Sampson's guilt. The editor of the *El Reno News* even embellished the story with lurid details and claimed that the "distorted" story that McGeisey and Sampson were innocent had caused a "knee jerk" reaction in Congress. And the *Tecumseh Republican*, responding to Soper's statement that evidence firmly established McGeisey's innocence, asked this question: if federal authorities could try white Oklahomans for lynching, why could they not catch the Indian killer of a white woman?[60]

That same question and other problems nagged at Soper and Speed. Soper told the press that the guilty Indian was at large in Oklahoma Territory and out of reach of Indian Territory officials.[61] To whom he referred is uncertain, and his statement may have been made simply to cover the fact that there had been practically no effort since the summer of 1898 to find the real killer. Prosecution of the mob had been Speed and Soper's first priority. Of the mob leaders, however, they had brought only Mathis to trial. During the next year they would work not only to bring the others before the court but to discover who really killed Mary Leard.

TEN

Justice on the Balance

When the court session ended at Muskogee in early June 1899, the three men that Speed and Soper considered the major leaders in the burning and the ones they wanted to try the most—Sam Pryor, H. Clay Roper, and George Bird Ivanhoe—were still at large because, Soper thought, their friends in Oklahoma and the Chickasaw and Choctaw Nations protected them. A grand jury impaneled during the session just past had returned a new indictment against them for kidnapping, and the search began again.[1] Reports had placed Pryor variously at San Antonio, in the Choctaw Nation, and at other places. Ivanhoe was with him, living under an alias. Though Roper's whereabouts were unknown, he, too, was hiding in south Texas, probably in Atacosa County, where Pryor had lived. Speed believed that authorities could not take them by ordinary means; they were "desperadoes," fugitives from justice, who would put up a fight if given a chance. Thus Speed asked for rewards as an incentive for people to turn them in. Had Speed known about the family relationships between Leard, Pryor, and Roper, tracking them down might have been easier. He desperately wanted them and believed they deserved to hang, but the most he could hope for was a sentence of twenty-one years for kidnapping and twenty for arson if they could be caught. "Their conviction," he wrote, "will be favored by every other defendant save perhaps Julius Laird." A conviction, he believed, "would make mobs impossible—certainly unpopular—for years to come in that locality."[2] Unfortunately, Speed's hopes far outstripped the realities that would unfold as he and Soper sought to bring these last mob leaders to justice and to seek out the killer of Mary Leard.

The offer of a reward of $250 brought results. Pryor and Roper, both of whom had large families, had become homesick and returned to the Indian Territory. Roper was the first brought in. He was captured in a cornfield near his house at Center, Chickasaw Nation, on the night of July 9. Richard Coleman Couch, the local deputy U.S. marshal, lay in wait in the field as Roper came to visit his wife and family. Couch took him to Muskogee and lodged him in jail, where he remained under bond. Pryor was the next brought in. Robert E. Wood, the Shawnee attorney who had represented some of the burners in both Tecumseh and Muskogee, delivered Pryor to Marshal Leo E. Bennett in Wewoka on September 25. Pryor gained immediate release on bond to appear in Muskogee for the court session in December. On December 5, he pleaded guilty to kidnapping Lincoln McGeisey and was held in the Muskogee jail to await sentencing at the January 1900 session of the court. Meanwhile, Roper, who had also said that he would plead guilty, changed his mind and now demanded a trial, which would be held in January, and gained release on bond. In December, Marshal Bennett brought in Ivanhoe. J. H. Thornton of Comanche, Texas, delivered him to Bennett at Denison and claimed the reward. Bennett lodged Ivanhoe in the Muskogee jail to await trial.[3]

As the trials of Roper and Ivanhoe approached, Speed assisted Pliny Soper. Trial was delayed until May, however, because of an outbreak of smallpox. Speed and Soper had built solid cases against Roper and Ivanhoe, and other defendants still under indictment in the burning cases had grown anxious to testify as government witnesses. Speed was willing to give them immunity because he had believed all along that it was "better to demoralize the mob than to convict many and have the remainder bitter."[4] Still, with so much time having elapsed since they had originally gathered their evidence, Speed and Soper felt it necessary to prepare their cases again before the May session. In February, Speed had become U.S. attorney for Oklahoma Territory once more, but he arranged his workload so he could return to Pottawatomie County and the Seminole Nation to talk to witnesses again. From communication with Ivanhoe's attorney, R. E. Wood, Speed believed that Ivanhoe would ultimately plead guilty, leaving only Roper to try. Thus he focused his efforts on Roper.[5]

Speed considered Roper in most ways the worst of the lot and disliked him intensely. In Pottawatomie County, he sought evidence that would show conclusively "beyond any doubt as to his active participation in that work, and his general diabolical and worthless character." Speed had seen the underside of human character in the course of these cases, and it irked him that people could still refer to the burners as men "generally of law abiding character." Speed believed that Roper might try to intimidate witnesses and felt it imperative to go over the same ground with prosecution witnesses once more. "I do not wish to trust those witnesses after Roper has had an opportunity to talk with them," Speed said.

Speed set up appointments to see his informants and others. They included Mrs. F. B. Malven from Roper's old Pottawatomie County neighborhood, to whom Roper had made statements about kidnapping and burning McGeisey and Sampson; John C. Wellborn, who had ridden in the surrey that took McGeisey and Sampson into Oklahoma; and Mike J. Lawless, the former Earlsboro saloonkeeper who, like Wellborn, had moved from Earlsboro, fearing retaliation.[6] Speed asked Eugene Arnett, the Earlsboro merchant and banker, to set up meetings with P. B. Staggs and Ed Nix. Perhaps concerned that the nerve of some of his witnesses might be failing, Speed wrote, "I do not think the Oklahoma people do right to protect these men [Roper and Ivanhoe], but they should show the part those people took. These two men used our people for their own purposes after this trouble began, and have never helped them, and I do not think that our people ought to hesitate to tell the truth in regard to them."[7] Speed also met attorney Wood at Shawnee to discuss possible plea bargains in the cases and asked Deputy U.S. Marshal John A. Jones of Tecumseh to travel with him for protection through Pottawatomie County and the Seminole Nation. At the same time, Jones could serve subpoenas to witnesses on the Oklahoma side of the line.[8]

Though his immediate purpose was to create a firmer case against Roper and Ivanhoe, Speed also wanted to follow some leads on the identity of Mary Leard's murderer. Those who still supported the burners based their support, in part, on the belief that McGeisey and Sampson were guilty of raping and killing her. United States officials were not the only ones who believed McGeisey and Sampson were innocent. In 1899 detectives allegedly worked in the Seminole Nation for months, trying to build a case against a suspect and hoped for an arrest by the start of 1900.[9] If detectives were, in fact, in the Seminole country, they were not agents of the Justice Department but were probably privately hired, perhaps by Thomas McGeisey, who had never given up the effort to prove his son's innocence. The lack of conclusive identification of the killer nagged at Speed. Using leads furnished by whites, Indians, and blacks, he had followed up reports and rumors, but with little success: "The members of the mob did not wish to say anything that would furnish a clue to any other persons than those who were burned, and the Indians did not wish any other persons disturbed since the mob had taken the matter into its own hands and had burned two Indians." Several sources in 1898 had implicated Keno in the killing. In January 1900, Speed received four letters from Seminoles who claimed Keno and one or two other Seminoles knew the facts and were perhaps guilty. Those leads and others needed investigation, for neither Indians nor whites would be satisfied until they knew who killed Mary Leard.[10]

To Speed, the strongest "evidence" against McGeisey and Sampson had been their alleged confession. However, he had been uncertain whether it were "a real confession" or "merely a story which they thought if given on the stand, would prevent the mob from killing them." He had arrived at this latter theory because the mob had asked other Seminole captives for confessions "under suggestions of protection," and two of the burners had intimated to Speed that after they had "confessed," McGeisey and Sampson expected the mob to take them to jail at Tecumseh. The new leads cast still more doubt on the guilt of the two Seminole teenagers.[11] The leads pointed consistently to Keno, captured by the marshals in the summer of 1898 but subsequently released.

Speed asked Chief John F. Brown to put pressure on the Seminoles to cooperate. Thomas McGeisey had sent Speed copies of letters from Jim Powell, a Seminole who claimed to know something about the murder. These letters, in addition to the ones he had received in January, gave Speed the names of seven Seminoles who were supposed to have information and asked Brown to use his influence to make them talk.[12]

Information obtained from the seven Seminoles placed Keno near the Leard farm on the day of the killing. Cumming (Commy) Tiger, Loby Cosa (Lopy Cosar), Mossa (Mosar), and Toby had seen Keno, Thomas Jefferson, and another Seminole riding together on the day of the murder. The identity of the third man was conflicted but could have been Jim Powell, brother-in-law of Lopy Cosar. Two women, Kachee Chupco and Jennie, also supposedly had information. Who these two women were is uncertain. Commy Tiger and his nephews Mosar and Toby lived between Passack Harjo's settlement and Leard's farm, as did Lopy Cosar and Jim Powell. "I have no question," Speed told Brown, "that something or other happened at that time which makes these people refer so often to Keno." Also, he said,

"Naquechee [Nakochee?], the medicine man has been repeatedly referred to as having made medicine at the request of Keno's father, immediately after this woman was murdered."[13] One version of the rumor said that Condulee gave Naquechee a good pony to make the "murder medicine" to prevent Mary Leard's ghost from haunting his son.[14] In urging Brown to use his influence with the Seminoles he had named, Speed strongly hinted that, in return, he would work especially hard during the ensuing year, in his capacity as U.S. attorney, to suppress the whiskey trade on the western Seminole border, which Brown was urging him to do. Speed wanted Brown to lay the groundwork for his inquiries when he arrived at Wewoka.[15]

Speed left Guthrie on April 29 and spent twelve days in Pottawatomie County and the Seminole Nation, firming up his case against Roper and Ivanhoe. At Earlsboro, Eugene Arnett helped him obtain a great deal of new information about Roper. He had lined up witnesses who could account for Roper's and Ivanhoe's movements from the time the mob strung up Lincoln McGeisey on Sunday night until they and other mob members passed through Earlsboro on Saturday morning following the burning.[16] Speed thanked Arnett: "Whatever may be said upon the subject, I do think that you and Bob Wood have done the defendants more good than sympathizers or counsellors have ever done."[17] Wood had continued to urge his clients to plead guilty and bargain for lighter sentences. Speed encouraged his efforts, for, as he said, his mind was "heartily sick of those cases." Speed met Roper in Shawnee to urge him to plead guilty but found him insufferable. Apparently unaware of the extensive evidence against him, Roper lied about his role in the mob and contradicted whatever Speed said. Thus Speed left the interview without letting Roper know just what evidence he had, more determined than ever to convict him.[18]

Roper's defiance may have been a bluff, for about this time, Julius Leard appealed to Speed in Roper's behalf. Speed responded very frankly that it was no use to defend Roper, who had erred by refusing to plead guilty, due in part, Speed believed, to meddlers: "Commonly in such cases foolish men who have no interest, try to make themselves conspicuous by running around giving advice after the fashion of Parson [James D.] Hodges, and men in trouble are very apt to take up as their lawyers the worthless fellows who promise everything, but who can do them no good." Speed was willing to show his evidence to Roper's lawyers, just as he had offered to Mathis's and Ballard's, but only if they were "men fit to be trusted and act like fair-minded lawyers should."[19]

The trial, scheduled for May 28, did not take place. That afternoon, perhaps after they saw which witnesses were arriving, counsel for the defendants notified Speed and Soper that their clients would plead guilty. Judge Joseph A. Gill sentenced Pryor and Ivanhoe to three years in Leavenworth but later changed their place of confinement to the Ohio State Penitentiary. Ivanhoe's sentence began retroactively on January 16, 1900, his original trial date, and Pryor's on December 4, 1899, the date of his plea. Roper, however, successfully begged to have his sentencing delayed because his family was destitute, and Gill allowed him to go home to make a crop for them. It was not until March 1, 1901, that Judge Thomas sentenced him to three years at Leavenworth, the sentence to begin retroactively on May 28, 1900, the date of his guilty plea. The court also dismissed all other cases pending against the burners at Muskogee, except two counts against James Jones. Those cases pending at Tecumseh would be dismissed when that court next met.[20]

With these developments, Speed put his work concerning the Seminole burning behind him. Rumors had circulated that he had received $10,000 to convict the burners. However, Senator Matthew Quay, who had agreed to pay him $1,000 per conviction, had paid him only $3,000 out of his personal account. But Quay had temporarily lost his Senate seat, and Speed, unwilling to ask the aging senator for more money, billed the federal government for an additional $2,500 for salary and expenses during his work. Speed believed he could justify the bill because of the convictions and guilty pleas. In addition, there remained some danger of retaliation. Though he said publicly that those whom he had prosecuted were not bitter, he refused to give the names of his paid informants because two of them "might be in very serious danger if their names by any possibility became known." As evidence of the good feeling among the mob members, he cited a letter from J. Ed Nix of Earlsboro, thanking him for his help and congratulating him on the fine work he had done.[21] But Speed did not tell the attorney general that Nix had been one of the informants whom he had early on agreed not to prosecute in exchange for information. And Speed's concerns that his informants might meet with violence if their identities became known made his statement that the mob members were not bitter sound hollow.

As he had prepared for Roper's and Ivanhoe's trials, Speed seemed quite interested in ferreting out the real killer of Mary Leard. He wrote Julius Leard quite frankly that the murderer remained at large and that he believed

Keno was the killer. From evidence he obtained in the Seminole Nation, he traced for Leard Keno's movements at the time of the murder. Two days before the murder, Keno had been near the Leard home, riding west toward Maud on a sorrel or light bay pacing pony whose mane had been clipped but was growing out. He had no saddle but had thrown something that looked like a quilt over the horse's back. Speed believed that Keno was going after whiskey as he rode toward Maud. Two days later, he was at Violet Springs where he had bought whiskey, and about ten o'clock in the morning on the day of the killing, he left Violet Springs and rode in the direction of Leard's farm. The daughter of Keno's aunt, who lived near Leard, said that Keno had been at their house. This last point was critical. Because the Seminoles were reluctant to talk about the event, Speed had not determined if the visit had occurred when Keno returned from Violet Springs the day of the murder or two days earlier when he left for Maud. Still, in Speed's mind the evidence suggested Keno's guilt: "He is the only person in the Seminole country that answers the description first scattered about that neighborhood of the murderer. He then was and ever since has been a desperate, lawless boy." Speed clearly assumed that Leard knew something about Keno as well, for he said that if other leads produced information, he would go to see Leard in the summer to talk to him about Keno.[22]

During the succeeding months, the Seminoles worked on the case, but Speed's interest in it flagged. In August he received a letter from Cheparney Chutkey (Chepon Chotke), who lived between Passack Harjo and Leard, saying that he had new information. Speed asked Cheparney Chutkey to have Chief Brown or "some other good man" write a full account of the new information and send it by first mail. Cheparney Chutkey was still trying to get Speed to come to the Seminole Nation the following March.[23] But Roper was sentenced that month, and after that, Speed apparently dropped all efforts to pursue new leads.

Why Speed, who had at times seemed almost obsessed with the case, now laid it aside is uncertain. As United States attorney for Oklahoma Territory, he had a heavy workload. He may simply have been weary. He had worked on the burning cases for more than two years. Finally, Speed truly may have believed that he had made his point. He told the attorney general that the convictions and guilty pleas had been a lesson to Pottawatomie County and would thereafter thwart mob action there.[24] That belief may explain why Speed expended a good deal of effort during the next few years to reduce the jail time of some of those he had worked so hard to convict.

The light sentences given to Sam Pryor, Bird Ivanhoe, and H. Clay Roper and the leniency of including time already served or out on bond seem startling in comparison to the sentences of those who went to trial. Though these results were the work in part of their attorney, Robert E. Wood, Soper and Speed had agreed to the terms. Moreover, after working long and hard to bring the mob members to trial, they supported efforts to reduce the sentences of Mont Ballard and Andrew J. Mathis, using as justification, in part, the light sentences given the mob leaders. These efforts after two years of difficult investigation and prosecution raise a question: Was justice served? If placed on the balance, to what extent did the fifty years of aggregate jail time form a counterweight to the injustice done both Seminole Nation citizens and the local white community during the first week of 1898?

Long before the courts disposed of the last cases, efforts were under way to undo the work of the trials. Pottawatomie County citizens circulated a petition in the fall of 1899, asking the president to pardon Mont S. Ballard. Sarah Jane Ballard led the effort. Only days after Roper's and Ivanhoe's guilty pleas, Judge John Thomas and Pliny Soper joined James M. Givens, Ballard's attorney, in an effort to gain a pardon for Ballard. Speed, however, would not support a pardon. He did not consider Ballard as guilty as Pryor, Roper, Ivanhoe, and other active leaders in the mob, but he placed him in the ranks of the "sub-leaders." In Ballard's favor, however, was that he had expected the mob not to burn the Indians but to hang them. Thus Speed was willing to support a plea for commutation to time equal to that served by Pryor, Roper, and Ivanhoe.[25]

For five years, Speed and Judge Thomas expended a great deal of effort in Ballard's behalf. Speed wrote a number of letters supporting commutation. In early 1901, with the recommendation of Speed, Soper, and Thomas, applications for commutation for both Ballard and Mathis reached President Theodore Roosevelt, who refused to approve them. Later that year, Speed told Julius Leard, who made a plea for Ballard, "The trouble is the President and the Attorney General cannot excuse the burning to death of a human being, and the evidence shows that Mont Ballard was there with his gun on several occasions, and was present at the time the men were burned." Thomas, who had left the bench, wrote letters and, like Speed, made trips to Washington and visited the Justice Department several times. According to Speed, Thomas had "taken a very warm interest in the matter," and in the fall of 1905 Speed encouraged Mrs. Ballard to seek the former judge's assistance.[26] Mont Ballard gained his release the following spring.

Similar efforts had begun for A. J. Mathis in 1900. When Mathis's application reached Speed in late 1900, he was not sympathetic. He considered Mathis a man who did not have a "strong mind" or "mental power" or "a good disposition." What struck Speed about Mathis was his admission during the trial that at the time he was praying he felt no pity in his heart for McGeisey and Sampson. Speed considered him disreputable and believed time in prison would do him good, though he was willing to consider commutation so that Mathis would spend about as much time in jail as Ballard. In a later application for a pardon, Mathis charged that the three witnesses most responsible for his conviction were "persons of unsavory reputation" and that the jury that convicted him "was composed largely of professional jurymen and negroes." His sentence was excessive, he believed, in comparison to those given Pryor, Roper, and Ivanhoe. Mathis presented himself as a pitiable character, whose family needed him. A sad case, indeed, but what probably disgusted Speed was Mathis's presenting himself as a Christian who felt duty-bound, when called upon, to pray for McGeisey and Sampson, "trusting that it might benefit those unfortunate men who were about to be ushered into eternity."[27] In the fall of 1905, when Mathis asked Speed to reopen his case, Speed told him, "It will be useless to re-open it while the Department holds its present attitude as to both yourself and Mont Ballard." If Ballard's sentence was commuted, Mathis's would be too.[28]

If Speed was unsympathetic to Mathis, he was even more so to Pryor and Roper. As soon as the judge pronounced sentence on Pryor, Robert E. Wood began efforts to gain his pardon. As with Ballard and Mathis, Speed was not willing to agree to a pardon. Because Wood had got such a huge reduction in Pryor's sentence at the time of the plea and at the date of the sentence, by the summer of 1900, when Wood began his efforts, Pryor had less than two years to serve. Commutation was the best Wood could hope for, and Speed would not agree to that.[29] Wood made similar requests for Roper. When Mrs. Roper appealed to Speed for assistance in 1901, he responded that he, Wood, and several others had done all they could. "It is not because we have not tried," he said, "that he is not pardoned, it is because the burning of a person is so horrible that it is hard to get any sympathy for anyone who assists in the burning."[30]

Julius Leard also appealed to Speed to intervene in behalf of Pryor and Roper. Leard apparently felt some guilt or, perhaps, the sting of accusations that he or his friends had somehow betrayed his cousins' husbands. Acrimony had apparently erupted within the Lewis family, some accusing others of informing on family members. Shortly before he was to go to trial, Roper had not realized how well Speed had documented his role in the mob. He was likely surprised to see the lineup of witnesses who were privy to his words and deeds. He must have wondered how Speed had managed to get his information without help from the inside. Roper and Pryor believed that Joseph M. Edwards, the husband of their wives' aunt, had informed on them.[31] Always skirting the law, the Lewises had stayed one step ahead of officials through their solidarity. Their tendency was to cast out those who would not go along with the majority, as they had done with Hiram Early and perhaps David Leard in the late 1870s. Edwards, an Arkansan, and his wife, Ophelia Lewis Edwards, had lived in the Choctaw Nation until the Choctaws expelled them. Edwards had tried homesteading when the Cherokee Outlet opened in 1893, but failing that, he returned with his family to Franklin County, Arkansas, where he ultimately acquired several hundred acres. Living apart from the majority of the family was enough to create suspicion in the likes of Roper and Pryor, but an even more likely cause of their distrust was that Edwards served as a deputy sheriff in Arkansas until he moved back to the Choctaw Nation in 1898.[32]

They also apparently pointed a finger at Leard, for Speed wrote to him, "As to Pryor and Roper, and all the rest of their mob, I have only to say that they escaped very cheaply for an inhuman piece of work. As to your giving them away, or the rest of your crowd giving them away, or giving anybody else away except Nelson Jones, that was preposterous folly as you and they certainly very well know." A number of people, Indian and white, he said, had fixed their identities, and he had retained a reserve of evidence that he had not used, but would have, if they had been tried for murder instead of kidnapping.[33]

Speed's statement that "Pryor and Roper, and all the rest of their mob" had "escaped very cheaply for an inhuman piece of work" put the Seminole burning and its aftermath in perspective. It was perpetrated and carried out by those two and other mob leaders, who played upon the emotions of the local population. The demand for vengeance by Julius Leard and Ed Martin fed their malevolence. A deep-seated racism fed the drive for vengeance, for the mode of lynching they chose was one reserved in recent times for blacks. On the surface, it appeared to be another in a long history of mass lynchings, and federal authorities either ignored or failed to recognize the fact that this case lacked the underlying motives of economic, political, or social control common to mass lynchings. Somehow, they overlooked the personal element: the apparent vendetta by Leard and his relatives against Passack

Harjo's settlement. Had they realized the family relationship between Leard and the major mob leaders, they might have taken the event out of a broader social context and looked at it for what it was—an exercise in vengeance based on personal grudges, more cold and calculated in its execution than mass mob action. It was, indeed, "an inhuman piece of work" for which the perpetrators paid little.

They had paid little, in part, because legal realities had overridden justice in the selection of candidates for trial. Leard and Martin, whom Speed believed he could never convict because of public sympathy, were at least as culpable as Pryor and Roper because they knew from the start that McGeisey was innocent, and they knew at the last that Sampson did not fit the description of the killer given by Frank Leard. In the end, Speed and Soper urged plea bargaining in the last three cases because they were tired of them and because it was the quickest and least expensive way of disposing of them. But Speed believed that he had achieved his original purpose: to try no more than ten, to make the trials a showcase, and to teach the region a lesson about lynching. The only failure in his original plan was the trial of James Jones, whom he considered one of the most culpable but who escaped punishment altogether except for the time served while he was awaiting trial. Speed had taken some comfort in his belief that Jones would serve time for grand larceny in Pottawatomie County. However, because of a legal technicality, Pottawatomie County courts dismissed the case on November 23, 1900.[34] Still, Speed gave lip service to the idea that justice had prevailed. He was convinced that his work had resulted in "the complete whipping of the mob and the mob spirit in this section of the country—the first time a mob was ever whipped in the southwest."[35]

There are serious doubts as to whether he taught the rank-and-file mob members a lesson. Some, without question, regretted their role in the burning, but their prosecution or the threat of it for the most part convinced the community at large that the federal government was meddling in a local affair and was using its power to persecute the mob members. There persisted a general refusal to admit that the burning was wrong, that the victims might have been innocent, or that lynching should not be an extralegal means of maintaining law and order. Certainly there is no evidence that the mob leaders felt any remorse, if H. Clay Roper was typical. More than forty years later, as Roper looked back on the burning, he considered his hiding from the law a job, calling it "about the hardest work he ever did." He continued to deny the truth, still maintaining that McGeisey and Sampson were guilty and insisting that they were adults, not teenagers, and said that "he was not ashamed or sorry that he had taken part in the burning of the boys." But to avoid appearing racist, he said that "if they had been white boys he would have helped mob them just the same."[36] No doubt he would have.

Though these cases may have represented the first successful prosecution of lynchers in the Southwest, Speed overrated his success. The effect was short-lived. In late 1900 Johnson Miller, a Creek, killed a white cowboy about five miles southeast of Holdenville and attempted to burn the body. The local residents believed the murder was retaliation for the burning of McGeisey and Sampson. In early 1901, a mob killed Miller. Implicated in the affair was Thomas P. King, a close friend of the Martins and a member of the mob at Leard's farm. Later that year, Bill Campbell was lynched at Pond Creek, Oklahoma Territory, and in July 1906, John Fullblood was hanged and burned at Womack. That fall, the Anti-Lynch Law Bureau was founded at Guthrie.[37] The following March, after a lynching at Durant, Bureau president W. H. Twine, editor of the *Muskogee Cimeter*, reminded his readers of the Seminole burning. "Some years ago," he wrote, "a hell hound from Texas and some from Arkansas mobbed two Indians near Wewoka. They were arrested and prosecuted to the bitter end. . . . We expect the government to do the same in this case."[38] However, the grand jury failed to indict anyone. A few months later, after a lynching in the Osage reservation, federal authorities again stepped in as they had in the Seminole burning case because the lynching occurred on Indian land. Ironically, one of the prosecutors was John W. Scothorn, who had assisted in indicting the burners at Tecumseh in 1898. Prosecution in the Osage case had no more effect than the earlier one, and the roll call of lynching victims continued and rapidly grew in Oklahoma with the cessation of federal authority in the territories and the rise of local authority in the state.[39]

Setting aside the question of whether any jail sentence could atone for the burning of a human being at the stake, one must conclude that the American legal system failed to achieve justice for the Seminoles. No one went to trial for the murder of Lincoln McGeisey and Palmer Sampson. No one went to trial for kidnapping Sampson or for the indignities suffered by John Washington, George Harjo, and others during the first week of 1898. The legal system failed the families of McGeisey and Sampson, who believed, as did federal officers, that their relatives were innocent. Leaving that innocence unproved created a legacy of anger and bitterness that persists among the Seminoles today.

If there was any justice, it might have been the sort called poetic in the failure of the Lewis family's fraudulent claim to Choctaw citizenship. Rejected in 1896, they had appealed to the federal courts, and only a few days after the burning the court at South McAlester affirmed their claim, placing them among more than 3,500 so-called Choctaw and Chickasaw "court citizens," most of whom the tribes knew had no rights. Each share was estimated to be worth $4,800; thus the value of the claim by nearly seventy of the Lewis clan represented a virtual fortune. With "legal" access to the Choctaw and Chickasaw public domain, they could open improvements, rent land to others, and engage in other economic enterprises. Those in Pottawatomie County, except one, used their "court citizenship" status as an excuse to leave Oklahoma and reenter the Indian Territory. However, the tribes secured passage of legislation that allowed them to appeal the court's decisions. The president appointed three judges as a Choctaw-Chickasaw Citizenship Court to hear the appeals. The Choctaws hired the able firm of Mansfield, McMurray, and Cornish to represent them. In the Lewis case, they demonstrated that the claim was an intentional fraud, that the Lewises paid witnesses to fabricate their claim to Choctaw blood, and that they had altered documents to suit their purposes. When the judges completed their work in December 1904, they had admitted only 161 of the claimants to the tribal rolls. They had rejected all of the Lewises.[40]

By the time this decision came down, Edward Martin and Leard were dead, leaving their descendants with the terrible legacy of memories. For the Leard children, it was memory of the night they spent with their mother's corpse lying in the yard and an incomplete or distorted understanding of what had happened in the aftermath of the murder. A cynic might be tempted to say there was justice in the terrible legacy the Seminole burning left for the mob members and their descendants in Pottawatomie County, particularly the Maud community. How many children knew that their fathers and other relatives had involved themselves in some dark, dire affair that night and grew up believing the lies and half-truths their elders told to hide the reality of what they had done? How many wives could not forget the stench of wood smoke and burned flesh that clung to their men's clothing as they returned home that January morning? And how many of those men could erase from their memories the image of Bird Ivanhoe, stick in hand, screaming wildly as the brains boiled from a charred skull he had just cracked? Yet they felt compelled to perpetuate through succeeding generations the false accounts of what had happened in order to make their actions seem "right." The community had been betrayed into this defensive posture, in part, by the failure of its moral and religious leadership—the ministers of the Gospel such as Jesse Guinn, James D. Hodges, A. E. Butterfield, Hiram Holt, and T. H. Day—who participated in the mob actions, later counseled a conspiracy of silence, or both. Throughout the community, *silence* was the watchword when it came to the truth about the Seminole burning.

Thus the mob members, not the Seminoles, investigators, prosecutors, or judges, established the historical legacy, which in most instances has wandered far from the truth. It began with the lies Leard, Martin, and the other leaders gave to the local press shortly after the burning. Over time, the alleged brutality of McGeisey and Sampson loomed larger in embellished accounts of the burning, while the role of mob members became sanitized. The county history sanctioned by the Pottawatomie County Historical Society in 1936 attempted to mitigate the action of the mob by making it appear that only a short time elapsed between the killing and the burning, thus taking emphasis from the deliberateness of the act and making it appear more like other mass lynchings of the time that somehow reinforced social standards of the community. It also made Thomas McGeisey a part of the howling mob and asserted that ten of the mob members agreed to go to trial "to take the 'rap' for the whole group," insinuating a nobility of self-sacrifice. Informants for the chapter included people whose relatives had been in the mob or who had been active in protecting the mob members and raising funds for their defense.[41] In subsequent years, the event has been sensationalized with emphasis on the murder, on the alleged rape and necrophilia, and on the "guilt" of McGeisey and Sampson.

The burning became popularly known as "The Mont Ballard Case" rather than "The McGeisey and Sampson Case," despite the fact that the town's hero, so warmly welcomed home from prison in 1906, was gunned down in Maud a decade later after shooting at a fellow townsman he accused of making amorous advances to Mrs. Ballard. Thus popular accounts obscure what happened in the borderlands of the Seminole Nation and Oklahoma Territory in the early days of 1898. They take the emphasis from what the Seminole burning really was—a wanton display of racial vengeance on the part of a few "old reservation habituees," as Speed called Leard and his relatives, who sought revenge and took advantage of United States territorial and Indian policy, hiding their cold-blooded deeds behind the popularity of lynching as a means of seeking American "justice."

Notes

Chapter 1. A Celebration

1. *Maud Democrat*, May 12, 1906; *New-State Tribune*, May 24, 1906. See also *Muskogee Times-Democrat*, May 23, 1906, and Smith, "Violence," 106–7, citing *Mangum Star*, May 17, 1906, and *Shawnee News*, May 21, 1906.

2. *Maud Democrat*, May 12, 1906.

3. Ibid.

4. Ibid.

5. Brundage, *Lynching*, 8–12.

6. Ibid., 12.

7. Ibid., 18–19.

8. Ibid., 28–31.

9. Ibid., 36–41.

10. Ibid., 40–41.

Chapter 2. Borderlands

1. *Cherokee Advocate*, April 3, 1897; *Muskogee Phoenix*, March 6, 1895; Commissioner to the Five Civilized Tribes, *Laws*, 12–13.

2. Wardell, *Political History*, 318–19; Brown, "Establishment"; Debo, *And Still the Waters Run*, 32–38; Spoehr, *Kinship System*, 33:42, 45.

3. See, e.g., Croffut, "Tempting Theory"; McAdam, "Indian Commonwealth." Such press reports are typical of the tone and content of the assault on tribal autonomy during the 1890s.

4. *Report of the Governor of Oklahoma Territory, 1893*, 9–10.

5. Ibid., 10; see also, *Report of the Governor of Oklahoma, 1894*, 12; *Report of the Governor of Oklahoma, 1896*, 16.

6. *Muskogee Phoenix*, March 6, 1895; Debo, *And Still the Waters Run*, 18–19; "Important Case." For a recent appraisal of the relationship between federal court jurisdiction and dissolution of the tribal nations, see Burton, *Indian Territory and the United States*.

7. *Daily Oklahoman*, April 14, 1907. For a description of the Seminole criminal code, see Burton, *Indian Territory and the United States*, 80–81. See also

Oklahoma City Daily Oklahoman, July 31, 1921, B2, and July 24, 1932, C10; *Indian-Pioneer History*, interviews with Carrie Cyrus (21:400), Frank Grall (16: 269–70), Lile Chupco (51:264–65), and John Alexander Frazier (91:460–61).

8. *Daily Oklahoman*, April 14, 1907, and February 12, 1922, B5; *Indian-Pioneer History*, interview with Carrie Cyrus (21:400); Burton, *Indian Territory and the United States*, 96–97.

9. McAdam, "Indian Commonwealth," 888.

10. McReynolds, *Seminoles*, 323–30.

11. An account of the disorder and violence surrounding the opening of the Cherokee Outlet is in Turner, "Order and Disorder." For a detailed account of the territory's struggle against lawlessness, see Shirley, *West of Hell's Fringe*.

12. Shirley, *West of Hell's Fringe*, 283–301, 390–411; Fortson, *Pott Country*, 19; *Oklahoma Times-Journal*, January 26, 1894; *County Democrat*, August 4, 1894.

13. *County Democrat*, May 5, 1894; Shirley, *West of Hell's Fringe*, 287–88; Fortson, *Pott Country*, 19–22; *Indian-Pioneer History*, interviews with Marion M. Young (66:513) and R. B. Schooley (101:86); Ragland, "Potawatomi Day Schools," 270–71.

14. *County Democrat*, June 23 and August 4, 1894; *Tecumseh Leader*, June 11 and December 30, 1897; Shirley, *West of Hell's Fringe*, 288; Fortson, *Pott Country*, 19–24; *Oklahoma Times-Journal*, January 26, 1894.

15. See, e.g., *Topeka Commonwealth*, February 4, 1885.

16. Atchison, Topeka & Santa Fe Railroad Company, *Beautiful Oklahoma and Indian Territory*.

17. *County Democrat*, January 21, 1898.

18. *County Democrat*, May 25, 1895. See also, *County Democrat*, November 2 and 9, 1895, and February 15, 1896.

19. *County Democrat*, January 21 and April 15, 1898.

20. "Laws and Acts of the National Council, 1897–1906," Seminole Nation Records, vol. 5, 1–5 (Film SMN1); *Tecumseh Leader*, May 7, 1897; *Indian-Pioneer History*, interviews with J. P. Montgomery (37:20) and John Alexander Frazier (91:459–60).

21. Contrasts between the northern and southern sections of the nation can be seen in McKennon, "Letters Home." McKennon, a member of the team that surveyed the Seminole Nation in 1895 and 1896, gives graphic descriptions of the landscape; his descriptions are verified by the detailed maps the surveyors made. The typescript was prepared by Sandra McKennon Bjork of Tulsa, Oklahoma, who owns the original letters. Copies of the maps can be seen at the Area Office of the Bureau of Indian Affairs, Muskogee, Okla.

22. *Indian-Pioneer History*, interviews with Henry Cotten (20:515), Joe M. Grayson (26:372), and J. P. Montgomery (37:21); Mooney, *Localized History of Pottawatomie County*, 88–89.

23. McKennon, "Letters Home."

CHAPTER 3. LANDLORDS,
RENTERS, INTRUDERS, AND FRAUD

1. McAdam, "Indian Commonwealth," 886. For figures on the numbers of Americans in Indian Territory, see Burton, *Indian Territory and the United States,* 178.

2. McAdam, "Indian Commonwealth," 891; Welsh, "Road to Assimilation," 87; *Fifty-ninth Annual Report of the Commissioner of Indian Affairs, 1890,* 91; *Indian-Pioneer History,* interviews with John Alexander Frazier (91:463) and Mary Elizabeth Morris (108:446).

3. *Cherokee Advocate,* March 31, 1882.

4. "State of Affairs"; Vestal, "First Families of Oklahoma," 10.

5. *Sixty-first Annual Report of the Commissioner of Indian Affairs, 1892,* 248; *Letter of the Cherokee Delegation,* 8–9.

6. McAdam, "Indian Commonwealth," 892.

7. *Letter of the Cherokee Delegation,* 9.

8. McAdam, "Indian Commonwealth," 891.

9. See, e.g., *El Reno News,* June 27, 1901; *Alva Review,* June 27, 1901.

10. Bond of Thomas McGeisey, August 9, 1882, and Testimony in *United States vs. Mack Geesey,* August 23, 1892, Jackets 127 and 278, Records of the U.S. District Court, Fort Smith Division (this file is hereafter cited as Fort Smith Criminal Cases); Document 39510-C, *Seminole-Miscellaneous,* Seminole Nation Records; *Indian Journal,* July 27, 1894; Statement of Thomas S. McGeisey, March 23, 1898, in consolidated file 666–98, General Records of the Department of Justice (records from this consolidated file are hereafter cited as File 666–98); Seminole Enrollment Cards 271 and 440, Enrollment Cards for the Five Civilized Tribes; 1900 Census, Enumeration District 71, Sheet 25; Statement of Nelson Jones, Exhibit D, 18, in C. H. Thompson to Attorney General, March 12, 1898, in File 666–98.

11. Statement of McGeisey, March 23, 1898, in File 666–98.

12. Testimony of Julius Leard, Testimony in the United States Court for the Northern District of Indian Territory, Kidnapping Case No. 4786, 272–73, hereafter cited as *Case 4786.*

13. Opinion of the Court, December Term 1904; Testimony of Thomas Lewis, Affidavit of Thomas P. Lewis, Affidavit of Edward M. Lewis, Cross-examination of Edward M. Lewis, and Testimony of Zora Early, September 1904, *Case 58* [Zora P. Lewis, et al.], Case Files-South McAlester, Choctaw-Chickasaw Citizenship Court, Records of the Bureau of Indian Affairs, Record Group 75 (NA-Southwest, Microcopy 7RA324). This file is hereafter cited as *Case 58.*

14. See, e.g., various documents in Jackets 62, 79, 116, 118, 119, and 242, Fort Smith Criminal Cases.

15. Cross-examination of Edward M. Lewis and Testimony of Thomas P. Lewis, September 1904; Affidavit of Sarah Lewis, October 21, 1878; Memorandum for Argument, February 1904; Opinion of the Court, December Term 1904, *Case 58.* See also, Affidavit of Susan A. Early, undated; Affidavit of Jane F. Page, October 28, 1903; and Affidavit of H. H. Early, undated, Case 58, Case Files, Melven Cornish Collection. This file is hereafter cited as *Cornish Case 58.*

16. Cross-examination of Edward M. Lewis, September 1903; Cross-examination of Preston Early, August 1903; Depositions of Willis Folsom and Jane Page, August 18, 1897, *Case 58,* and Testimony of Peter B. Krebs and Joseph Ward, February 4, 1904, *Cornish Case 58.*

17. Testimony of Thomas Lewis, Cross-examination of Lewis, and Testimony of Preston Early, September 1903, and Affidavit of Early, August 4, 1897, *Case 58.*

18. Testimony of Early, Testimony of Benjamin H. Bailey, Cross-examination of Thomas P. Lewis, and Cross-examination of Edward M. Lewis, September 1903, *Case 58.*

19. See list of claimants, Bible records, and birth and death records of the Lewis family in *Case 58*; Testimony of Hiram H. Early, February 1904, *Cornish Case 58.*

20. Cross-examination of Edward M. Lewis, Testimony of Thomas Lewis, and Cross-examination of Thomas P. Lewis, September 1904; and Homestead Certificate 5684, *Case 58.*

21. *Sixtieth Annual Report of the Commissioner of Indian Affairs, 1891,* 248. See Complaint of R. B. Creekmore, September 1, 1891, Bass Reeves to Jacob Yoes, September 11, 1891, and Testimony of Thomas Reed, October 12, 1891, Jacket 258; Testimony in *United States vs. Virgil Cowart,* July 21, 1891, and related documents, Jacket 242; Complaint of Charles Barnhill, November 29, 1884, Jacket 166; Testimony in *United States vs. Clay Roper,* November 24, 1891, Appeal for Witnesses, February 2, 1892, and related documents, Jacket 299, Fort Smith Criminal Cases. See also *Shawnee and Pottawatomie County Directory, 1898,* 222.

22. Testimony of Preston Early, Testimony of Zora Early, and Cross-examination of Edward M. Lewis, September 1903; Affidavit of Thomas P. Lewis, August 28, 1896; Affidavit of George McKibbon, August 26, 1896; and Affidavit of Herschel Leard, August 18, 1896, *Case 58.* See also Pottawatomie County History Book Committee, *Pottawatomie County Oklahoma History,* 37, and *Shawnee and Pottawatomie County Directory, 1898,* 173, 175, 186.

23. 1900 Census, Enumeration District 145, Sheet 30.

24. 1900 Census, Enumeration District 145, Sheet 37; Thomas W. Martin, Appeal for Witnesses, April 23, 1899, and John S. Martin, Appeal for Witnesses, April, 1899, Cases 4702 and 4706, Criminal Case Files, Records of the

U.S. Court for the Bureau of Indian Territory, Muskogee, National Archives–Southwest Region. See also, list of claimants, Bible records, and birth and death records of the Lewis family, *Case 58*.

25. Brown, "Choctaw-Chickasaw Court Citizens," 425–26.

26. See various affidavits dated August 1896 in *Case 58*. See also, Affidavit of S. M. Smart, February 24, 1904; G. Rosenwinkel to Mansfield, McMurray and Cornish, February 26, 1904; Affidavit of Hettie Hicks, June 5, 1903; Statements of J. S. Bender, Eliza B. Mathis, and Jesse B. Mathis, undated, *Cornish Case 58*.

27. Affidavit of H. H. Early, undated, and Decree of Court, December Term 1904, *Cornish Case 58*.

28. Brown, "Choctaw-Chickasaw Court Citizens," 429; Choctaw-Chickasaw Citizenship Commission Records, *Choctaw Volume 434*, 322, Choctaw Nation Records.

29. Brown, "Choctaw-Chickasaw Court Citizens," 430; *Choctaw Volume 434*, 322.

30. Testimony of Julius Leard, *Case 4786*, 272.

31. Statement of Thomas S. McGeisey, March 23, 1898, in File 666–98.

32. Untitled typescript by Louella Leard, July 8, 1993, author's file, copy provided by Herman Kirkwood and Guy Guinn; Pottawatomie County History Book Committee, *Pottawatomie County Oklahoma History*, 319–20.

CHAPTER 4. MURDER AND RIDERS AFTER VENGEANCE

1. Statement of Nelson Jones, and Statement of David O'Bright, Exhibit D, 12–13, 37–38, in C. H. Thompson to Attorney General, March 18, 1898, in File 666–98.

2. Testimony of Julius Leard, *Case 4786*; untitled typescript by Louella Leard, July 8, 1993, author's file, copy provided by Herman Kirkwood of Oklahoma City and Guy Guinn of Edmond, Oklahoma. The account of events during the next week in Smith, "Violence," 1–10, is error-ridden because it is drawn primarily from newspaper accounts and assumptions made from a reading of *Case 4786*.

3. Statement of Nelson Jones, and Statement of David O'Bright, Exhibit D, 13, 37–38, in File 666–98.

4. *Washington Post*, January 10, 1898, 1:7; *Tecumseh Republican*, January 14, 1898.

5. Statement of David O'Bright, Exhibit D, 36, in File 666–98.

6. Ibid.; Testimony of Bert Catron, *Case 4786*, 108; Statement of Kinda Palmer, March 23, 1898, in File 666–98; *Tecumseh Republican*, January 14, 1898.

7. Testimony of Thomas S. McGeisey, John Stankewitz, Julius Leard, and Peter Osanna, *Case 4786*, 3, 31, 139, 241, and 274.

8. Statement of Billy Coker, Cobley Wolf, and Chippey Coker, March 23, 1898, and Statement of Billy Coker [Transcript of Vinita Grand Jury], in File 666–98.

9. Statement of Kinda Palmer, March 23, 1898, and Statement of Palmer and Statement of David O'Bright, Exhibit D, 37, 77, in File 666–98.

10. Testimony of Thomas S. McGeisey, *Case 4786*, 3, 27, 31, 32.

11. Statement of Louis Graham [Transcript of Vinita Grand Jury], in File 666–98.

12. Statements of George P. Harjo, Samuel P. Harjo, Duffy P. Harjo, Johnson McKaye, Sever, Parnoka, and Cobley Wolf, March 23, 1898, and Statements of Sam P. Harjo, James Harjo, Louis Graham, Billy Coker, Moses Tiger, Pinoka, and David Coker [Transcript of Vinita Grand Jury] in File 666–98.

13. Ibid.; Testimony of Thomas S. McGeisey, George Harjo, and Louis Graham, *Case 4786*, 3, 13–14, 67–68, 76; Statements of David O'Bright, Sam Harjo, and George Harjo, Exhibit D, 36, 80, 85, in File 666–98.

14. Statement of Kinda Palmer, March 23, 1898, and Statement of Palmer, Exhibit D, 77, in File 666–98; Testimony of Louis Graham, *Case 4786*, 70.

15. Statement of Nelson M. Jones, Exhibit D, 8–9, and Testimony of James Jones and Louis Graham [Transcript of Vinita Grand Jury] in File 666–98.

16. Statement of Nelson M. Jones, Exhibit D, 8, 9–10, 11, and Testimony of James Jones [Transcript of Vinita Grand Jury] in File 666–98.

17. Statement of Nelson M. Jones, Exhibit D, 11–12, 13–14, 16, in File 666–98.

18. Ibid., 15.

19. Ibid., 10–11; Testimony of N. M. Jones [Transcript of Vinita Grand Jury] in File 666–98.

20. Statement of Billy Thlocco, March 25, 1898, and Testimony of Thlocco [Transcript of Vinita Grand Jury] in File 666–98.

21. Testimony of N. M. Jones [Transcript of Vinita Grand Jury] and Statement of Jones, Exhibit D, 11, in File 666–98.

22. Statement of Nelson Jones, Exhibit D, 1–2, in File 666–98; Bent Turner to Friend Cash, May 8, 1883, and related documents and J. H. Mershon to John Caral, March 16, 1886, and related documents, Jacket 108, Fort Smith Criminal Cases.

23. Statement of George P. Harjo, et al., March 23, 1898, and Testimony of Moses Tiger [Transcript of Vinita Grand Jury] in File 666–98.

24. Statement of Albert Washington, Exhibit D, 70–71, in File 666–98; Testimony of Albert Washington, *Case 4786*, 114–15.

25. Statement of Billy Thlocco, March 25, 1898, and Testimony of Thlocco [Transcript of Vinita Grand Jury] in File 666–98.

26. Testimony of A. J. Vincent and other witnesses, *Case 4786*, 5, 86, 140, 172.

27. Testimony of Peter Osanna, *Case 4786*, 240–42. Smith draws some erroneous conclusions regarding the involvement of the lighthorse police, reflecting a lack of understanding of jurisdictional issues. See, e.g., her "Violence," 26–27, 91.

28. 1900 Census, Enumeration District 71, Sheet 18; *Indian-Pioneer History*, interview with Louis Graham (4:144–45.27).

29. Testimony of Thompson Brown [Transcript of Vinita Grand Jury] and Statement of Brown, Exhibit D, 68, 69, in File 666–98; Testimony of Thomas S. McGeisey, *Case 4786*, 4, 10.

30. Statement of Thompson Brown, Exhibit D, 68–69, in File 666–98.

31. Ibid., 69; Testimony of Thompson Brown [Transcript of Vinita Grand Jury] in File 666–98.

32. Testimony of James Alfred Smallwood, Thomas S. McGeisey, and other witnesses, *Case 4786*, 5, 35, 37, 47, 172.

33. Testimony of James Alfred Smallwood, A. J. Vincent, Bert Catron, and George Brown, *Case 4786*, 36–42, 82–83, 98–99, 149. The others identified were Smallwood, Vincent [Vinson], Catron, Brown, B. Dyer, Ben Lovelady, and Bob Tripp.

34. Testimony of Thomas S. McGeisey and James Alfred Smallwood, *Case 4786*, 34, 42–43, 50, 60.

35. Testimony of Thomas S. McGeisey, *Case 4786*, 28–29.

36. Testimony of Julius Leard, *Case 4786*, 280–81. Edwin C. McReynolds speculates that the mob took McGeisey because of his father's position in the Seminole government as a means of making a racial statement because of the frustration they felt over their failure to find the killer. McReynolds was unaware of the personal connections among the mob members and between various mob members and the Seminoles. See *Seminoles*, 338–39.

37. Statement of Shawnee Barnett, March 24, 1898, in File 666–98.

38. Testimony of N. M. Jones [Transcript of Vinita Grand Jury], Statement of Jones, Exhibit D, 29, and Affidavits of Stoke Martin and T. W. Martin, February 15, 1898, Exhibit C, in File 666–98.

39. Testimony of N. M. Jones [Transcript of Vinita Grand Jury] and Statement of Jones, Exhibit D, 5–7, 24, in File 666–98; Testimony of Thomas S. McGeisey, *Case 4786*, 6, 8–9.

40. Statement of John Palmer, March 24, 1898, in File 666–98.

41. Statements of Thomas Thompson, George Kernel, and John Washington, Exhibit D, 62, 65–66, 87; Statement of Washington, March 24, 1898; and

Statement of Washington [Transcript of Vinita Grand Jury] in File 666–98; Testimony of George Brown, *Case 4786*, 252–53; *Cherokee Advocate*, April 9, 1898.

42. Testimony of Moses Tiger and George Harjo [Transcript of Vinita Grand Jury], Statement of Harjo, Exhibit D, 85, and Statement of Harjo, March 23, 1898, in File 666–98; Testimony of Harjo, *Case 4786*, 13–15.

43. Testimony of Louis Graham [Transcript of Vinita Grand Jury] and Statement of Sam Harjo, Exhibit D, 81, in File 666–98; Testimony of Graham, *Case 4786*, 72, 77.

44. Testimony of Graham [Transcript of Vinita Grand Jury], in File 666–98; Testimony of Graham, *Case 4786*, 68, 71.

45. Statement of Sam Harjo, Exhibit D, 81–82, in File 666–98.

46. Statement of Indian Sam, Exhibit D, 79; Statement of Sam Ela, March 23, 1898, in File 666–98.

47. Testimony of N. M. Jones and George Harjo [Transcript of Vinita Grand Jury]; Statement of Harjo, March 23, 1898; and Statement of Jones, Exhibit D, 16–17, in File 666–98.

48. Statement of John Washington, March 24, 1898; Testimony of Washington [Transcript of Vinita Grand Jury]; Statement of Washington, Exhibit D, 88, and Affidavits of Stoke Martin and T. W. Martin, February 15, 1898, Exhibit C, in File 666–98; Testimony of George Cash, *Case 4786*, 176–77; *Cherokee Advocate*, April 9, 1898.

49. Statement of John Washington, Exhibit D, 88, in File 666–98; *Cherokee Advocate*, April 9, 1898.

50. Testimony of N. M. Jones [Transcript of Vinita Grand Jury] and Statements of Jones, Thomas Thompson, and George Kernel, Exhibit D, 17, 24, 62, 66–67, in File 666–98; Testimony of George Harjo, *Case 4786*, 18–19.

51. Statement of Billy Thlocco, March 25, 1898, and Statement of John Palmer, March 24, 1898, in File 666–98.

52. Testimony of Louis Graham, *Case 4786*, 78; Statement of Sam Ela, March 23, 1898, and Testimony of Moses Tiger and Thomas Thompson [Transcript of Vinita Grand Jury] in File 666–98.

53. Statement of John Washington, March 23, 1898, in File 666–98; *Cherokee Advocate*, April 9, 1898.

54. Testimony of George Harjo, George Cash, and Julius Leard, *Case 4786*, 184, 276–77; Testimony of N. M. Jones and James Jones [Transcript of Vinita Grand Jury] and Statement of Nelson Jones, Exhibit D, 24, in File 666–98.

55. Testimony of N. M. Jones [Transcript of Vinita Grand Jury] and Statement of Jones, Exhibit D, 18–19, in File 666–98.

56. Statement of Nelson Jones, Exhibit D, 19–21, and Testimony of Jones [Transcript of Vinita Grand Jury] in File 666–98. McGeisey's story is verified,

for example, in Statement of Sam Harjo, Exhibit D, 80–81, in File 666–98. Sam Harjo said that at least twenty others could also verify it.

57. Statement of Nelson Jones, Exhibit D, 16.

58. Ibid., 18, 34.

59. Ibid., 21–22; Testimony of N. M. Jones [Transcript of Vinita Grand Jury] in File 666–98.

60. Testimony of N. M. Jones [Transcript of Vinita Grand Jury] and Statements of Jones and J. G. Morrow, Exhibit D, 22–23, 26–27, 34–35, 92–93, in File 666–98. Among those who confronted Jones were "Parson" Butterfield, James D. Hodges, George Pettifer, Stoke Martin, Chesley R. Guinn, Jim Morrow, Ward Chievers, Philip H. Cooper, Charley Woodward, and Robert Ogee, all, except Guinn and Martin, from Maud.

61. Testimony of N. M. Jones [Transcript of Vinita Grand Jury] in File 666–98.

62. Ibid., and Statement of Jones, Exhibit D, 23, 27, 31, in File 666–98.

63. Testimony of James Jones, N. M. Jones, and George Harjo [Transcript of Vinita Grand Jury] and Statements of Nelson Jones and George Harjo, Exhibit D, 31, 32, 35, 85–86, in File 666–98; Testimony of George Harjo, *Case 4786*, 21–22.

64. Affidavits of Stoke Martin, T. W. Martin, and E. L. Martin, February 15, 1898, Exhibit C, and Affidavit of Julius Leard, February 19, 1898, Exhibit B, in File 666–98.

65. Ibid.; Statement of Nelson Jones, Exhibit D, 34, in File 666–98; Testimony of John Stankewitz, *Case 4786*, 127–28.

Chapter 5. Seminole Burning

1. *Cherokee Advocate*, April 9, 1898. Smith, "Violence," 34, indicates erroneously that local mob members were in control. Her account of events during the day of the burning is riddled with factual errors; see 13–15.

2. 1900 Census, Enumeration District 79, Sheets 13 and 33; 1910 Census, Enumeration District 113, Sheet 36; Testimony of George Pettifer, *Case 4786*, 159–60.

3. Horace Speed to Attorney General, June 7, 1899, in File 666–98.

4. Speed to Attorney General, December 28, 1898, in File 666–98.

5. 1900 Census, Enumeration District 186, Sheet 1; Testimony of Ward Chievers and George Pettifer, *Case 4786*, 159–60, 164; Speed to Attorney General, June 9, 1899, in File 666–98; *Indian-Pioneer History*, interview with Thomas P. King (32:320–21).

6. Pottawatomie County History Book Committee, *Pottawatomie County Oklahoma History*, 37; *Shawnee and Pottawatomie County Directory, 1898*, 173,

275, 186; *Tecumseh Leader,* January 24, 1896; Speed to Pliny Soper, November 14, 1900, *Horace Speed, United States Attorney, General Correspondence from August 23, 1900 to February 21, 1901,* 194, Records of the U. S. District Court, Western District of Oklahoma, hereafter cited as *Speed Correspondence.*

7. 1900 Census Enumeration District 120, Sheet 28; *Land Record Book 3,* 468, County Clerk's Office, Pottawatomie County, Shawnee, Okla.; *Indian-Pioneer History,* interview with H. C. Roper (42:313–18).

8. A. J. Mathis to C. M. Barnes, March 22, 1903, with enclosures, Governors —Oklahoma Territory—Pardons and Paroles, Record Group 12–2, Oklahoma Department of Archives; Speed to Pliny Soper, November 14, 1900, *Speed Correspondence,* 194–95; 1900 Census Enumeration District 195, Sheet 1.

9. See, e.g., Testimony of various witnesses, *Case 4786,* 5, 37, 47, 52, 140, 172; *Tecumseh Republican,* March 10, 1899; *Tecumseh Leader,* January 8 and 15, September 9, and December 30, 1897; *County Democrat,* January 2, 1897; Complaint of Jeff D. Mynott, June 28, 1894, and related papers, Jacket 347, Fort Smith Criminal Cases; Cases 178, 184, 236, 377, Criminal Felony Court Case Files (File 717 and 718), Court Clerk's Office, Pottawatomie County, Okla.; Smith, "Violence," 81.

10. Testimony of Louis Graham, *Case 4786,* 73. For an analysis of lynching rituals, see Harris, *Exorcising Blackness,* esp. 11–28; Brundage, *Lynching,* ch. 1.

11. Statement of J. M. Gloer and J. H. Ingram, Exhibit D, 49–55, in C. H. Thompson to Attorney General, March 18, 1898, in File 666–98; Testimony of Mike Lawless, *Case 4786,* 192–93; Speed to Attorney General, September 27, 1898, with newspaper clipping enclosed, and Speed to Attorney General, December 18, 1898, in File 666–98.

12. Statements of Younger Bowlegs, Thomas Coker, and Harry Brown, Exhibit D, 43, 56, 60–61, in File 666–98; Testimony of Albert Washington, *Case 4786,* 116.

13. Statements of Coker, George Kernel, and Brown, Exhibit D, 39–42, 56–57, 64–65, in File 666–98.

14. Statement of Coker, Exhibit D, 57–59, in File 666–98; Testimony of Julius Leard, *Case 4786,* 278.

15. Statements of Brown and Bowlegs, Exhibit D, 44, 61, in File 666–98.

16. Statement of J. Herman Patton, Exhibit D, 94, in File 666–98.

17. Statement of Nelson Jones, Exhibit D, 32; Testimony of Jones [Transcript of Vinita Grand Jury], and Affidavit of T. W. Martin, February 15, 1898, Exhibit C, in File 666–98.

18. Statement of Jones, Exhibit D, 32, in File 666–98; Testimony of Jones and James Jones [Transcript of Vinita Grand Jury] in File 666–98.

19. Statement of Nelson Jones, Exhibit D, 27, 32–33; Testimony of Jones [Transcript of Vinita Grand Jury] in File 666–98.

20. *Cherokee Advocate*, April 9, 1898; Statement of Jacob Harrison (Unasey), March 25, 1898, in File 666–98.

21. Statement of Nelson Jones, Exhibit D, 27, 29–30; Testimony of Jones [Transcript of Vinita Grand Jury] in File 666–98.

22. Statement of Jones, Exhibit D., 27–38, 33, in File 666–98; Application for Witnesses, Nelson and David Jones, April 17, 1899, Cases 4702 and 4706, Records of the U.S. Court for Indian Territory, Muskogee.

23. Testimony of Albert Washington, Woodson Ballard, and Julius Leard, *Case 4786*, 124, 261, 276; Speed to Attorney General, September 17, 1898, with enclosed newspaper clipping, in File 666–98; Witnesses, Registers, 1892–97, Grand Jury, December 1898 Session, Records of the U.S. Court for the Indian Territory, Muskogee; *Indian-Pioneer History*, interview with H. C. Roper (42:314–15).

24. Testimony of Albert Washington, *Case 4786*, 124.

25. Statement of Sukey Sampson, April 6, 1898; Speed to Attorney General, September 27, 1898, with enclosed newspaper clipping; and Testimony of Albert Washington [Transcript of Vinita Grand Jury] in File 666–98; *Indian-Pioneer History*, interview with H. C. Roper (42:315).

26. Speed to Attorney General, September 27, 1898, with enclosed newspaper clipping, in File 666–98; Tilghman, *Marshal*, 236.

27. Testimony of James Jones [Transcript of Vinita Grand Jury], in File 666–98.

28. Testimony of Jesse Guinn, *Case 4786*, 254; Speed to Attorney General, September 27, 1898, with enclosed newspaper clipping, and Testimony of James Jones [Transcript of Vinita Grand Jury] in File 666–98.

29. Brundage, *Lynching*, 39–40.

30. Testimony of George Brown and Jesse Guinn, *Case 4786*, 244–45, 257; Testimony of James Jones [Transcript of Vinita Grand Jury] in File 666–98.

31. Testimony of James Jones [Transcript of Vinita Grand Jury] in File 666–98. No other source verifies either the statement or its substance. Much of Jones's testimony regarding the event is unreliable and was refuted by Nelson M. Jones. This may be, however, a factual rendering of a statement that Pryor and Leard forced Sampson to make.

32. Records Relating to *United States vs. Palmer Sampson*, May 14, 1894, Jacket 270, Fort Smith Criminal Cases; Cases 357 and 361, Criminal Felony Court Case Files, Court Clerk's Office, Pottawatomie County, Okla.; *Kansas State Penitentiary, Expiration and Discharge Record (Prisoner Ledger C)*, 19, 130, 185, and *Prisoner Ledger H*, 161–62, Kansas State Archives, Kansas Historical Society; *Tecumseh Leader*, January 1, 1897; T. F. McMechan to M. S. Quay, March 18, 1898, *Seminole Indians—Murders*, Vertical File, Oklahoma Historical Society.

33. Lincoln McGeisey was the son of Passack Harjo's daughter Seney. Billy Coker was the husband of his daughter Anna. Kinda Palmer was a brother of his wife, Jennie, and Osanna Harjo (Peter Osanna) was his daughter Lowiza's husband. There were other connections to Passack Harjo through his former son-in-law, Thomas McGeisey. Lowiza, Peter Osanna's wife, was the mother of McGeisey's daughter Martha. Billy Coker was the son of David Coker and Hettie Bean, who was McGeisey's cousin and whose improvements the Williams family, prominent in the mob, were renting. Riders had attacked Chippy Coker, Billy's brother. Hettie Coker's sister Lucy, also McGeisey's cousin, was the wife of George Moppin, who lived in Passack Harjo's settlement and went with Nelson Jones to Leard's on his first trip there. Lucy's daughter Selda Davis was the wife of David Jones. Louis Graham, who was picked up three times by the mob, also lived at Passack Harjo's settlement. Shawnee Barnett, Billy Thlocco, and Albert Washington—all arrested by the mob—had been visitors at Passack Harjo's. Sepa Palmer was his near neighbor. See Seminole Enrollment Cards 105, 109–11, 134, 271, 440, and 588, Enrollment Cards for the Five Civilized Tribes, 1898–1914.

34. Speed to Attorney General, September 27, 1898, with enclosed newspaper clipping, in File 666–98. The story of the saddle comes from Herman Kirkwood, interview, Oklahoma City, August 6, 1993.

35. Speed to Attorney General, September 27, 1898, with enclosed newspaper clipping, in File 666–98; Case 361, Criminal Felony Court Case Files, Court Clerk's Office, Pottawatomie County, Okla.; *County Democrat*, January 23, 1897; *Tecumseh Leader*, January 1, 1897; *Prisoner Ledger H*, 161–62; Statement of Seber Palmer [Transcript of Vinita Grand Jury] in File 666–98.

36. *Indian-Pioneer History*, interview with Jim Guinn (80:224–25); *Cherokee Advocate*, April 9, 1898; *Indian Chieftain*, February 10, 1898; *New York Herald*, June 16, 1899, Sec. 6, p. 8. For discussions of clans and kinship terminology among the Seminoles, see Spoehr, *Kinship System of the Seminole*, 33:52ff. Edwin C. McReynolds in *The Seminoles*, 339, speculates that Sampson's alleged confession and implication of McGeisey may have resulted from a misunderstanding of his response to questions because he did not speak English. McReynolds, however, was unaware of the determination of Leard to have revenge and of Pryor to burn someone.

37. Brundage, *Lynching*, 32–33.

38. Testimony of James Jones [Transcript of Vinita Grand Jury] and Speed to Attorney General, September 27, 1898, with enclosed newspaper clipping, in File 666–98.

39. Testimony of John Stankewitz, James Alfred Smallwood, and Mike Lawless, *Case 4786*, 58, 136, 193; Testimony of C. P. Lynn [Transcript of Vinita Grand Jury] in File 666–98.

40. Testimony of George Cash, Mike Lawless, and A. J. Vincent, *Case 4786,* 83, 103, 189, 194.

41. Speed to Soper, November 14, 1900, *Speed Correspondence,* 194; *Muskogee Evening Times,* February 12, 1898.

42. Testimony of George Cash, John Stankewitz, and George Pettifer, *Case 4786,* 142, 157, 177; Brundage, *Lynching,* 40–41.

43. Testimony of Lawless, Julius Leard, and George Pettifer, *Case 4786,* 158, 201, 183.

44. Testimony of James Alfred Smallwood, Bert Catron, and George Cash, *Case 4786,* 44–45, 99–101, 175, 177; Soper to Attorney General, June 7, 1899, in File 666–98; *Daily Oklahoman,* July 27, 1897.

45. Testimony of James Jones [Transcript of Vinita Grand Jury], in File 666–98.

46. Speed to Soper, November 14, 1900, *Speed Correspondence,* 194; Testimony of George Brown, Pettifer, Stankewitz, and Lawless, *Case 4786,* 130, 133, 136–37, 142–43, 154–55, 157, 160, 195; Speed to Attorney General, June 9, 1899, in File 666–98; *Indian-Pioneer History,* interview with H. C. Roper (42:315).

47. Testimony of George Pettifer, *Case 4786,* 158, 159, 160; Speed to Attorney General, June 9, 1899, in File 666–98.

48. Testimony of Lawless, *Case 4786,* 195, 202; Testimony of C. P. Lynn [Transcript of Vinita Grand Jury] in File 666–98.

49. McMechan to Quay, March 18, 1898, *Seminole Indians—Murders;* 55th Congress, 2nd Session, *Senate Document 99,* Pt. 3, p. 3.

50. 55th Congress, 2nd Session, *Senate Document 99,* Pt. 3, p. 3; *Cherokee Advocate,* February 12, 1898; *Tahlequah Arrow,* February 12, 1898; Speed to Attorney General, June 9, 1899, in File 666–98; *Indian-Pioneer History,* interview with H. C. Roper (42:315).

51. McMechan to Quay, March 18, 1898, *Seminole Indians—Murders;* 55th Congress, 2nd Session, *Senate Document 99,* Pt. 3, p. 3; *Cherokee Advocate,* February 12, 1898; *Tahlequah Arrow,* February 12, 1898; Speed to Attorney General, September 27, 1898, with enclosed newspaper clipping, and Speed to Attorney General, June 9, 1899, in File 666–98; Testimony of Vincent, Stankewitz, and Neal Brown, *Case 4786,* 93, 134, 225–26; *Guthrie Daily Leader,* February 9 and March 5, 1898; *Indian-Pioneer History,* interview with H. C. Roper (42:315–16).

52. Speed to Attorney General, June 9, 1899, in File 666–98.

53. Statement of Peter Osanna, March 23, 1898; Statement of John Palmer, Exhibit D, 72, and Statement of Kinda Palmer [Transcript of Vinita Grand Jury] in File 666–98; Testimony of John Davis and Testimony of Peter Osanna, *Case 4786,* 230–31, 233–36, 238–39.

54. Testimony of Julius Leard and Osanna, *Case 4786*, 237–38, 281; Statement of John Davis, Peter Osanna, and Kinda Palmer, Exhibit D, 73–74, 75–76, 78, in File 666–98; Testimony of Jasanna Harjo and Statement of John Davis [Transcript of Vinita Grand Jury] in File 666–98.

55. Speed to Soper, November 14, 1900, *Speed Correspondence*, 194; Speed to Eugene Arnett, May 14, 1900, *Speed Correspondence*, 140; Statement of J. H. Ingram, Exhibit D, 54–55, in File 666–98.

56. Statement of J. Herman Patton, Exhibit D, 95, in File 666–98.

57. Testimony of C. P. Lynn, [Transcript of Vinita Grand Jury] in File 666–98; *Tahlequah Arrow*, January 15, 1898.

58. Statement of J. Herman Patton, Exhibit D, 95, and Testimony of Lynn [Transcript of Vinita Grand Jury] in File 666–98; *Tahlequah Arrow*, January 22, 1898.

59. Statement of Nelson Jones and George Harjo, Exhibit D, 30, 34, 32–33, 34, 85, and Testimony of John Washington, [Transcript of Vinita Grand Jury] in File 666–98.

60. Testimony of Lynn [Transcript of Vinita Grand Jury] in File 666–98; Tilghman, *Marshal*, 237; *Guthrie Daily Leader*, March 5, 1898.

Chapter 6. Defense of Burning

1. Mooney, *Ghost-Dance Religion*, 500.

2. *Tecumseh Republican*, January 7, 1898.

3. *Washington Post*, January 9, 1898, 9:4; *Washington Post*, January 10, 1898, 1:7; *Guthrie Daily Leader*, January 11, 1898; *El Reno News*, January 14, 1898; *Tahlequah Arrow*, January 15, 1898.

4. *Washington Post*, January 10, 1898, 1:7.

5. *El Reno News*, January 14, 1898; *Guthrie Daily Leader*, January 14, 1898; *Tahlequah Arrow*, January 22, 1898; Statement of Thomas S. McGeisey, March 23, 1898, in File 666–98; W. S. Field to W. A. Jones, January 18, 1898, Letters Received by the Office of Indian Affairs, Record Group 75, National Archives.

6. Testimony of Jasanna Harjo [Transcript of Vinita Grand Jury] in File 666–98.

7. *Tecumseh Leader*, January 13, 1898; *Tecumseh Republican*, January 14, 1898; *El Reno News*, January 14, 1898; *Washington Post*, January 12, 1898, 1:3; *Guthrie Daily Leader*, January 13, 1898; Field to Jones, January 12, 1898, Letters Received by the Office of Indian Affairs; *El Reno Evening Star*, January 12, 1898; *New-York Tribune*, January 12, 1898, 1:5; *Muskogee Evening Times*, January 12, 1898; *Daily Oklahoman*, July 26, 1931, C6.

8. *New-York Tribune*, January 14, 1898, 3:3; *Tahlequah Arrow*, January 15, 1898; *Muskogee Phoenix*, January 20, 1898; *El Reno News*, January 14, 1898; *Indian Chieftain*, January 27, 1898.

9. *Guthrie Daily Leader*, January 14, 1898; Leo E. Bennett to Attorney General, January 12, 1898, in File 666–98.

10. *Tecumseh Republican*, January 14, 1898.

11. C. N. Bliss to C. M. Barnes, January 12, 1898, and Bliss to Secretary of War, January 12, 1898, 55th Congress, 2nd Session, *Senate Document 98*, 2; *Washington Post*, January 12, 1898, 1:3; *Muskogee Evening Times*, January 12, 1898; *Tecumseh Republican*, January 14, 1898; *New-York Tribune*, January 14, 1898, 3:3; Bennett to Attorney General, January 12, 1898, in File 666–98.

12. Barnes to Bliss, January 15, 1898, 55th Congress, 2nd Session, *Senate Document 98*, 2–3; *Tecumseh Leader*, January 13, 1898; *Tecumseh Republican*, January 14, 1898; *New-York Tribune*, January 28, 1898, 3:3.

13. *Guthrie Daily Leader*, January 15, 1898; 55th Congress, 2nd Session, *Congressional Record—Senate*, 31:612.

14. *Tecumseh Republican*, January 14, 1898.

15. Bliss to President of the Senate, January 26, 1898, 55th Congress, 2nd Session, *Senate Document 98*, 1; *Congressional Record*, 31:783.

16. Joseph McKenna to C. R. Brooks, January 21, 1898, Brooks to Attorney General, January 21 and 23, 1898, and McKenna to United States Attorney, January 22, 1898, 55th Congress, 2nd Session, *Senate Document 99*, 5–6.

17. Brooks to Attorney General, January 22, and January 26, 1898, in File 666–98.

18. T. F. McMechan to Brooks, January [?], 1898, in File 666–98.

19. Brooks to McKenna, January 26, 1898, 55th Congress, 2nd Session, *Senate Document 99*, Pt. 2, 1–2; *Indian Chieftain*, February 10, 1898.

20. C. H. Thompson to Attorney General, January 26, 27, and 28, 1898, in File 666–98; *New-York Tribune*, January 28, 1898, 3:3.

21. Thompson to Attorney General, April 4, 1898, and Brooks to Attorney General, February 14, 1898, in File 666–98; *Tecumseh Leader*, January 27, 1898; *Indian-Pioneer History*, interview with John Alexander Frazier (91:44–46); Shirley, *West of Hell's Fringe*, 266, 413.

22. Thompson to Attorney General, March 12 and May 20, 1898, and Statement of Sam Harjo, Sever Palmer, Billy Thlocco, George Harjo, and John Washington, Exhibit D, 80, 83–85, 87, in File 666–98; Testimony of James Alfred Smallwood, 45, *Case 4786*.

23. Thompson to Attorney General, April 29 and May 20, 1898; Brooks to Attorney General, February 14, 1898, in File 666–98.

24. *Tecumseh Republican*, January 21, 1898.

25. Ibid.

26. Ibid.

27. Quoted from *Tecumseh Republican*, January 21, 1898.

28. Ibid.; *Tecumseh Republican*, January 28 and February 4, 1898; *Daily Oklahoman*, November 22, 1898; *Oklahoma Times-Journal*, November 22, 1894.

29. *Indian Chieftain*, February 10, 1898; *Muskogee Evening Times*, January 28, 1898.

30. *Tahlequah Arrow*, February 12, 1898; *Muskogee Evening Times*, February 8, 1898; *County Democrat*, February 11, 1898; *New-York Tribune*, February 6, 1898, 1:1, and February 8, 1898, 4:1; *Tecumseh Leader*, February 10, 1898; *Shawnee Daily News*, February 7, 1898; *Cherokee Advocate*, February 12, 1898; *Guthrie Daily Leader*, February 9, 1898; Brooks to Attorney General, January 31, 1898, 55th Congress, 2nd Session, *Senate Document 99*, Pt. 3, 1–2; Brooks to Attorney General, February 8, 1898, and T. F. McMechan to Brooks, February 12, 1898, in 666–98; Tilghman, *Marshal*, 237. See also, Smith, "Violence," 58–60. The fifteen brought in were John Malloy, W. H. Vansickle, Jesse Guinn, Mont S. Ballard, Woodson W. Ballard, Hardy Williams, Russell Guinn, George Pettifer, Thomas King, W. H. Davis, Poliet Smith, Edward Nix, Mike Lawless, Sam Norton, and Hiram Holt.

31. *Guthrie Daily Leader*, February 24, 1898; *Tecumseh Republican*, February 18, 1898; *Cherokee Advocate*, February 12, 1898; *Muskogee Evening Times*, February 12, 1898; *Shawnee Daily News*, February 9 and 10, 1898; McMechan to Attorney General, February 9, 1898, McMechan to Brooks, February 12, 1898, and Brooks to Attorney General, February 25, 1898, in File 666–98; Testimony of James Alfred Smallwood and A. J. Vincent, *Case 4786*, 56, 94–95; Tilghman, *Marshal*, 237. The men arrested, besides those listed above, were Samuel Adams, Lincoln Blair, John T. Bullock, George Brown, E. R. Cartmill, George Cash, James Castleberry, Joe Cherry, Ward Chievers, Philip H. Cooper, Pete Curley, Delbert Denim, J. M. Dickerson, J. H. Dodson, I. J. Dooherty, W. R. Foyil, J. M. Franks, E. J. Gardner, J. T. Gilmore, Chesley R. Guinn, David Guinn, George Guinn, J. A. Guinn, J. R. Guinn, William Guinn, J. D. Hodges, Burt Hodges, James Jones, David Jones, Nelson Jones, Edward King, Daniel Kirkendall [Kuykendall], Julius Leard, Herschel Leard, V. Larabee, Edward L. Martin, Stoke Martin, Thomas W. Martin, George Moppin, G. W. Morris, Richard Null, Robert Ogee, Fred Owens, William Poff, Henry Powers, P. B. Staggs, A. J. Vinson, J. O. Wellborn, James Woodard, and R. C. Woodard.

32. *Shawnee Daily News*, February 7 and 12, 1898; Thomas McGeisey to Commissioner of Indian Affairs, March 6, 1898, Letters Received by the Office of Indian Affairs.

33. Vouchers, February 9 and February 12, 1898, U.S. Department of Justice and Marshal's General Correspondence, Records of the U.S. District Court, Western District of Oklahoma; Thompson to Attorney General, May 20, 1898,

in File 666–98; Deposition of Thompson Brown, February 25, 1899, and Sam Ela to Thompson, March 25, 1899, District Court Correspondence, Western District of Oklahoma.

34. *Tecumseh Leader*, February 10, 1898; *County Democrat*, February 25, 1898; *Tecumseh Republican*, February 11, 1898.

35. *Cherokee Advocate*, February 12, 1898; *Tahlequah Arrow*, February 18, 1898.

36. *Muskogee Evening Times*, February 12, 1898.

37. S. J. Scott to Thompson, February 17, 1898, and Scott to Brooks, February 18, 1898, Department of Justice and Marshals' General Correspondence; and Brooks to Scott, February 19, 1898, *C. R. Brooks, United States Attorney, General Correspondence from December 4, 1896 to June 20, 1898*, 602, Records of the U.S. District Court, Western District of Oklahoma. This source is hereafter cited as *Brooks Correspondence*.

38. *Cherokee Advocate*, February 12, 1898; *Tahlequah Arrow*, February 12, 1898; 55th Congress, 2nd Session *Senate Document 99*, Pt. 3, 1–3; *Tecumseh Republican*, February 11, 1898.

39. *Guthrie Daily Leader*, February 9, 1898; *New-York Tribune*, March 1, 1898, 14:2; *Muskogee Phoenix*, March 3, 1898; *Cherokee Advocate*, March 5, 1898; *Guthrie Daily Leader*, January 12, 1898; *County Democrat*, February 4, 1898; T. F. McMechan to M. S. Quay, March 18, 1898, *Seminole Indians—Murders*.

40. *Tecumseh Leader*, February 17, 1898.

41. Brundage, *Lynching*, 3–8, 98–102; Grant, *Anti-Lynching Movement*, 1–7, 8–13; Brown, "Legal and Behavioral Perspectives," 96, 102, 105; Harris, *Exorcising Blackness*, 15–24.

42. Brown, "Legal and Behavioral Perspectives," 96, 105, 106.

43. Brundage, *Lynching*, 19–28; Brown, "Legal and Behavioral Perspectives," 101, 104–5; "An Outrage" (newspaper clipping), 1890, vol. 1, Frank A. Root Collection; *Norman Transcript*, July 2 and November 17 and 24, 1893; *Kingfisher Free Press*, September 24, 1896; *El Reno News*, September 25, 1896, and January 29, 1897; *Watonga Republican*, November 22, 1893; *Stillwater Gazette*, November 24, 1893, and June 24, 1897; *Guthrie Daily Leader*, November 1, 1893; *Daily Oklahoma State Capital*, November 22, 1893; *Eagle-Gazette*, April 6, 1894; *Edmond Sun-Democrat*, March 29, 1895; *Hennessey Clipper*, February 27, 1896.

44. Newton and Newton, *Racial and Religious Violence*, 241, 251, 267, 270, 273, 279, 280, 283. See also, for details, *Eagle-Gazette*, September 27, 1894; *Langston City Herald*, November 2, 1895; *Edmond Sun-Democrat*, January 24, 1896; *El Reno News*, September 25 and December 25, 1896.

45. *Norman Transcript*, July 2, 1893; *Daily Leader*, July 2, 1893; *Daily Oklahoman*, April 20, 1894; *Daily Oklahoma State Capital*, April 21, 1894; *Oklahoma*

Daily Press-Gazette, April 21, 1894; *El Reno News,* March 5, 1897. See the following examples from the *Langston City Herald*: June 22 and 29, July 6 and 27, August 24, November 9, 16, and 30, and December 7, 14, and 21, 1895; January 4, February 1 and 8, and April 4, 1896; February 6, 1897.

46. *County Democrat,* July 13, 1895; *Tecumseh Leader,* January 31 and February 7, 1896; May 21, October 14, and November 18, 1897; *Edmond Sun-Democrat,* October 23, 1896; *Stillwater Gazette,* May 27, 1897.

47. *Tecumseh Leader,* March 6, 1896; *County Democrat,* March 7, 1896; *Langston City Herald,* March 21, 1896.

48. *Tecumseh Leader,* February 17, 1898.

49. Ibid.

50. *Tecumseh Republican,* and March 11, 1898; "Notice!" *Tecumseh Leader,* March 10 and 31, 1898; Horace Speed to D. T. Flynn, February 17, 1900, in File 666–98; Smith, "Violence," 67–68.

51. *Tecumseh Leader,* March 10, 1898.

52. *Tecumseh Republican,* February 25, 1898.

53. Ibid.

54. *Tecumseh Leader,* March 31, 1898; *County Democrat,* February 4, 1898.

55. *Tecumseh Republican,* February 25 and March 4, 1898; *Guthrie Daily Leader,* January 12 and 15, 1898; *Purcell Register,* February 10, 1898; *Washington Post,* January 12, 1898, 1:3.

56. *Tecumseh Republican,* March 4, 1898; Shirley, *West of Hell's Fringe,* 377–78.

57. *Sunday Globe,* February 12, 1898.

58. Ibid. See also, Smith, "Violence," 63–64, on the *Globe* and political implications of the prosecution.

59. *County Democrat,* January 21 and April 29, 1898.

60. 55th Congress, 2nd Session, *Senate Document 56,* 1–4; *Senate Document 78,* 7–10; *Senate Document 105,* 1–4.

61. *Stillwater Gazette,* January 21, 1897.

62. *Tecumseh Leader,* March 10, 1898; *Muskogee Phoenix,* March 17, 1898.

63. C. R. Brooks to Attorney General, February 25, 1898, and John W. Scothorn to John W. Griggs, April 7, 1898, in File 666–98; "District Court," *Tecumseh Republican,* April 8, 1898.

CHAPTER 7. A MATTER OF JURISDICTION

1. John W. Scothorn to John W. Griggs, April 7, 1898, in File 666–98.

2. *El Reno News,* March 5, 1897; Debo, *Road to Disappearance,* 255; Shirley, *Law West of Fort Smith,* 150; Littlefield, *Chickasaw Freedmen,* 94–98; *Muskogee Phoenix,* January 13, 1898. For sentiment similar to that in Oklahoma, see, for example, *Indian Chieftain,* January 13, 1898.

3. *Tahlequah Arrow*, January 15, 1898.

4. *Tahlequah Arrow*, January 22, 1898.

5. *County Democrat*, January 21, 1898.

6. Littlefield, "Utopian Dreams." Though this article deals primarily with the Cherokees, it places Cherokee removal efforts in the context of Mexican emigration plans of other tribes, including the Seminoles.

7. *Muskogee Evening Times*, January 27, 1898.

8. *El Reno Evening Star*, January 13, 1898.

9. *Purcell Register*, January 20, 1898.

10. Testimony of C. P. Lynn [Transcript of Vinita Grand Jury] in File 666–98.

11. Leo E. Bennett to Attorney General, January 10, 1898, in File 666–98; 55th Congress, 2nd Session, *Senate Document 99*, 3–5.

12. C. N. Bliss to John F. Brown, January 11, 1898, and Bliss to Commissioner of Indian Affairs, January 24, 1898, in 55th Congress, 2nd Session, *Senate Document 98*, 4; *Tahlequah Arrow*, January 22 and February 5, 1898; Thomas Ryan to Attorney General, April 6, 1898, with enclosures, in File 666–98; *Muskogee Evening Times*, March 19, 1898; *Muskogee Evening Times*, March 30, 1898; *New-York Tribune*, March 31, 1898, 1: 2; *Cherokee Advocate*, April 9, 1898.

13. *Who Was Who*, 4:885; Soper to Attorney General, January 16, 1898, and Leo E. Bennett to Attorney General, January 26, 1898, in File 666–98; 55th Congress, 2nd Session, *Senate Document 99*, 2, 4.

14. *Indian Chieftain*, January 20 and February 10, 1898. See testimony of these witnesses [Transcript of Vinita Grand Jury] in File 666–98. Witnesses included John Washington, Thompson Brown, Sam Harjo, George Harjo, Billy Thlocco, Peter Osanna, Billy Coker, Mose Tiger, Thomas Thompson, Albert Washington, Parnoka, Sepa Palmer, Kinda Palmer, James Harjo, Louis Graham, John Davis, Thomas Coker, David Coker, and Dr. C. P. Linn. Smith, "Violence," 56, says that little was learned from the Seminoles at Vinita. Quite the contrary was true.

15. *Guthrie Daily Leader*, February 5, 1898; Soper to C. R. Brooks, February 5, 1898, and Brooks to Attorney General, February 8, 1898, in File 666–98.

16. Brooks to Attorney General, February 8, 1898, in File 666–98; Attorney General to Soper, February 12, 1898, Letters Sent by the Department of Justice: Instructions to U.S. Attorneys and Marshals, 1867–1904 (National Archives Microfilm Publications 701), 92:451, 464, Record Group 60, National Archives.

17. Brooks to Soper, February 15, 1898, *Brooks Correspondence*, 594–95.

18. Soper to Attorney General, February 7, 1898, in File 666–98; Attorney General to Soper, February 7, 1898, Letters Sent by the Department of Justice: Instructions to U.S. Attorneys and Marshals, 1867–1904, 92:298; T. F. McMechan to Attorney General, February 9, 1898, and Court Report, February 10, 1898, Exhibit D, 53, in File 666–98.

19. T. F. McMechan to Brooks, February 12, 1898, in File 666–98; McMechan to M. S. Quay, March 18, 1898, *Seminole Indians—Murders.*

20. McMechan to Attorney General, February 9, 1898, in File 666–98; McMechan to Quay, March 18, 1898, *Seminole Indians—Murders;* McMechan to Brooks, February 12, 1898, in File 666–98.

21. McMechan to Attorney General, February 9, 1898, and McMechan to Brooks, February 12, 1898, in File 666–98; McMechan to Quay, March 18, 1898, *Seminole Indians—Murders.*

22. Soper to Attorney General, March 6, 1898, in File 666–98.

23. McMechan to Soper, February 14, 1898, *T. F. McMechan, Assistant United States Attorney, General Correspondence, 1895–1898,* 142–50, Records of the U.S. District Court, Western District of Oklahoma, hereafter cited as *McMechan Correspondence.*

24. McMechan to Soper, February 14, 1898, *McMechan Correspondence,* 142–50.

25. Ibid.; Shirley, *West of Hell's Fringe,* 221; *Muskogee Phoenix,* December 14, 1905.

26. McMechan to Soper, February 14, 1898, *McMechan Correspondence,* 142–50.

27. Brooks to Soper, February 26 and March 7 and 16, 1898, *Brooks Correspondence,* 614, 633, 645; Soper to Attorney General, March 6, 1898, in File 666–98.

28. McMechan to Soper, February 14, 1898, *McMechan Correspondence,* 145–46; Soper to Attorney General, March 6, 1898, and Brooks to Attorney General, February 14, 1898, in File 666–98.

29. Soper to Attorney General, March 6, 1898, in File 666–98.

30. Brooks to Griggs, February 18 and 26 and March 28, 1898, *Brooks,* 615, 622, 634; McMechan to Quay, March 18, 1898, *Seminole Indians—Murders;* Brooks to McMechan, March 18, 1898, *Brooks Correspondence,* 659; Doyle, "Supreme Court of the Territory of Oklahoma," 218.

31. *Shawnee Daily News,* April 6, 1898; Brooks to Soper, April 1, 1898, *Brooks Correspondence,* 672.

32. Attorney General to Brooks, March 1 and 3, 1898, Letters Sent by the Department of Justice: Instructions to U.S. Attorneys and Marshals, 1867–1904, 93:324, 358.

33. *Muskogee Phoenix,* April 7, 1898; *Cherokee Advocate,* April 16, 1898; S. C. Overstreet to Griggs, April 16 and 28, 1898, in File 666–98; Attorney General to Brooks, March 3, 1898, Letters Sent by the Department of Justice: Instructions to U.S. Attorneys and U.S. Marshals, 1867–1904, 93:382; Scothorn to Griggs, April 20, 1898, in File 666–98; *El Reno Evening Star,* April 23, 1898; *Shawnee Daily News,* April 8, 1898; Overstreet to Griggs, April 28, 1898, enclosing *United States vs. Nelson Jones, et al.,* Indictment for Conspiracy to Commit

Offenses Against the United States and the Laws Thereof, in File 666–98; *Muskogee Evening Times*, April 22, 1898; *Tecumseh Republican*, April 29, 1898. Those indicted were Nelson Jones, Edward Martin, Jesse Guinn, Thomas King, Rube Newport, Julius Leard, Ward Chievers, Joseph Williams, Poliet Smith, Herschel Leard, George Pettifer, W. H. Vansickle, Mont S. Ballard, W. H. Davis, John Mallow, Cap Guinn, James Jones, Stoke Martin, and Hiram Holt.

34. Quoted from *Cherokee Advocate*, April 9, 1898.

35. McMechan to Quay, March 18, 1898, *Seminole Indians—Murders; Cherokee Advocate*, April 16, 1898; *El Reno Evening Star*, January 14, 1898; *El Reno News*, January 14, 1898.

36. James Lyman to Attorney General, April 21, 1898, in File 666–98.

37. *County Democrat*, April 15, 1898. Legislation to pay indemnities to the Seminoles was approved July 1, 1898. *Annual Reports of the Department of the Interior, 1898*, 625.

38. *County Democrat*, April 29, 1898; *Shawnee News*, February 11, 1898.

39. Overstreet to Griggs, April 28, 1898, in File 666–98.

40. *Daily Oklahoman*, June 18, 1898.

41. *Stillwater Gazette*, June 2, 1898; *El Reno News*, June 3, 1898; Seminole Enrollment Cards 563 and 597, Enrollment Cards for the Five Civilized Tribes, 1898–1914; Tilghman, *Marshal*, 238–39.

42. *Tecumseh Leader*, June 2, 1898.

43. *Tecumseh Leader*, June 9, 1898.

44. *Tecumseh Republican*, June 3, 1898.

45. Quoted in *Tecumseh Leader*, June 9, 1898.

46. Ibid.

47. Overstreet to Griggs, July 29, 1898, in File 666–98.

48. *Tecumseh Leader*, August 18, 1898.

49. *Tecumseh Republican*, August 19, 1898.

50. Testimony of George Harjo [Transcript of Vinita Grand Jury] in File 666–98.

CHAPTER 8. HORACE SPEED, SPECIAL PROSECUTOR

1. S. L. Overstreet to John W. Griggs, April 16 and 28, 1898, *Brooks Correspondence*, 653, 664.

2. Louise J. Speed, "Horace Speed" (typescript), Horace Speed Collection, Archives and Manuscripts Division, Oklahoma Historical Society; Foreman, "Horace Speed"; Peery, "First Two Years," 320, 424; *Daily Oklahoman*, November 22, 1901; *Daily Times-Journal*, May 12, 1894; *Norman Transcript*, April 27, 1894.

3. Horace Speed to D. T. Flynn, February 17, 1900, in File 666–98; Attorney General to Samuel L. Overstreet, April 11, 1898, Letters Sent by

the Department of Justice, General and Miscellaneous, 1818–1904, 32: 261.

4. Griggs to Speed, April 20, 1898, Horace Speed Collection; Speed to Pliny L. Soper, May 30, 1898, and Soper to Attorney General, July 28, 1898, in File 666–98; Louise J. Speed, "Horace Speed."

5. Speed to Soper, May 30, 1898, in File 666–98.

6. Soper to Attorney General, June 2, 1898, in File 666–98.

7. Soper to Attorney General, July 3 and 28, 1898; Speed to Attorney General, September 27, 1898, with enclosures; Speed to Flynn, February 17, 1900, in File 666–98.

8. Speed to Attorney General, September 27, 1898, with enclosures, in File 666–98.

9. Speed to Attorney General, July 18, 1898; Overstreet to John W. Griggs, August 18, 1898; and William B. Johnson to Attorney General, August 16, 1898, in File 666–98.

10. Soper to Attorney General, July 18, 1898, Speed to Attorney General, September 17, 1898, C. H. Thompson to Attorney General, October 26 and November 16, 1898, in File 666–98; Griggs to Speed, August 11, 1898, Horace Speed Collection.

11. Speed to Mrs. Horace Speed, September 12, 1898, Horace Speed Collection; Speed to Attorney General, September 27, 1898, with enclosed newspaper clipping, in File 666–98.

12. Speed to Mrs. Horace Speed, September 14, 1898, Horace Speed Collection; Speed to Eugene Arnett, April 18, 1900, Speed to M. J. Lawless, April 18, 1900, Speed to Mrs. F. B. Malven, April 18, 1900, and Speed to John C. Wellborn, April 18, 1900, *John W. Scothorn, United States Attorney, General Correspondence from December 28, 1899 to April 20, 1900*, 463, 484, 485, 488, 489, Records of the U.S. District Court, Western District of Oklahoma, hereafter cited as *Scothorn Correspondence*; *Daily Oklahoman*, January 24, 1938.

13. Speed to Mrs. Horace Speed, September 16, 1898, Horace Speed Collection.

14. Speed to Attorney General, September 27, 1898 with enclosed newspaper clipping, and Speed to Attorney General, December 28, 1898, in File 666–98.

15. Ibid.

16. Ibid.; Soper to Attorney General, July 18, 1898, in File 666–98; *Tecumseh Republican*, December 9, 1898; *Muskogee Phoenix*, December 22, 1898.

17. Witnesses, Registers, 1892–1907, December Term, 1898, Records of the U.S. Court for the Indian Territory, Muskogee; Speed to Attorney General, December 28, 1898, in File 666–98.

18. Thompson to Attorney General, January 7, 1899, in File 666–98; Testimony of William Tilghman and Neal Brown, *Case 4786*, 222–23, 224; *Tecumseh Republican*, January 27, 1899.

19. Speed to Attorney General, February 5, 1899, and John S. Hammer to Attorney General, February 7, 1899, in File 666–98; Department of Justice, District Court Records, Register of U.S. Prisoners in County Jails [1898–1904], 9, 10, 12, 13, 16, Records of the U.S. District Court, Western District of Oklahoma; 1900 Census, Enumeration District 120, Sheets 10, 20, and 71 and Enumeration District 145, Sheet 37, and Enumeration District 102, Sheet 19. Those arrested from Pottawatomie County included Mont and W. W. Ballard, George Cash, Jesse Guinn, Ward Chievers, George Brown, and Chesley R. Guinn. In early March, John Malloy, George Pettifer, William Guinn, and Joseph Williams were brought in.

20. Littlefield, *Chickasaw Freedmen*, 94–98; *Tecumseh Republican*, February 3, 1899; *El Reno News*, February 17, 1899.

21. *Tecumseh Republican*, February 3 and 17, 1899; *El Reno News*, February 24, 1899.

22. *Tecumseh Republican*, March 10, 1899; Testimony of David Jones, *Case 4786*, 219–20.

23. Soper to Attorney General, April 12, 1899, in File 666–98; Department of Justice, District Court Records, Register of U.S. Prisoners in County Jails [1898–1904], 12; *Tecumseh Republican*, April 14 and 21, 1899; *Muskogee Phoenix*, May 11, 1899.

24. Speed to Attorney General, April 28, 1899, in File 666–99.

25. Ibid.

26. Ibid.

27. Ibid.

28. Ibid.

29. Ibid.

30. Ibid.

31. Subpoena for John Washington, April 22, 1899, Cases 4702 and 4706, Criminal Case Files, Records of the U.S. Court for the Indian Territory, Muskogee; Testimony of Albert Washington, George Cash, and W. H. Vansickle, *Case 4786*, 117, 179, 209–10.

32. Speed to Attorney General, April 28, 1899, in File 666–99.

33. *Daily Chieftain*, March 25, 1899.

34. *Fort Gibson Post*, May 25, 1899; *Muskogee Phoenix*, May 11, 1899; *Daily Chieftain*, May 12, 1899.

35. "Important Case."

CHAPTER 9. THE TRIALS

1. *Muskogee Phoenix*, January 13, 1898.

2. Harman, *Hell on the Border*, 158–61; Motion for a New Trial in *United States vs. Nelson M. Jones*, June 27, 1899, Case 4786, Criminal Case Files, Records of

the U.S. Court for the Indian Territory, Muskogee. This file is hereafter cited as Criminal Case Files, Muskogee.

3. *Muskogee Phoenix*, January 20, 1898; Statement of Nelson Jones, Exhibit D, 31, in C. H. Thompson to Attorney General, March 18, 1898, in File 666–98; Testimony of C. P. Lynn [Transcript of Vinita Grand Jury] File 666–98; Herman Kirkwood (interview), Oklahoma City, August 6, 1993; Guy Guinn to Daniel F. Littlefield Jr., February 9, 1994, Author's Files.

4. Affidavit of Nelson Jones, February 17, 1898, Exhibit A; Statement of Nelson Jones, Exhibit D, cover sheet, in File 666–98.

5. Testimony of Nelson M. Jones [Transcript of Vinita Grand Jury]; Affidavits of Stoke Martin, T. W. Martin, and E. L. Martin, February 15, 1898, and Julius Leard, February 19, 1898, Exhibits B and C, and Statement of Nelson Jones, Exhibit D, 3, 22–23, 34, in File 666–98.

6. Statement of Nelson Jones, Exhibit D, 29–30, in File 666–98.

7. Ibid., 2, 29, 35.

8. *Tecumseh Republican*, April 21, 1899; *Muskogee Phoenix*, May 11 and 18, 1899; *Daily Chieftain*, May 19, 1899; Motion for a New Trial in *United States vs. Nelson Jones*, June 27, 1899, Case 4786, Criminal Case Files, Muskogee.

9. Application for Witnesses by Nelson Jones and Dave Jones, April 17, 1899, and Subpoena for James Burgess, George Harjo, and Lelia Johnson, April 22, 1899, Cases 4702 and 4706, Criminal Case Files, Muskogee.

10. Motion for a New Trial in *United States vs. Nelson Jones*, Case 4786, Criminal Case Files, Muskogee.

11. Instructions to the Jury, *United States vs. Nelson M. Jones*, Case 4786, Criminal Case Files, Muskogee; Common Record Book No. 11, 578–79, Records for the United States Court for Indian Territory, Muskogee; *Muskogee Phoenix*, May 25, 1899; Horace Speed to Mrs. Speed, May 12, 13, and 15, 1899, Horace Speed Collection, Archives and Manuscripts Division, Oklahoma Historical Society; *El Reno News*, May 26, 1899.

12. *Muskogee Phoenix*, May 18, 1899.

13. Speed to Mrs. Speed, May 19, 1899, Horace Speed Collection.

14. Speed to Julius M. Leard, May 17, 1900, *Speed Correspondence*, 170; Harman, *Hell on the Border*, 510, 607, 627.

15. Speed to Soper, November 14, 1900, *Speed Correspondence*, 194–95.

16. Extract of a Letter from Judge John R. Thomas, May 23, 1899, Correspondence, 1899, Grant Foreman Collection, Archives and Manuscripts Division, Oklahoma Historical Society.

17. Common Record Book No. 11, 583–86, Records of the U.S. Court for the Indian Territory, Muskogee.

18. *Muskogee Phoenix*, May 25, 1899.

19. *Tecumseh Republican*, May 26, 1899.

20. Testimony of James Jones and Testimony of Nelson M. Jones [Transcript of Vinita Grand Jury], in File 666–98.

21. Application for Witnesses in *United States vs. James Jones*, April 24, 1899; Cases 4702 and 4706, Criminal Case Files, Muskogee, and Common Record Book No. 11, 590–97; *Muskogee Phoenix*, May 25 and June 1, 1899; Speed to Attorney General, May 24, 1899, in File 666–98; Speed to Mrs. Speed, May 18, 1899, *Horace Speed Collection*.

22. Instructions to the Jury, *United States vs. James Jones*, Case 4786, Criminal Case Files, Muskogee.

23. Soper to Attorney General, June 7, 1899, and Speed to Attorney General, June 9, 1899, in File 666–98; Speed to Mrs. Speed, May 28, 1899, *Horace Speed Collection*.

24. Common Record Book No. 11, 599; Speed to Attorney General, May 24, 1899, in File 666–98; Speed to Mrs. Speed, May 30, 1899, *Horace Speed Collection*; *Muskogee Phoenix*, June 1, 1899.

25. Speed to Leard, May 17, 1900, and Speed to Soper, July 13, 1900, *Speed Correspondence*, 170, 413; "Sarah Jane Eddy," Typescript (1963?), Author's File, copy provided by Herman Kirkwood of Oklahoma City and Guy Guinn of Edmond; 1900 Census Enumeration District 217, Sheet 7A; Tecumseh Genealogy Club, *Pottawatomie County Cemetery Inscriptions*, 1:37.

26. Testimony of various witnesses, *Case 4786*, 5, 12, 16, 17, 33, 35–40, 42–43, 47, 53, 61, 62–63, 68, 79, 98, 108, 116, 117, 126, 128, 129, 131, 134, 135, 139, 142, 150, 153, 156, 157. For another interpretation of the Ballard trial, see Smith, "Violence," 89–103.

27. Testimony of James Alfred Smallwood, *Case 4786*, 35–56.

28. Testimony of A. J. Vincent, *Case 4786*, 82–93; Tecumseh Genealogy Club, *Pottawatomie County Cemetery Inscriptions*, 2:22.

29. Testimony of Bert Catron, *Case 4786*, 97–111.

30. Testimony of George Brown, Ward Chievers, and George Cash, *Case 4786*, 148–52, 163–64, 169–85; Mooney, *Localized History of Pottawatomie County*, 222.

31. Testimony of Mike Lawless, *Case 4786*, 192–201.

32. Testimony of George Pettifer, *Case 4786*, 156–58.

33. Testimony of John Stankewitz, *Case 4786*, 125–47.

34. Testimony of Vincent, *Case 4786*, 92.

35. Testimony of various witnesses, *Case 4786*, 44, 49, 54, 58, 84, 89, 90, 98, 101, 104, 110, 111, 155, 164, 166, 170, 171, 178, 185, 187.

36. Testimony of Smallwood, *Case 4786*, 56, 63–64.

37. Testimony of Vincent, *Case 4786*, 94–95.

38. Testimony of various witnesses, *Case 4786*, 4, 6, 7, 15, 26–27, 28, 30–33, 51–52, 68, 175, 181; Thomas's ruling, *Case 4786*, 7, 105, 158–59. See also 69.

39. Thomas's ruling, *Case 4786*, 10–11.

40. Testimony of Thomas McGeisey and Bert Catron, *Case 4786*, 106.

41. Testimony of various witnesses, *Case 4786*, 22–23, 74, 111, 151, 153, 161–62, 167, 179, 200, 107–8, 218–20, 227–29, 251, 269–70.

42. Testimony of Albert Washington, *Case 4786*, 117–24, 254, 261–62.

43. Testimony of William Tilghman, *Case 4786*, 221–22.

44. Testimony of Neal Brown, *Case 4786*, 224–25.

45. Testimony of various witnesses, *Case 4786*, 117–20, 138, 141, 152, 246–49, 252, 265, 261–62, 275, 277; Testimony of Jesse Guinn, *Case 4786*, 254, 257.

46. Affidavit of Julius Leard, February 19, 1898, Exhibit B, Affidavit of T. W. Martin, February 15, 1898, Exhibit C, and Statement of Nelson Jones, Exhibit D, 30, in File 666–98; Testimony of Julius Leard, *Case 4786*, 275.

47. Testimony of Catron, Cash, Vincent, James D. Hodges, and Chesley R. Guinn, *Case 4786*, 90–91, 112, 188, 191, 167–69, 170–71.

48. Testimony of Jesse Guinn, *Case 4786*, 256, 258–59.

49. Testimony of Leard, *Case 4786*, 275, 276, 278, 279.

50. Testimony of David Jones, *Case 4786*, 216–17.

51. Testimony of Jesse Guinn, *Case 4786*, 254, 257–58.

52. Testimony of Mary Guinn, *Case 4786*, 266.

53. *Muskogee Phoenix*, June 8, 1899.

54. Instructions to the Jury, *United States vs. Mont Ballard, Case 4786*.

55. Ibid.

56. Common Record Book No. 12, 4–8, Records of the U.S. Court for the Indian Territory, Muskogee; *Muskogee Phoenix*, June 8, 1899.

57. *Muskogee Phoenix*, June 8, 1899.

58. Testimony of Jesse Guinn, *Case 4786*, 255.

59. Bonds of Chesley R. Guinn, Ed L. Martin, Charles Woodard, Thomas W. Martin, Julius Leard, Stoke Martin, Herschel Leard, John Malloy, George Brown, Joseph Williams, Jesse Guinn, W. W. Ballard, George Pettifer, and Ward Chievers, June 5, 1899, Case 4702, Criminal Case Files, Muskogee; Common Record Book No. 12, 9, 10–11, 14, 57; Sentences of Nelson Jones, Andrew J. Mathis, and Mont Ballard, June 5, 1899, Judgments and Sentences, 1890–1907; and Certified Copy of Judgment, Sentence, and Order of Commitment, *United States vs. Mont Ballard*, September 21, 1899, Motion for a New Trial, *United States vs. Nelson M. Jones*, and Motion for a New Trial, *United States vs. Mont Ballard*, Case 4786, Criminal Case Files, Muskogee; and Common Record Book No. 11, 592. See also *Muskogee Phoenix*, June 1 and 8, 1899; *Cleveland County Leader*, June 17, 1899.

60. "Lynchers on Trial," *El Reno News*, June 30, 1899; *Tecumseh Republican*, June 16, 1899; *Edmond Sun Democrat*, June 16, 1899.

61. *Tecumseh Republican*, June 16, 1899.

CHAPTER 10. JUSTICE ON THE BALANCE

1. Indictment, *United States vs. Texas Ranger, et al.*, May, 1899, Case 4790, Criminal Case Files, Muskogee; Pliny L. Soper to Attorney General, June 7, 1899, in File 666–98. Smith presents a sketchy, error-ridden account of the disposition of these last three cases, "Violence," 74–75, 105–6.

2. Soper to Attorney General, June 7, 1899, and Horace Speed to Attorney General, June 9, 1899, in File 666–98.

3. Thomas Vernon Cowart, Typescript (Untitled, undated), Author's Files, copy provided by Herman Kirkwood of Oklahoma City and Guy Guinn of Edmond, Oklahoma; *Indian-Pioneer History*, interview with H. C. Roper (42:316–18) and statement of James Riley Couch (77:491); Leo E. Bennett to Attorney General, July 14 and 29, 1899, and John S. Hammer to Attorney General, June 26 and July 25, 1899; Bennett to Attorney General, November 26 and December 26, 1899, and January 3, 1900, Speed to Attorney General, December 7, 1899, R. E. Wood to Attorney General, December 29, 1899, in File 666–98; Common Record Book No. 12, 59, 208; *Cleveland County Leader*, October 7, 1899.

4. Speed to Attorney General, December 7, 1899 and January 23, 1900, and Speed to D. T. Flynn, February 17, 1900, in File 666–98; Common Record Book No. 12, 337–38, 366.

5. Speed to Soper, March 17 and April 9, 1900, and Speed to Wood, April 9, 1900, *Scothorn Correspondence*, 333, 439, 444.

6. Speed to Soper, March 17, 1900; Speed to Mrs. F. B. Malven, April 14 and 18; Speed to John C. Wellborn, April 18, 1900; and Speed to M. J. Lawless, April 18, 1900, *Scothorn Correspondence*, 333–34, 463, 484, 485, 487, 488.

7. Speed to Eugene Arnett, April 18, 1900, *Scothorn Correspondence*, 489; Speed to Arnett, April 24, 1900, *Speed Correspondence*, 19.

8. Speed to Wood, April 24, 1900, and Speed to John A. Jones, April 18, 1900, *Speed Correspondence*, 18, 20; Speed to Jones, April 18, 1900, and Speed to U.S. Marshal, April 19, 1900, *Scothorn Correspondence*, 486, 492.

9. *New York Tribune*, November 6, 1899, 1:3.

10. Speed to Attorney General, March 23 and April 24, 1900, in File 666–98.

11. Speed to John F. Brown, April 19, 1900, *Scothorn Correspondence*, 502.

12. Speed to Thomas McGeisey, March 23, 1900, and Speed to Brown, April 14, 1900, *Scothorn Correspondence*, 372, 465.

13. Speed to Brown, April 19, 1900, *Scothorn Correspondence*, 501–2; Seminole Enrollment Cards 126, 137, 139, 465, 589.

14. Tilghman, *Marshal of the Last Frontier*, 238.

15. Speed to Brown, April 19, 1900, *Scothorn Correspondence*, 502.

16. Speed to Jones, April 24, 1900, Speed to Thomas McGeisey, April 24,

1900, Speed to Brown, April 24, 1900, Speed to Arnett, May 14, 1900, and Speed to United States Attorney, May 16, 1900, *Speed Correspondence*, 18, 22, 23, 140, 157.

17. Speed to Arnett, May 14, 1900, *Speed Correspondence*, 140.

18. Speed to Julius M. Leard, May 17, 1900, *Speed Correspondence*, 171.

19. Speed to Leard, May 17, 1900, *Speed Correspondence*, 170–71.

20. Speed to Attorney General, May 31, 1900, in File 666–98; *Daily Chieftain*, May 30, 1900; Common Record Book No. 13, 52–54, 423, Records of the U.S. Court for the Indian Territory, Muskogee (Film USC8); Sentences of Bird Ivanhoe and Sam Pryor, May 28, 1900, and Sentence of Henry Clay Roper, March 1, 1901, Judgments and Sentences, Records of the U.S. Court for the Indian Territory, Muskogee.

21. *El Reno News*, December 28, 1899; *Woodward News*, December 29, 1899; Speed to Attorney General, May 14 and 31, 1900, with enclosures, in File 666–98.

22. Speed to Leard, May 17, 1900, *Speed Correspondence*, 170–71. See also Tilghman *Marshal of the Last Frontier*, 236–37; though written nearly fifty years later, the facts related concerning Keno generally agree with Speed's evidence.

23. Speed to Chee parney (Chutkey), August 24, 1900, *Speed Correspondence*, 11, and Speed to Chee parney (Chutkey), April 1, 1901, *Speed Correspondence*, 183; Seminole Enrollment Card 157.

24. Speed to Chee parney (Chutkey), April 1, 1901, *Speed Correspondence*, 183; Speed to Attorney General, May 31, 1900, with enclosures, in File 666–98.

25. *New-York Tribune*, November 6, 1899, 1:3; *Indian Chieftain*, February 15, 1900; Speed to James M. Givens, June 7, 1900, and Speed to Pliny L. Soper, July 13, 1900, *Speed Correspondence*, 237, 413.

26. Speed to Julius Leard, September 25, 1902, 126; Speed to Sarah J. Ballard, June 27, 1904, 75; Speed to Mont Ballard, June 30, 1905, 359; Speed to Mrs. J. S. [sic] Ballard, September 18, 1905, and Speed to R. E. Wood, September 18, 1905, 134, 135, *Speed Correspondence*.

27. Speed to Eugene Arnett, March 22, 1900, *Scothorn Correspondence*, 359; Speed to Soper, November 14, 1900, *Speed Correspondence*, 194–95; *Brooklyn Daily Eagle*, February 2, 1902, 1:2; A. J. Mathis to C. M. Barnes, with enclosures, March 22, 1903, Governors—Oklahoma Territory—Pardons and Paroles.

28. Speed to Mathis, August 2, 1905, 458; Speed to Mathis, September 29, 1905, 180, *Speed Correspondence*.

29. Speed to Wood, July 31, 1900, *Speed Correspondence*, 433.

30. Speed to Mrs. H. C. Roper, September 18, 1901, *Speed Correspondence*, 244.

31. Speed to Leard, September 25, 1902, *Speed Correspondence*, 126. Accusations against Joseph Edwards are stated in Thomas Vernon Cowart, Typescript

(untitled, undated), author's files, copy provided by Herman Kirkwood of Oklahoma City and Guy Guinn of Edmond, Oklahoma.

32. Testimony of Joseph Edwards, February 4, 1904, Case 58, Melven Cornish Collection; Testimony of Ophelia Edwards, September 1903, *Case 58*.

33. Speed to Leard, September 25, 1902, *Speed Correspondence*, 126.

34. Common Record Book No. 12, 399; Speed to Soper, February 24 and April 5, 1900, *Scothorn Correspondence*, 229, 435; Case 504, Criminal Felony Court Case Files, Court Clerk's Office, Pottawatomie County, Okla.

35. Speed to D. T. Flynn, February 17, 1900, in File 666–98.

36. *Indian-Pioneer History*, interview with H. C. Roper (42:316–318).

37. *Stillwater Gazette*, May 30, 1901; *Stillwater Advance*, May 30, 1901; *Indian Journal*, July 6, 1906; *Tecumseh Democrat*, July 6, 1906; *Indian-Pioneer History*, interview with Thomas P. King (32:321–22); *Muskogee Cimeter*, November 9, 1906.

38. *Muskogee Cimeter*, April 5, 1907; *Muskogee Times-Democrat*, June 15, 1907.

39. *Muskogee Cimeter*, April 12, June 21, July 19 and 26, and December 6 and 13, 1907; *Daily Oklahoman*, July 18, 19, and 25, 1907; *Muskogee Times-Democrat*, July 18, 27, and 30 and December 26, 1907; *Muskogee Daily Phoenix*, December 25 and 27, 1907; *Times-Record*, February 5, 1914; Newton and Newton, *Racial and Religious Violence*, 304, 306, 326, 329, 330, 331, 337.

40. Brown, "Choctaw-Chickasaw Court Citizens," 430–42; Judgment, Central District Court, January 19, 1898, Case 101, Decree of Court, Case 58, December Term 1904; and Opinions delivered by the Choctaw and Chickasaw Citizenship Court, Cornish Case 58. See also, Choctaw-Chickasaw Citizenship Commission Records, *Choctaw Volume 434*, 322–27, Choctaw Nation Records.

41. Fortson, *Pott Country*, 16–18.

Bibliography

Alva (Okla.) Review, 1901.

Atchison, Topeka and Santa Fe Railroad Company. *Beautiful Oklahoma and Indian Territory*. Chicago: Pool Brothers, 1892.

Brooklyn (N.Y.) Daily Eagle, 1902.

Brown, Loren N. "The Choctaw-Chickasaw Court Citizens." *Chronicles of Oklahoma* 16 (December 1938): 425–43.

———. "The Establishment of the Dawes Commission for Indian Territory." *Chronicles of Oklahoma* 18 (June 1940): 92–101.

Brown, Richard Maxwell. "Legal and Behavioral Perspectives on American Vigilantism." In *Perspectives in American History*, vol. 5, edited by Donald Fleming and Bernard Bailyn. Cambridge: Harvard University Press, 1971.

Brundage, W. Fitzhugh. *Lynching in the New South: Georgia and Virginia, 1880–1930*. Urbana: University of Illinois Press, 1993.

Burton, Jeffrey. *Indian Territory and the United States: Courts, Government, and the Movement for Oklahoma Statehood, 1866–1906*. Norman: University of Oklahoma Press, 1995.

Cherokee Advocate (Tahlequah, Cherokee Nation), 1882, 1897, 1898.

Choctaw Nation Records (maintained by the Archives and Manuscripts Division, Oklahoma Historical Society). Records of the Bureau of Indian Affairs (Record Group 75). National Archives, Washington, D.C.

Cleveland County Leader (Lexington, Okla.), 1899.

Commissioner to the Five Civilized Tribes. *Laws, Decisions and Regulations Affecting the Work of the Commission to the Five Civilized Tribes, 1893 to 1906*. Washington, D.C.: Government Printing Office, 1906.

Congressional Record. 55th Cong., 2d sess.

Cornish, Melven, Collection. University of Oklahoma, Western History Collections, Norman, Okla.

County Democrat (Tecumseh, Okla.), 1894, 1895, 1896, 1897, 1898.

Cowart, Thomas Vernon. Typescript, Untitled, Undated.

Criminal Felony Court Case Files. Court Clerk's Office. Pottawatomie County Courthouse, Shawnee, Okla.

Croffut, Bessie B. "A Tempting Theory in Practice." *North American Review* 157 (November 1893): 637–38.

Daily Chieftain (Vinita, Cherokee Nation), 1899.

Daily Oklahoma State Capital (Guthrie, Okla.), 1893, 1894.

Daily Times-Journal (Oklahoma City, Okla.), 1894.

Debo, Angie. *And Still the Waters Run: The Betrayal of the Five Civilized Tribes.* Princeton: Princeton University Press, 1972.

———. *The Road to Disappearance: A History of the Creek Indians.* Norman: University of Oklahoma Press, 1941.

Doyle, Thomas H. "The Supreme Court of the Territory of Oklahoma." *Chronicles of Oklahoma* 13 (June 1935): 212–18.

Eagle-Gazette (Stillwater, Okla.), 1894

Edmond (Okla.) Sun-Democrat, 1895, 1896, 1899.

El Reno (Okla.) Evening Star, 1898.

El Reno (Okla.) News, 1896, 1897, 1898, 1899, 1901.

Enrollment Cards for the Five Civilized Tribes, 1898–1914. Microcopy M1186. National Archives Microfilm Publications, Washington, D.C.

Foreman, Grant, Collection. Oklahoma Historical Society, Archives and Manuscripts Division, Oklahoma City, Okla.

Foreman, Grant. "Horace Speed." *Chronicles of Oklahoma* 25 (Spring 1947): 5–6.

Fort Gibson (Cherokee Nation) Post, 1899.

Fortson, John. *Pott Country and What Has Come of It.* Shawnee: Pottawatomie County Historical Society, 1936.

Genealogical Charts of the Cowart, Leard, and Lewis Families. Author's files.

General and Miscellaneous Letters Sent, 1818–1904, Department of Justice. Microcopy M699. National Archives Microfilm Publications, Washington, D.C.

Governors—Oklahoma Territory—Pardons and Paroles. (Record Group 12–2). Oklahoma Department of Archives, Oklahoma City, Okla.

Grant, Donald L. *The Anti-Lynching Movement: 1883–1932.* San Francisco: R and E Research Associates, 1975.

Guthrie (Okla.) Daily Leader, 1893, 1898.

Harman, S. W. *Hell on the Border: He Hanged Eighty-Eight Men.* 1898. Reprint, Lincoln: University of Nebraska Press, 1992.

Harris, Trudier. *Exorcising Blackness: Historical and Literary Lynching and Burning Rituals.* Bloomington: Indiana University Press, 1984.

Hennessey (Okla.) Clipper, 1896.

"An Important Case," *Twin Territories* 1 (April 1899): 90.

Indian Chieftain (Vinita, Cherokee Nation), 1898, 1900.

Indian Journal (Eufaula, Creek Nation), 1894, 1906.

Indian-Pioneer History. Oklahoma Historical Society, Archives and Manuscripts Division, Oklahoma City, Okla.

Instructions to U.S. Attorneys and Marshals, 1867–1904. Department of Justice. Microcopy M701. National Archives Microfilm Publications, Washington, D.C.

Kingfisher (Okla.) Free Press, 1896.

Kirkwood, Herman, and Guy Guinn. Correspondence with Daniel F. Littlefield, Jr., 1994. Author's files.

Land Records. County Clerk's Office. Pottawatomie County Courthouse, Shawnee, Okla.

Langston (Okla.) City Herald, 1895, 1896, 1897.

Leard, Louella. Typescript, Untitled, July 8, 1993. Author's files.

Letter of the Cherokee Delegation to the President of the United States, Relating to Intruders in the Cherokee Nation. Washington, D.C.: Gibson Brothers, 1896.

Letters Received by the Office of Indian Affairs. Records of the Bureau of Indian Affairs (Record Group 75). National Archives, Washington, D.C.

Littlefield, Daniel F., Jr. *The Chickasaw Freedmen: A People Without a Country.* Westport, Conn.: Greenwood Press, 1980.

———. "Utopian Dreams of the Cherokee Fullbloods: 1890–1934." *Journal of the West* 10 (July 1971): 404–27.

Marriage Records. Court Clerk's Office. Pottawatomie County Courthouse, Shawnee, Okla.

Maud (Okla.) Democrat, 1906.

McAdam, Rezin W. "An Indian Commonwealth." *Harper's New Monthly Magazine* 87 (November 1893): 884–97.

McKennon, Paul. "Letters Home," Typescript, 1993, author's file.

McReynolds, Edwin C. *The Seminoles.* Norman: University of Oklahoma Press, 1957.

Mooney, Charles W. *Localized History of Pottawatomie County, Oklahoma, to 1907.* Midwest City, Okla.: The Author, 1971.

Mooney, James. *The Ghost-Dance Religion and Wounded Knee.* 1896. Reprint, New York: Dover, 1973.

Muskogee (Creek Nation) Cimeter, 1906, 1907.

Muskogee (Creek Nation) Evening Times, 1898.

Muskogee (Creek Nation) Phoenix, 1895, 1898, 1899.

Muskogee (Creek Nation) Times-Democrat, 1906, 1907.

New-State Tribune (Muskogee, Creek Nation), 1906.

New York Herald, 1899.

New-York Tribune, 1898, 1899.

Newton, Michael, and Judy Ann Newton. *Racial and Religious Violence in America: A Chronology.* New York: Garland, 1991.

Norman (Okla.) Transcript, 1891, 1893, 1894.

Oklahoma City Daily Oklahoman, 1894, 1897, 1898, 1901, 1907, 1921, 1922, 1931, 1932, 1938.

Oklahoma Daily Press-Gazette (Oklahoma City, Okla.), 1894.

Oklahoma Historical Society, Library. Vertical Files. Oklahoma City, Okla.

Oklahoma Times-Journal (Oklahoma City, Okla.), 1894.

Peery, Dan W. "The First Two Years." *Chronicles of Oklahoma* 7 (September 1929): 281–322, and 7 (December 1929): 419–57.

Pottawatomie County History Book Committee, comp. *Pottawatomie County Oklahoma History*. Claremore, Okla.: Country Lane Press, 1987.

Purcell (Chickasaw Nation) Register, 1898.

Ragland, Hobert D. "Potawatomi Day Schools." *Chronicles of Oklahoma* 30 (Autumn 1952): 270–78.

Records of the Bureau of Indian Affairs (Record Group 75). National Archives-Southwest Region, Fort Worth, Texas.

Records of the Department of Justice (Record Group 60). General Records, Central Files, Year Files. National Archives, Washington, D.C.

Records of the Kansas State Penitentiary. Kansas State Historical Society, Topeka.

Records of the Office of the Pardon Attorney (Record Group 204). National Archives, Washington, D.C.

Records of the U.S. Court for the Indian Territory, Muskogee (Record Group 21). National Archives-Southwest Region, Fort Worth, Texas.

Records of the U.S. District Court, Fort Smith Division. (Record Group 21). National Archives-Southwest Region, Fort Worth, Texas.

Records of the U.S. District Court, Western District of Oklahoma. University of Oklahoma, Western History Collections, Norman, Okla.

Roll, Patricia. Correspondence with Daniel F. Littlefield, Jr., 1994. Author's file.

Root, Frank A., Collection. Oklahoma Historical Society, Archives and Manuscripts Division, Oklahoma City, Okla.

"Sarah Jane Eddy," Typescript (regarding Mont Ballard), 1963. Author's file.

Seminole Nation Records (maintained by the Archives and Manuscripts Division, Oklahoma Historical Society). Records of the Bureau of Indian Affairs (Record Group 75). National Archives, Washington, D.C.

Shawnee and Pottawatomie County Directory, 1898. Shawnee, Okla.: Shawnee Directory, 1898.

Shawnee (Okla.) Daily News, 1898.

Shirley, Glenn. *West of Hell's Fringe: Crime, Criminals and the Federal Peace Officer in Oklahoma Territory, 1889–1907*. Norman: University of Oklahoma Press, 1978.

———. *Law West of Fort Smith: Frontier Justice in the Indian Territory, 1834–1896*. New York: Collier, 1957.

Smith, Geraldine M. "Violence on the Oklahoma Territory-Seminole Nation Border: The Mont Ballard Case." M.A. thesis, University of Oklahoma, 1957.

Speed, Horace, Collection. Oklahoma Historical Society, Archives and Manuscripts Division, Oklahoma City, Okla.

Spoehr, Alexander. *Kinship System of the Seminole.* Anthropological Series, Field Museum of Natural History, vol. 33. Chicago: Field Museum Press, 1942.

"State of Affairs in Indian Territory," *Red Man* 9 (October 1889): 7.

Stillwater (Okla.) Advance, 1901.

Stillwater (Okla.) Gazette, 1893, 1897, 1898, 1901.

Sunday Globe (Oklahoma City, Okla.), 1898.

Tahlequah (Cherokee Nation) Arrow, 1898, 1906.

Tecumseh Genealogy Club. *Pottawatomie County Cemetery Inscriptions.* 3 vols. Tecumseh, Okla.: Tecumseh Genealogy Club, 1980–81.

Tecumseh (Okla.) Leader, 1896, 1897, 1898.

Tecumseh (Okla.) Republican, 1898, 1899.

Testimony in the United States Court for the Northern District of Indian Territory. Sitting at Muskogee. May Term A.D. 1899. *U.S. vs. Mont Ballard.* Kidnapping. No. 4786. Transcript of Testimony and Judge's Instructions to the Jury (Film B-110). University of Oklahoma, Western History Collections, Norman, Okla.

Tilghman, Zoe A. *Marshal of the Last Frontier: Life and Services of William Matthew (Bill) Tilghman for Fifty Years One of the Greatest Peace Officers of the West.* Glendale, Calif.: Arthur H. Clark, 1949.

Times-Record (Blackwell, Okla.), 1914.

Topeka (Kans.) Commonwealth, 1885.

Turner, Alvin O. "Order and Disorder: The Opening of the Cherokee Outlet." *Chronicles of Oklahoma* 71 (Summer 1993): 154–73.

U.S. Bureau of the Census. 1900. Microcopy M623. National Archives Microfilm Publications, Washington, D.C.

———. 1910. Microcopy T624. National Archives Microfilm Publications, Washington, D.C.

U.S. Department of the Interior. *Annual Reports of the Department of the Interior for the Fiscal Year Ended June 30, 1898: Indian Affairs.* Washington, D.C.: Government Printing Office, 1898.

———. Commissioner of Indian Affairs. *Fifty-ninth Annual Report of the Commissioner of Indian Affairs to the Secretary of the Interior, 1890.* Washington, D.C.: Government Printing Office, 1890.

———. Commissioner of Indian Affairs. *Sixtieth Annual Report of the Commissioner of Indian Affairs to the Secretary of the Interior, 1891.* Washington, D.C.: Government Printing Office, 1891.

————. Commissioner of Indian Affairs. *Sixty-first Annual Report of the Commissioner of Indian Affairs to the Secretary of the Interior, 1892.* Washington, D.C.: Government Printing Office, 1892.

————. *Report of the Governor of Oklahoma Territory for the Fiscal Year Ending June 30, 1893.* Washington, D.C.: Government Printing Office, 1893.

————. *Report of the Governor of Oklahoma to the Secretary of the Interior, 1894.* Washington, D.C.: Government Printing Office, 1894.

————. *Report of the Governor of Oklahoma to the Secretary of the Interior, 1896.* Washington, D.C.: Government Printing Office, 1896.

U.S. Senate. 55th Cong., 2d sess., S. Docs. 56, 75, 98, 99, and 105.

Vestal, Stanley. "The First Families of Oklahoma Come from Many Tribes." *American Indian* 1 (January 1927): 10–11.

Wardell, Morris L. *A Political History of the Cherokee Nation.* Norman: University of Oklahoma Press, 1977.

Washington Post, 1898.

Watonga (Okla.) Republican, 1893.

Welsh, Michael E. "The Road to Assimilation: The Seminoles in Oklahoma, 1839–1936." Ph. D. diss., University of New Mexico, 1983.

Who Was Who in America with World Notables. 10 vols. to date. Chicago: Marquis-Who's Who, 1942–.

Woodward (Okla.) News, 1899.

Index

on McGeisey's innocence, 48, 68;
and law enforcement, 49; Sampson
captured by, 71–72; Sampson charged
by, 73–74; Seminoles threatened
by, 83–84; lies told by, 84, 102; as
fugitive, 136; capture of, 137; death
of, 171; mentioned, 27, 28, 31, 34,
78, 106, 124, 135, 138, 144, 145, 148,
167, 168

Leard, Madison, 27

Leard, Mary Martin: murder of, 34,
88; killer of, 35, 40–41, 45, 134, 158,
161–63, 165; funeral of, 47; alleged
rape of, 89; mentioned, 29, 31, 33, 82

Leard, Nannie, 29, 35

Leard, Roena Guinn, 31

Leard, Rufus, 28

Leard, Sudie, 29, 35

Leard, Susannah Lewis, 27, 28

Ledbetter, James F. (Bud), 92

Lewis, David, 26, 27

Lewis, Edward, 26, 28

Lewis, James M., 25

Lewis, John B., 26

Lewis, Marcus, 26, 27, 30

Lewis, Sarah, 26, 27, 30

Lewis, Thomas, 26, 27, 28

Lewis, Zora P., 25, 30

Lewis family: history of, 25–30;
criminal activities of, 26; claims of,
26–27, 29–30, 171; as intruders, 26;
in Oklahoma, 28–29; and whiskey
traffic, 28; as mob leaders, 61; as
fugitives, 136; mentioned, 63, 65,
167, 168

Lincoln, Peter, 86

Linn, C. P., 86, 116, 126–27

Little, John S., 97

Loby Cosa (Lopy Cosar), 162, 163

Lowiza, 24

Lynching: history of, 6, 170; in
Oklahoma, 103–04; newspaper
support for, 104; in Indian Territory,

112–13; mentioned, 107, 110. *See also*
Burning; Mobs

McColgan, Joseph, 106

McFarland, Jesse, 64, 139

McGeisey, James, 24

McGeisey, Lincoln: innocence of, 40,
46, 58, 68, 74, 100, 102, 120, 125,
144, 158; capture of, 46; as prisoner,
46–50; interrogation of, 46–47;
torture of, 47–48; warrant for, 50; in
U. S. custody, 53–54, 55–56; alibi
for, 56–57, 77; promised release of,
70; grudges against, 76; burning of,
82–83; remains of, 86–87; alleged
confession of, 105–06; exhumation
of, 116; Roper's comments on,
169–70; mentioned, 24, 25, 38, 52,
59, 61, 62, 63, 69, 72, 73, 76, 79, 84,
150, 151, 170

McGeisey, Martha, 24

McGeisey, Nora, 24

McGeisey, Thomas S.: family of, 24–25,
46; improvements of, 25; warrants
sworn by, 50; indemnities to, 116–17;
mentioned, 31, 35, 36, 37, 46, 47, 69,
71, 90, 99, 100, 123, 152, 153, 161,
172

McGeisey, William, 24

McGeisey family: vendetta against, 75

McGlothlin, Israel C., 104–05

McKaye, Johnson, 38, 75, 77

McKenna, Joseph, 93, 94, 108, 123

McKennon, Paul, 18

McMaster, Evan: editorials by, 108–09

McMechan, Thomas F.: investigations
by, 94–95, 119–20; report by, 101–02;
and Luman F. Parker, 120–22;
background of, 122; mentioned, 94,
100, 101, 108, 143

McPhail, Jim, 35

Mallosey, 24

Malven, Mrs. F. B., 133, 161

Marcum, Calvin, 54

background of, 63; as burner, 84; threats by, 87, 99; as fugitive, 138; capture of, 160; guilty plea of, 160; pardon sought for, 167; mentioned, 38, 71, 72, 74, 78, 85, 111, 124, 133, 134, 135, 136, 145, 146, 152, 159, 160, 166, 168, 169

Purcell Register: editorial stand of, 115

Quay, Matthew S.: motives of, 109–10; mentioned, 93, 109, 123, 130, 164

Queen, D. T., 106

Racism, 98, 109, 114–15
Reed, J. Warren, 141, 142–43, 147
Reeves, Bass, 28
Renters: character of, 21–23; origin of, 22, 23; racism among, 23–24; and lawlessness, 24
Riddle, Elias, 3, 106
Roper, Henry Clay: as mob leader, 59–60, 81, 139; as fugitive, 136, 138; capture of, 160; case against, 161; guilty plea of, 164; sentencing of, 164; pardon sought for, 167; lack of remorse in, 169–70; mentioned, 28, 40, 47, 51, 52, 55, 71, 74, 85, 111, 124, 133, 134, 135, 145, 146, 159, 163, 166, 168
Roper, Zora Cowart, 64

Sampson, Palmer: as suspect, 69, 75; capture of, 71–72; alleged confession of, 73–74, 77–78, 79, 105–06; background of, 75; grudges against, 76–77; torture of, 77; burning of, 82–83; remains of, 86–87; innocence of, 102, 125; exhumation of, 116; Roper's comments on, 169–70; mentioned, 84, 138, 150, 154, 170
Sampson, Sukey: indemnities to, 116–17; mentioned, 72, 75
Sarber, Billy, 75, 77
Sasakwa, Seminole Nation, 49
Scothorn, John W., 108, 123, 170

Scott, S. J., 97, 98, 101
Seminole Nation: code of law in, 13–14; description of, 17–18; renters in, 21; whites in, 21; blacks in, 24; court jurisdiction in, 44
Seminoles: and racism, 24; alleged uprising by, 90–92
Seney, 24
Sever, 38, 135
Smallwood, James Alfred, 48, 150, 152
Smith, Poliet, 68, 99, 119
Soper, Pliny: investigation by, 117–19; and Oklahoma officials, 120–23; as prosecutor, 130–40, 142–57 *passim*; and trial site, 131; trial strategy by, 135; pardons sought by, 166; mentioned, 94, 160
Speed, Horace: biographical sketch of, 129–30; as special prosecutor, 130–40 *passim*; investigations by, 132–34, 160–63, 164–65; case broken by, 133; prosecutions determined by, 138–39; trial tactics by, 139–40; prosecutions by, 142–57 *passim*; as U. S. attorney, 165; pardons opposed by, 166–68; success of, 170
Staggs, P. B., 151, 161
Stankewitz, John, 151, 152
Statehood: debate on, 115–16
Stauber, C. A.: editorials by, 100, 101, 107

Taylor, Henry, 42, 86, 116
Thlocco, Billy, 42, 44, 54, 135
Thomas, Heck, 95, 102, 136
Thomas, John R.: as trial judge, 142–57 *passim*; jury charged by, 145–46, 148–49, 156–57; pardons sought by, 166; mentioned, 117, 122, 164
Thompson, Canada H., 95, 96, 98, 99, 100, 119, 123
Thompson, Thomas, 51, 52